Family Man

The art of surviving domestic tranquility

Family Man

The art of surviving domestic tranquility

ROB JENKINS

Dogwood Publishing
Lawrenceville, Georgia

Published by Dogwood Publishing
 Published in the United States by Dogwood Publishing, a division of More Than Books, Inc., Georgia.

Library of Congress Cataloging-in-Publication Data is available upon request from the publisher.

ISBN: 0978774485
ISBN-13: 978-0-9787744-8-6

Manufactured in the United States of America.

9 8 7 6 5 4 3 2 1

First Edition: September 2012

Cover Design by Matt Smartt

To Bonnie, Jennifer, Robert, Michael, and Nathan,
without whom I quite literally could not have written this book.

CONTENTS

PART TWO:

The Associative Property of Multiplication

PART THREE:

It's Not an Adventure It's Just a Job

PART FOUR:

The Family That Spends Time Together Could Probably Think of a Better Rhyme Together

PART FIVE:

Other Duties as Assigned

Introduction

Don't let the title fool you: this book is not just for family men. It's also for their wives and others who know and love them, such as children, parents, siblings, and friends; for those who know but don't particularly like them, including their employers and co-workers; and for future family men, former family men, men (or women) raised by wolves, and anyone else who cares to read it, particularly if you paid retail.

But this book is especially for family men — guys in their thirties or forties, with a wife, two or more kids, a job (or, if they're lucky, a "career," defined as a job that occupies all their waking hours and doesn't pay overtime), a mortgage, a couple of car payments, half a dozen credit cards. If you fit that description, then this book is for you in a way that few books have ever been.

Perhaps, like me, you've always wondered what it would feel like to be grown up. Well, you can stop wondering. This is it. You're not a kid anymore, although you may at times act like one. If you don't believe me, just try doing something you did all the time when you were young, like eating three Big Macs in one sitting, or playing pick-up basketball for two hours, or coaxing a smile from that pretty young girl in the checkout line. Feel free to explain to your wife that you're merely testing my theory.

Yes, you have become what you feared most: not just an adult, but that variety of adult most maligned in our society, the family man. This is a man who, depending on which version of television sitcom reality you believe, is either never home or tied to his wife's apron strings, overbearing or subservient, a tyrant or a blowhard. You know, and I know, that such dichotomies are unfair and misleading. A family man is all of those things, and more.

Like all good family men, you probably spend most of your time trying to figure out how to balance everything — all the expectations of your wife, your children, your job, your home, your community. I hope this book will help. Failing that, I hope at the very least it will enable you to laugh at yourself occasionally. Why shouldn't you? Everyone else has been laughing at you for years.

Perhaps I should at this point issue the following disclaimer: I am not a psychiatrist, a psychologist, or a family counselor. About the only thing I have in common with the professionals is that I probably don't know what I'm talking about most of the time.

What I *am*, however, is a Family Man. I have one wife, four children, a huge mortgage, two cars (one of which is a minivan), two cats, and an undisclosed amount of credit card debt. I have a challenging and rewarding career (hope the boss is reading this), a nearly non-existent social life, and an income that ten years ago would have seemed astronomical but today barely covers my expenses.

If any of this sounds familiar, then perhaps you, too, are a family man — whether or not you've ever applied that label to yourself or even thought in those terms. And Lord willing, you're going to be one for a while. Get used to it. Embrace it. Being a family man is certainly better than the alternatives, such as being eaten alive by wolverines.

Actually, at times, it's a lot like being eaten alive by wolverines.

PART ONE:

Love, Honor, and Cherish and Other Great Motown Hits

Your most important relationship is the one you have with your wife, for at least a couple of very good reasons. The first is that you will ultimately spend more time with her than with anyone else. Unless your family is the result of secret government cloning experiments, you knew her before any of your kids were born, and after the last of the kids leaves home the two of you may have twenty or thirty more years to trim each other's ear hair. It just makes sense, then, that this is a relationship you would want to cultivate.

The other reason is — well, you know.

Look, we need to talk frankly for a moment. It's been my intention from the beginning to make this a "family" book and thus keep the subject matter on a relatively high moral plain. Still, it is written for adults — which does not, however, make it an "adult book." If it were, it would have far fewer words and more pictures.

But the truth of the matter, as I once observed to a friend of mine about to enter the bonds of matrimony, is that all marital interactions are predicated upon the fact that, on average, men need physical intimacy more than women. This means that although you are free to disagree with your wife, and may occasionally even put your foot down, you will eventually come to see things her way.

Nor am I alone in this opinion. Aristophanes made the same point thousands of years ago in his play *Lysistrata*, about a group of women who make a pact to ignore their husbands' physical needs until the men put an end to what the women regarded as a silly war. Not exactly *Cliff's Notes*, but it'll have to do. Guess what? (Spoiler alert.) The war ended.

Those ancient Greeks, despite their funny clothes, knew a thing or two about human nature. And I believe most modern men, even those who think an Oedipus complex is a downtown office development, can identify with the guys in *Lysistrata*.

Not surprisingly, though — to get back to my story — after offering my friend what I thought was extraordinarily levelheaded advice, I was soundly rebuked by my wife for being "so cynical." Obviously, I disagreed with her on this point. For several days. Ultimately, though, I came to see that she is right, and that I am a cynical, insensitive, misogynistic son of a gun who barely deserves to live. You may therefore disregard everything I've just said, if you haven't already.

Don't get me wrong. I'm not saying that sex is the most important issue in marriage. That would be control. Or money. Or control of the money. In this section I intend to examine all of those topics and more. And remember, honey: I'm only kidding.

Chapter 1

Sharing the Pants

One of the most significant issues in any relationship, aside from who gets to take first shower, is who's in charge. The traditional view is that the husband is the head of the household and that the wife is subservient to him. This is an excellent position for you to take, as long as your wife doesn't know about it.

A supposedly more modern and enlightened view is that marriage is a 50-50 proposition, with equal give and take on both sides. Others might argue that marriage must be, not 50-50, but 100-100, with both partners giving all their attention and resources to make the marriage work. This is particularly attractive if your wife has more resources than you to begin with.

My own advice is that you find some way to share the responsibility in your marriage. That way, when things go south, you can also share the blame. With a little practice, you can even become adept at shifting the *majority* of the blame onto your wife, by saying things like, "I only went along with that because I knew it was what you wanted." This both gets you off the hook and makes you seem deceptively selfless.

Of course, if you're reading this book, you and your wife have probably resolved the control issue long ago. If you hadn't, then you wouldn't still be a family man. You'd be a Single Dad, which is another book, and one I never hope to write.

And anyway, everyone knows that in any family the real power lies with the one who makes the most noise — usually an infant or a teenager (i.e., a really large infant). Just ask yourself who has the most influence over the really important decisions in your life, such as:

- where you go, and when
- when you go to sleep, and how much sleep you get
- what you watch on television
- what kind of breakfast cereal you buy

If you answered "myself" to any of these, put this book down immediately. Go out and get married, have a child or two, then resume reading.

The point is that no real family man has control over his own destiny, much less his household. But it is vital that he *appear* to be in control — or, more accurately, that he and his wife appear to be in control. Nothing is more devastating to the tender young psyche of a child than to find out that he or she is actually running the show. That's just the sort of traumatic realization that can cause a child to become a psychopathic killer, or perhaps a U.S. Senator.

This means that, at all costs, you and your wife must present a united front. Any power struggles between the two of you must never become apparent to the offspring, who already understand instinctively the divide-and-conquer strategy. Recognize that the real power struggle is not between you and your wife, but between the two of you and *them*. As Abraham Lincoln once said, "Nothing unites like a common enemy." (Or was it, "Nothing unties like a common enema"? I can never remember.)

Once you and your wife have united in your efforts to establish an artificial control over your household, you must then begin to develop strategies to maintain that control. Perhaps you will find the following suggestions useful.

The Wise Ruler

One excellent strategy is to make completely arbitrary, totally ridiculous rules. You remember these — your parents used to make them all the time. And it worked for them, didn't it? That's because nothing says "control" like power exercised for its own sake. A good arbitrary/ridiculous rule is characterized by being a) pointless, and b) impossible to remember, like the tax code and the rules of hockey.

For example, you can bring your children in and say to them, "Your mother and I have decided that there will be no more television on days of the week containing an 'r'." Or your wife could casually tell them over the dinner table, "Your father and I have decided that we will no longer allow malted milk balls in this house."

Please note that it's usually a good idea to include your wife in the unveiling of these rules. In fact, you may want to consider having her always be the one to break the news. Then your children will resent her more than they resent you, if only marginally.

Here are some other rules you may want to consider:

The toilet seat must be left up on even-numbered days and down on odd-numbered days. This rule has the added benefit of being politically correct, since it recognizes the differing hygiene needs of both male and female members of your household.

Peanut butter sandwiches may only be made with kumquat jelly. This may anger the marmalade producing nations, not to mention the Grape Growers Association of America, but that's just a chance you'll have to take.

All homework must be done before using the bathroom. Science has shown that nothing stimulates brainpower like a full bladder.

Anyone caught trespassing will be shot on sight. This isn't actually a good family rule, since it raises a potential point of contention over who will actually be doing the shooting. I just threw it in for the boomers.

An Eye for an Eye

Another sure indicator of power is the ability to inflict pain, either emotional or physical. When your children are small you are able to do this because you are bigger and know more psychological dirty tricks. Even as your children get older, you still have control over important resources such as money, the car, and the television remote. You can use all these resources to punish violators of the arbitrary rules established above. I will cover some of the more popular forms of punishment in the section of this book that deals with disciplining children. My point here, though, is that whatever you do, make sure you and your wife do it in concert. This will show unity and perhaps also be entertaining.

Humility is a Virtue

Another great way to show who's boss is to embarrass your children in public as often as possible. Such humiliation makes a number of clear statements to your children, such as "you're a worthless piece of scum" and "if you mess with me you'll regret it for a long, long time." In these days of inflated egos and exaggerated feelings of self-worth, such messages can have a long-term impact — although nothing years of therapy shouldn't be able to offset.

Public embarrassment sometimes works well on a one-on-one basis: for example, when you interrupt your son's baseball practice to discuss the onset of puberty, or when your wife takes your daughter with her to shop for lingerie. But nothing is as embarrassing to a child as being seen with his or her *whole family*.

These public outings, which I intend to discuss in more detail later, provide numerous opportunities for humiliating your children. Try taking your twelve-year-old along with his or her pre-school siblings to see *Barney Live!* Or you and your wife can simply join your teenagers at the mall for two hours of window-shopping. Or best of all: at a social gathering where your kids are present, tell potty training or "blossoming" stories (depending on their ages) loud enough for them to hear.

These are just a few of the strategies you and your wife can use to show that you are the ones who wear the pants in the family. (You may also want to allow your children to wear pants, when appropriate). Again, whatever you do, remember to present a united front — and make sure your fly is zipped.

Chapter 2

Romance and the Family Man

It is vital that you never stop romancing your wife. Well, okay, you should stop for a few minutes when the kids come into the room. But remember that ongoing romance is one of the key factors in making a relationship work. Many experts say so, and the fact that quite a few of them have been divorced at least once is probably irrelevant.

Think of your relationship with your wife as a tender young plant that must be constantly fed and nourished in order for it to bloom and grow. If you're one of those guys who has killed every green thing he's ever touched, then come up with your own metaphor. Or consider hiring a good lawyer.

I think romance is important to a marriage for several reasons. First, it strengthens the bond between husband and wife by enabling them to recapture the affection they felt for each other when newly in love. This can offset years of watching each other apply underarm deodorant.

Secondly, romantic attention from you will help your wife feel better about herself, which in turn can have a positive effect on the peace and tranquility of your home. I mean, what woman, having spent fourteen hours juggling the demands of insistent supervisors, screaming toddlers, and capricious teenagers, doesn't long at the end of the day for her husband's loving caress? (Note to my wife: don't answer that.)

Finally, romantic interludes (or "dates," as they used to be called before that term became a euphemism for having sex, which as a family man you know better than to cxpcct) simply provide a great excuse for getting out of the house. Add to that an opportunity to fortify your position in the us (parents) versus them (children) struggle for dominance — remember, leaving your children behind while you and your wife go out demonstrates unity and shows you have no qualms whatsoever about abandoning them — and you have an excellent reason to break free of the confines of home, entrusting your offspring to the care of a seventeen-year-old babysitter whom you've never met and who may, for all you know, belong to a Sun-worshipping cult.

However, like many men, you may have been accused of lacking romantic sensibilities. If you resent this accusation, despite the fact that it's probably true, let me give you some tips for improving your romance quotient (like that term? I just made it up), thus earning the undying love and devotion of your wife. At the very least, she probably won't leave you.

Dating: It's Not Just for Members of Congress

One of the best ways to inject romance into your marriage is to have a regular date night. Yes, I know this is what gets a lot of politicians in trouble, but if you restrict yourself to your *own* wife — which is the point of all this, after all — you ought to be able to avoid some of those pitfalls. And the time you spend together will provide the basis for a loving relationship for many years to come. If nothing else, you may get to see a movie with live action characters, portrayed by adults.

What I'm talking about is taking your wife *away* from the house and *away* from the children to some other location — just the two of you. This need not be as expensive as it sounds. Sure, it's nice occasionally to dress up, go out to dinner at a nice restaurant, take in a show. But fast food and a movie can be just as much fun. So can a simple walk in the park. Heck, if you have small children, going to the dentist together for his and her root canals qualifies as a date. The important thing is for the two of you to spend time alone with each other (is that an oxymoron?) on a regular basis.

The operative word here is *regular*, a term which, after one reaches the age of thirty-five, becomes very relative indeed, whether applied to dating or to bodily functions. Many experts recommend that you set aside a specific date night each week. However, those are probably the same experts who expect you to drink twelve glasses of water a day and make an itemized inventory of all your household belongings. I'd certainly advise you to go out at least monthly, as anything less frequent may lead your children to believe you're staying home for their sakes, which can cause a dangerous shift in the balance of power.

Ultimately, though, you and your wife must adjust your dating schedule to fit your own lifestyle and circumstances. For example, couples with more than two children under the age of ten should expect to go out together approximately once every five years. Couples with teenage children, on the other hand, may go out two or three nights a week, or simply go out and not come back.

Another important issue is destination. As I've already said, it doesn't really matter where you go, as long as the two of you enjoy being there together. Still, as a family man dedicated to romancing your wife, you may want to give some thought to your destination beforehand. This will make you seem confident and decisive, and may even keep you from having to see the latest Leonardo DiCaprio movie for the fourth time.

Here are some tips for planning a great date:

First, choose something your wife will enjoy. I don't know your wife, so I can't say with certainty that she won't go weak in the knees at the prospect of midnight ice-fishing. Chances are, though, if ice-fishing is your idea of a date, you may come to find that there are things much colder.

This doesn't mean, by the way, that you have to choose something you *don't* like, though you may occasionally want to compromise or even sacrifice in that regard. After all, what's four hours of *Harlequin Bodice Rippers: The Musical* compared to a lifetime of wedded bliss?

Secondly, remember that a cheap date can always be passed off as romantic if it involves anything artistic. If you spent your date money on ice-fishing gear, for example, you can always impress your sweetheart with a trip to the public art museum; crash a reception, and you may even manage several *hors d'oeuvres* before they throw you out. Another good idea is an arts and crafts festival, although in this case you'd better be prepared to buy something, most likely some *object d'art* of indeterminate origin and dubious utility that won't fit in your vehicle. (Interestingly, that's only the second time in my life I've used two French phrases in one paragraph. I can't tell you about the other time.)

Finally, be sure to determine how much money you'll need before you leave the house. Then ask your wife for that amount. If her reply is simply a cold stare, see if you still have the receipt from the bait and tackle shop.

Adventures in Babysitting

Another important issue when you're planning a date is getting a sitter. Finding a good babysitter may be one of the most difficult things in life, on a par with achieving financial independence or getting a straight answer out of a White House press secretary. If you do manage to find one (a babysitter, I mean, not an honest press secretary), I recommend that you do everything in your power to keep her, excluding, perhaps, abduction, except in extreme circumstances. You may even want to consider adopting her, if you can get her parents to agree to it — which, if she's a teenager, they probably will. (Excuse my perpetuation of sexual stereotypes here. I'm sure there are many fine male babysitters out there, working hard to pay their way through interior design school.)

If you are one of those families with built-in babysitters, in the form of relatives nearby or older siblings, consider yourself lucky. Any problems that may arise from living near other members of your extended family (and that's another book in itself, or maybe a Jerry Springer episode) are more than offset during the child rearing years by the proximity of readily available babysitting. Of course, not all grandparents live to entertain toddlers while their adult children amuse themselves, but even the most reluctant can usually be persuaded, especially if you threaten to withhold visitation rights.

One of the hardest things for a parent to do may be to leave young children with an older child. The question always arises, how old is old enough to babysit? Here's a simple and scientific formula: multiply the age of your oldest child by the number of months since your last date. If the product is at least 24, you have a babysitter. (Example: Your last date was two months ago. Your oldest child is twelve. *Viola!* Haven't been out in three months? An eight-year-old will do. Next month, my wife and I will be able to leave our three-year-old by himself.)

On the other hand, if you have both a teenager and a toddler at home, you may have been doing just a little too much "dating," in the euphemistic sense of the word. But that's your business. For all I know, you might have done this intentionally, just so you would one day have a built-in babysitter. If so, be sure to let your teenager know. It will be certain to raise her self-esteem.

One more tip regarding babysitting: if you want to appear as romantic as possible, then in addition to setting the agenda for your date, you should also be the one to arrange for a sitter. Then your wife will be worry-free, with nothing to do but get ready for the big night. While she's doing that, you can go to pick up the babysitter, or perhaps earn a Ph.D. in genetics and clone your own babysitter.

Mountain Bikes are Forever

Another way to improve your Romance Quotient (consider that term copyrighted) is to shower your wife with gifts. Note that this is different from giving your wife a shower, though that may have its own romantic implications. What I'm talking about here is gift-giving, for any and all occasions as well as for no occasion.

Again, this doesn't mean you always have to spend a lot of money. That depends on what you've done. No, I'm kidding. Seriously, never allow yourself to fall into the pattern of giving gifts only to apologize. If you do, you won't be able to give your wife anything without her wondering what you've done this time. She may be right to wonder, but it's definitely not to your advantage.

The best kind of gift is the one that is completely unexpected, given for no reason she knows of. Many men send roses for Valentine's, but how many bring home daisies at the end of an otherwise unremarkable day? For that matter, how many men know a daisy from a quadruped? It is this kind of thoughtfulness that will deposit into your relationship account copious amounts of goodwill, which you can later use to attend live sporting events.

Another characteristic of the ideal gift is that it is unique and specific to some personal interest or pleasure of your wife's. Retailers work hard to market the standard gift items designed for men who have no idea what their wives actually like — in other words, the vast majority. Don't be caught in that trap. Anyone can buy flowers or candy or jewelry. A unique and thoughtful gift will communicate to your wife that you are actually in tune with her deepest longings, whether you are or not.

For example, if your wife is into mountain biking, then you can't go wrong with cool bike accessories: a personalized miniature license plate, a ringer or bulb horn for the handle bars, a colorful wicker basket. None of this stuff is expensive, and it all looks great. Or you could spend a little more and go for the rear-mounting child seat. That way, you won't have to watch the toddler while she pursues her hobby.

If you're really lucky, maybe your wife is one of those women who collect small and relatively inexpensive items, such as porcelain figurines or stuffed animals. This can save hours spent agonizing over what to buy her and hours more standing in return lines. Be careful, though, not to limit your gift buying solely to these collectibles; there are some occasions for which a beanbag monkey just isn't appropriate.

You should also take care not to submit to the temptation of buying your wife only gifts you would like for yourself. I know many women would be thrilled with an NFL cable package, for instance, but your wife may not be one of them. Even lingerie can fall into this category, unless your idea of sexy nightwear is cotton flannel plaid pajamas.

Of course, you may need to select a more expensive gift on certain occasions, such as Christmas, landmark anniversaries, and returning from a four-day camping trip with your buddies. For these occasions, jewelry is almost always your best bet. A custom-made mountain bike can also make a nice gift, though it doesn't look nearly as stunning with an evening gown.

Ultimately, though, it isn't the price of the gift that counts, but rather the thought behind it. At least, that's what I tell my wife when I haven't spent much money. If you really want to appear the incurable romantic, what is most important is that you give gifts frequently — often, as I mentioned above, for no apparent reason — and that your wife never suspect your generosity is all part of an elaborate scheme to elicit sexual favors, even if that's exactly what you have in mind.

Real Men *Do* Cuddle

Finally, having used the "S" word, let me conclude this chapter with a few words about the role sex plays in a romantic relationship between two mature, married adults: it has no role. Okay, that's an exaggeration, but it is definitely important for you not to confuse romance with sex. In fact, there is an easy way to distinguish them: Sex is what you want. Romance is what your wife wants.

Understanding that, if you still want your wife to think you're romantic and not merely libidinous (which she already knew), you're going to have to make the occasional sacrifice — for example, substituting cuddling (defined for men as "stimulation without release") for the real thing. It's worth any sacrifice, though, when you hear your wife bragging to her friends about how thoughtful and romantic you are. At least, you hope she's talking about you.

Chapter 3

A Penny Saved is the Root of All Evil

Marriage counselors agree that financial problems are a chief source of stress in marriage, as well as a leading cause of divorce. Coincidentally, those same marriage counselors charge $125.00 an hour to come to such conclusions. In practical terms, this means you can spare yourself a great deal of grief if you and your wife agree early in your marriage on a basic approach to family finances. It would also be helpful if one or both of you could inherit large sums of money from deceased relatives.

Of course, we all know that money alone does not guarantee happiness. We know this because the people with money have told us so. Who would know better than they? True happiness, it seems, comes from accepting the fact that, no matter how seemingly adequate your salary, you will always be broke, only at progressively higher levels; that you will never be more than a scant half-dozen paychecks away, at best, from answering one of those late night television advertisements by sleazy bankruptcy lawyers who can't make a living chasing ambulances or over-billing flush mega-corporations, like honest attorneys. (If you're a sleazy bankruptcy lawyer who also happens to be a family man, please understand that I mean that in the most complimentary way possible.)

Regardless of how much or how little money you make, your task is to learn to manage it wisely and thus eliminate one potential source of contention between you and your wife. What follows in this chapter, then, are a number of suggestions for handling your finances.

Budgeting Made Easy

One of the best things you and your wife can do to ensure domestic tranquility is to agree upon a budget, which is an itemized list of what you would spend in a given month if you had any sense. Don't panic, though: remember the budget has nothing to do with what you actually spend.

In this regard, we can take inspiration from our glorious leaders in the nation's capital, who have created a concept so brilliant as to make the theory of relativity seem like the ravings of an imbecile. This concept is known as "off-budget." Simply put, it means any money you spend that you don't want to count against your projected expenses can conveniently be listed under "off-budget," a wonderful catch-all category which can include anything from extra groceries and household goods to big-screen TVs and sport utility vehicles.

You can even use this concept — again taking a page from Congress — to convince yourself that you are actually quite thrifty. For instance, if you budget $500.00 for food, and one month you spend only $480.00, you can claim to have saved $20.00, even though you spent $4,000.00 that same month — off budget, of course — on a handkerchief once sneezed into by Tom Brady. Save $20.00 a month in this manner for five months and you can proudly announce to your family a budget surplus of $100.00, even as the men are carrying out your furniture.

For those of you new to the budgeting process, I am including a sample budget, which, though necessarily general, should with some modification be applicable to most households. If, for example, your net monthly income is $5,000.00, you may want to construct your budget as follows:

<u>Budget</u>

RV payment	$ 550.00
Country club dues	$ 200.00
Greens fees	$ 300.00
Hair, nails, make overs	$ 200.00
Wife's hair, nails, make overs	$ 300.00
Eating out	$ 400.00
Movie rentals	$ 100.00
Pizza delivery	$ 200.00
Jewelry repair	$ 100.00
TV shopping network	$ 400.00
900 numbers	$ 300.00
Online gaming subscriptions	$ 300.00
Lottery tickets	$ 100.00
Magazine subscriptions (*Sports Illustrated, Redbook, Field & Stream, Cosmo, Mad*)	$ 50.00
Minimum credit card payments	$ 500.00
Books by Rob Jenkins	$ 200.00
Financial advisor	$ 400.00
Marriage counseling	$ 300.00
Total	$4,900.00

Off-budget

Home mortgage	$ 1,500.00
Car payments	$ 800.00
Food	$ 300.00
Electricity	$ 300.00
Gasoline	$ 300.00
Insurance	$ 600.00
Childcare	$ 800.00
Total	$ 4,600.00

Note that my proposed budget shows a surplus of $100.00 a month, or $1,200.00 a year (I did that math in my head). That's enough money for you to take your family to Disney World, or buy an aboveground pool. The off-budget figure may be mildly alarming at first glance, but don't worry. The total *expenditures* (not to be confused with *budget*) can be financed easily and indefinitely with credit cards. Which segues very neatly into my next topic.

Credit Where Credit Is Due

As a rule, credit cards should be used only in case of emergency, such as when you really want to buy something and don't have enough money to pay for it. According to a recent survey, the average American family has six credit cards, including gasoline and department store cards. These cards have interest rates that vary from about eight per cent to you-could-have-bought-two-for-what-you'll-end-up-paying. The combined balance of all six cards, on the average, equals approximately one first-born child.

Actually, credit cards do have their uses. Experts advise that you carry cards instead of cash when you travel, since stolen cards can easily be replaced, and most credit card companies have built in safeguards to protect you from having to pay for items bought with your stolen card. The fact that someone used your card to buy $1,000.00 worth of leather S&M gear, or to order the $89.95 "Best of Wayne Newton" CD collection from the Home Shopping Network, should be no more than an inconvenience. And you can enjoy the catalogs and phone solicitations for months to come.

And speaking of television shopping — not to mention shopping over the Internet — you certainly can't do that with cash. In fact, these days you can't even use cash to rent a car, even if you have enough cash on your person to *buy* the darned car (for example, if you're transporting drug money, although in that case you probably aren't a family man, unless you're actually a "Family" man, if you get my drift). So credit cards are clearly a necessary evil of modern life, like personal injury lawyers and text messaging.

If you don't want credit card debt to ruin your marriage, though, you'll need to take some steps to curb your spending. One suggestion is that you avoid using credit cards to pay for routine expenses, such as groceries, gasoline, and body waxings. Another is to make a rule that you and your wife must agree before making any major purchase on a credit card. If she won't agree to let you charge your pro wrestling season tickets, you can always pay cash and give them to her for her birthday.

Cute Checks

One of the keys to happiness in your marriage, as I've already stated, is for you and your wife to make all-important decisions *together* — and this certainly includes decisions about money. Some men have a difficult time with this concept, especially if their wives make less money than they do. For these men, my first piece of advice would be to refer back to the introduction to this section on marriage. If that's not enough to convince you, just remember that your wife is probably much smarter than you are. After all, *she's* never purchased season tickets to pro wrestling, or bought a used bass boat.

Of course, it's not just men who occasionally have problems with financial togetherness. Some working women go so far as to insist on separate checking accounts, perhaps to prevent their husbands from spending their money on used bass boats, or maybe just so they can have pictures of cats on their checks. In many cases the husbands are perfectly happy with this arrangement, so that a surprising number of couples not only keep separate accounts but divide all bills and expenses.

I don't recommend this approach. On a practical level, it's just more expensive to keep two accounts, and if your wife wants cats on the checks, well, it's not the end of the world. You can always doodle them into little effeminate-looking dogs. Moreover, dividing the expenses can be tricky at best. If you make more money, she'll never agree to a 50-50 split, even if she does occasionally use the bass boat. And, finally, think of the message you'll be sending your kids: are two parents who can't agree on how to spend money likely to agree on the aesthetic properties of nipple rings?

Speaking of kids (yet another beautiful segue; must be the journalistic training), some experts recommend that parents include older children in important financial decisions, such as whether or not to send them off to military school. I think this is a good idea, as it will help them learn about the budgeting process and the value of money. Just be sure never to reveal to your children exactly how much money you make. The IRS has been known to depose all members of the immediate family.

Retiring on Eggshells

The last subject I want to cover in this chapter is that of saving money for college tuition, retirement, etc. — often referred to as "building a nest egg." I like this metaphor because, although it's a bit of a cliché, it does manage to convey the fragile nature of the enterprise, in which the proceeds of your life's work can, in a moment, be dashed to smithereens or ripped from your grasp by scavengers. With that inspirational thought in mind, let us move forward to a discussion of why and how you should save your money.

The best reason to save money is so you'll have more of it later. And you're going to need it. Estimate the rate at which your routine expenses have increased over the last ten years, then multiply that figure by the gross national product of Uruguay to determine what those expenses will be ten years from now. Remember, too, that as your children get older you'll have more and more expenses that aren't included in your monthly budget, such as braces, automobile insurance, college tuition, and bail.

Then there's retirement. The great thing about retirement, as I understand it, is that you don't have to work; unfortunately, in one of life's little ironies, you don't get paid as much, either. So you're going to have to come up with some extra money somewhere, because even after retirement you're still likely to enjoy such luxuries as food and electricity.

Like many who entered adulthood prior to the Great Recession, you may have spent all of your working life assuming that those vast amounts of money taken out of your paychecks by the federal government in the form of Social Security payments would one day be returned to you with interest. Now you discover that the whole thing is a sham, like welfare reform or Yoko Ono's singing career. Apparently, unless you want your golden years to be fueled by the cat food *du jour*, you're going to have to save that money yourself.

Where are you going to get the money to save, you may well ask. Well, remember that if you follow the sample budget laid out above, you'll have a monthly surplus of $100.00. If you have the discipline to forego the Disney vacation and the in-ground pool, you can start your savings with that money. Just a brief note, though: if you intend to follow that budget to the letter, you may want to put those savings in your mother-in-law's name.

Exactly where to keep your savings is another important consideration. Most experts agree that you should avoid stowing your money under your mattress. Instead, they recommend porcelain crockery. Or you can take a more traditional approach and divide your savings into three parts: risk-free investments (traditional bank accounts, considered to be risk-free because they are insured by the federal government, which everyone knows is the epitome of solvency), low-risk investments (such as money market accounts, which can rise or fall only by a few dozen percentage points in a given day), and moderate risk investments (e.g. Israeli pork futures).

The point is that you need to have your savings invested somewhere, so that your money will work for you. We know this because the investment brokers have told us so, and our money certainly seems to be working for them. The bottom line is, if you don't invest your money, it will depreciate significantly over the years; if you do invest it, it will depreciate only moderately.

Of course there are a number of other options for retirement savings, such as employer-sponsored pensions, personal IRA accounts, and 401K plans. Any of these would probably be a good choice, since they all appear to be based on the same premise: namely, that having had your income reduced by several hundred dollars a month throughout your working life, you'll be better prepared to live on the measly pittance you'll receive after retirement.

In any case, whatever decisions you make about retirement and savings, you should make them together with your wife — just like all your other financial decisions. This will promote an atmosphere of peace and harmony in your home, and even though you may never own a bass boat, you'll have something much better: checks with cats on them.

Chapter 4

A Man's Place is in the Kitchen

If you really want to have a great relationship with your wife, one of the best things you can do is help her around the house. Be careful, though, not to use the word "help" when referring to this activity, as it is likely to elicit from your wife the following response: "What do you mean, *help*? Isn't this your house, too?" Or a variation: "What do you mean, *help with the kids*? Aren't they your kids, too?" She has a point there. As far as you know, they are.

Your wife is especially unlikely to appreciate such blatant insensitivity if she works full-time outside the home. I understand you may have grown up in a household where your mother worked all day, came home, fixed dinner, cleaned up afterward, then settled in for a relaxing evening of laundry and ironing; whereas your father worked all day, came home, sat down in his recliner, took off his shoes, had dinner served to him on a television tray, then watched the tube until falling asleep with his mouth open around 9:30. So what? Your house probably had avocado kitchen appliances, too. Things change.

My point is that women who work full-time outside the home, as well as women who work full-time *inside* the home raising small children and maintaining the domicile, have every right to expect their husbands to share some of the household responsibilities. They also have a right to remain silent, though most of them rarely choose to do so.

This doesn't mean you have to divide the housework 50-50. There are a lot of things to be done around the typical home, not all of them "housework" in the traditional sense of the term. One of the best ways to get out of housework, in fact, is to be busy doing yard work or exterior home maintenance.

Those are legitimate tasks, unlike extended testing of satellite reception, and your wife can hardly complain when you're hard at work cutting the grass or painting the trim. The drawback to this strategy is, well, you have to cut the grass or paint the trim. Neither is exactly fun, and this type of work can be especially inconvenient when the weather is bad. Even so, the fact that such chores are on your list of things to be done at some point in the indefinite future, when the weather is perfect and the alternative is folding socks, will probably get you out of some housework.

But not all of it. As a modern-day family man, you're going to need to know how to perform basic household functions, such as cooking, cleaning, laundry, and childcare. Fortunately for you, there is this book, in which I will tell you everything you need to know about these tasks — which is not to be confused with everything your wife would *like* you to know.

Basic Nutrition 101

Most family men these days are capable of at least elementary food preparation: boiling, thawing, toasting, microwaving, dialing. Using these basic processes, we are able when necessary to provide meals that are, if not enticing, at least minimally edible. The problem with this is that *we* generally have to eat these meals, too, unless we've managed to sneak a Quarter Pounder on the way home.

For this reason, most of us are content to let our wives do the cooking, just as they are content to let us take care of automobile maintenance. In fact, to many of us, this seems like a perfectly reasonable division of labor — which no doubt it would be, if we only ate once every three months or 3,000 miles.

The truth is, with a working wife, active children, and conflicting schedules, today's family man will be called upon frequently to prepare meals, and he had better be ready. This means more than picking up the occasional takeout, more even than having an ample supply of TV dinners and microwaveable pizza in the deep freeze, though no one disputes the wisdom of that, especially during football, basketball, baseball, and hockey seasons. But being truly prepared means following a few basic rules that will make the mom-less dining experience beneficial to your family and, if not pleasant, then at least tolerable.

Rule # 1: Eat something green.

Lime Jell-O doesn't count. Neither does anything that wasn't green before you put it in the refrigerator.

There are basically two types of green foods: dead and alive. Dead green foods include green beans, peas, okra, spinach — all those lumpy, slimy substances that stimulated your gag reflex as a child but which you have now learned to tolerate. This fact, by the way, makes dead green foods an excellent choice to serve your children, who will no doubt find them as nauseating as you once did. Nutritional value is an added benefit.

Live green foods include lettuce and fresh cucumbers. These are not bad, as long as they are completely covered in a thick dressing or a similar arterial coating compound. For this reason, live green food — also known as *salad* — is the green food of choice for those who don't wish to see a good meal ruined by something that resembles raw sewage.

Rule #2: Use at least three of the main food groups.

Most men recognize only two food groups: sweet and salty. A bit of sifting through your memory, though, may help you to recall what you learned in eighth-grade health class — no, not that, I'm talking about the basic food groups: meats, grains, fruits and vegetables, poultry, and dairy. In fairness to your children, you should try to include at least three of these in every meal, so as to provide balance in their diet. Otherwise, they might fall over.

This doesn't mean you can't be creative in the way you present these food groups. Ice cream, for example, is made from milk, a diary product. *Chocolate* ice cream contains cocoa beans, which are vegetables. A cone is baked from a flour base. Thus a chocolate ice cream cone can be seen as a nutritious meal unto itself. And how about pizza? A single take-out supreme has all five known groups plus at least four others.

Rule # 3: Provide alternatives.

If possible, try to prepare a menu with alternative choices to potentially unpopular items. For example, if spinach makes your children spew, you should still fix it for them and insist that they eat a few bites. This is no more than your duty as a father. However, after the fun is over, you may want to offer them a suitable alternative, such as collard greens. One quick note: Captain Crunch is *not* a suitable alternative in this instance. It's for you to eat after the kids go to bed.

Keeping It Clean

Let me say right up front that I'm not talking here primarily about cleaning up after yourself. That should be a given. It isn't, but it should be. What I'm talking about is helping your wife — excuse me, *working hand in hand* with your wife — to keep the house clean. I know this goes against the grain for many men, since house cleaning has traditionally been regarded as women's work. Then again, men have traditionally been responsible for supporting the family financially. Care to comment?

I didn't think so. And what your silence means is that you can expect to do some housecleaning. Maybe not much, but some.

I should mention at this point that one good way to get out of housework is to appear totally inept. For some of you this won't be difficult. And it doesn't really work with cooking, because you probably only cook when there's no other alternative. But you can avoid a great deal of cleaning, for example, just by acting dense as your wife explains some simple process over and over again. Why an otherwise intelligent woman would believe that a 38-year-old systems analyst can't figure out how to manipulate a vacuum cleaner is beyond me. But she will believe it — perhaps because she's predisposed to accept your ineptitude — and she'll eventually give up, much as you would with your children, who mastered this technique long ago.

Of course, the theme of this chapter, if I may recapitulate briefly, is not how to get out of housework but how to ingratiate yourself with your wife by appearing to be useful. So you may want to save the dumb act for days when there's a really good game on.

Once you recognize that some housework is inevitable if you wish to have a truly harmonious marriage, you'll need to identify the specific tasks you may be expected to perform. Two of the most objectionable are cleaning the kitchen and cleaning bathrooms.

If you're lucky, you may be able to avoid cleaning the kitchen except when you do the cooking, which is to say rarely. And on these occasions you can reduce your cleanup time dramatically by using only disposable utensils. Please keep in mind that your wife's great-grandmother's English china is not disposable, even if the dishwasher *is* full; you can, however, find plastic forks and spoons, paper plates, and Styrofoam cups at your local grocer, one aisle over from the frozen microwave pizza.

Still, there may be times when you find yourself actually having to clean a genuinely disgusting kitchen. Remember, too, that you can earn great good will and perhaps even other rewards by telling your wife, after she has prepared a particularly large and delicious meal, "You go lie down, honey. I'll take care of the kitchen." (Note: this principle does not apply on Thanksgiving and Christmas days, when it is your inalienable right as an American male to watch eight hours of football after gorging yourself. Just be sure to invite enough female relatives to help with the clean-up.)

When you do have to clean the kitchen, keep in mind the following tips:

Use the dishwasher. The one thing you should never do is wash a dish by hand. This is not only a complete waste of energy but also sets a bad precedent. You don't even need to rinse the dishes before putting them in the dishwasher, though you may allow your pets to remove the worst of the food residue. Anything too large to be put in the dishwasher should be hidden — behind the sofa, for example, or in your sock drawer. Once the dishwasher is full, any remaining dishes can be left "to soak" in a sink full of soapy water. With any luck, your wife will take care of them later.

Have your children do it. This will be a great learning experience for them, not to mention helping to justify their existence. Since dishwashers are built low to the ground, even toddlers can help (and you may find that great-grandma's china is disposable, after all). Older children can do all the work themselves and for a few dollars may even be willing to give you the credit.

Throw out any leftover food. Transferring food to storage containers is a waste of time and a tremendous pain in the buttocks. If it isn't already in such a container, throw it out. Yes, I know you'll probably be guilt-ridden, thinking of all those poor starving children in India your mother used to tell you about. If it helps, simply leave the food out on the counter for several hours, perhaps while you watch football. Once it's gone bad, you can throw it away with impunity. (Another possibility is to eat all the leftovers yourself, though this presents its own set of problems.)

I don't have nearly as much to say about cleaning bathrooms; in fact, I shudder just thinking about it. That may be because I have three boys, not counting myself. There may truly be nothing more disgusting than cleaning a bathroom that has been used regularly by four males, unless it's cleaning a bathroom that has been used regularly by five or more males. From a woman's point of view, though, I suppose there is a kind of sick poetic justice in making us deal with the consequences of our own, shall we say, poor aim.

Fortunately, we don't have to do it very often, because when it comes to cleanliness, no room is more important to a woman than the bathroom, and frankly they just don't trust us to do it right. This is where our natural incompetence really comes in handy.

If you do have to clean the bathroom — well, you're pretty much on your own, and you deserve what you get. But, since this book is supposed to be useful as well as hilariously funny, I suppose I should share a few quick pieces of advice: 1) Wear elbow-length rubber gloves and waders, unless you happen to own a bio-containment suit. 2) If you have sons, make them help. This may ultimately improve their aim and thus save wear and tear on the linoleum. 3) Apply liberal amounts of an ammonium-based disinfectant, being sure to leave the door open. And, 4) if you use a washcloth as a cleaning rag, do not hang it back on the towel rack over the sink.

REDECORATING TIPS FOR THE BOYS BATHROOM

Dirty Laundry

Speaking of incompetence, there is no area where it serves us better. Women may be inexplicably obsessive about clean bathrooms, but they are positively compulsive when it comes to laundry — perhaps because the consequences of screwing up can be both expensive and embarrassing, depending on where the stains are located.

Like many men, I learned to do laundry in college. Each week, I had to deal with the age-old question, "Do I wash clothes, or just buy new underwear?" At that time it cost about $2.50 to do two loads of laundry, whereas a three-pack of briefs went for $2.79 at the local Kmart. Clearly a no brainer. After five years, I graduated with a bachelor's degree, $53.75 in library fines, and 248 pairs of shorts.

Occasionally, of course, I did have to wash clothes, usually when my jeans began to move around the room by themselves during the night. The system I used most often was to divide my clothes into two loads — merely filthy and truly disgusting — and wash each with as much detergent as I could beg, borrow, or steal from whoever happened to be using the laundry room at the same time. Then I would take each load out of the dryer, put the shirts and slacks on hangers to prevent their becoming overly wrinkled (moderately wrinkled was par for the course), and dump the rest into an old pillowcase. This seemed to work well. I never once had a woman turn me down for a date because of the way my clothes looked or smelled. At least, that was never mentioned as a reason.

Unfortunately, the fact that this system worked just fine for me in college seems to mean nothing to my wife. (You know, women are supposed to be sentimental, but they're really not about the things that matter. They'll wait until you're on a business trip and then throw away the boxers you wore under your high school basketball uniform in a heartbeat.) Nowadays, laundry has to be sorted into 14 or 15 different piles using some arcane formula that would befuddle Ursula the Sea

Witch (if you don't know who that is, you're not a family man at all; you're an imposter!), then loaded first into the washer and later into the dryer on various settings, which my wife apparently knows by heart. Afterwards, it all has to be folded or — gasp! — *ironed* and then put away.

That's a lot of work. Fortunately, except for some occasional folding and ironing my own shirts — yes, I iron my own shirts, but only so that they will be ironed — I don't have to do very much of the actual laundry, unless my wife is out of town for an extended period of time. I suspect the same is true for you. If so, here's a brief, basic primer for doing the laundry when you have to:

First, divide it into no more than three loads. Leave your wife's dirty clothes in the hamper; if she's out of town, she doesn't need them anyway. Anything else that won't fit into three loads should be stuffed under your kids' beds, so you can pull it out later and upbraid them in your wife's presence for not getting their laundry in the hamper. (Whether it's actually theirs or not doesn't matter, as long as it's wadded up.) This will both lighten your workload and make you seem like a concerned father.

Second, be sure to wash everything on cold/cold, with no bleach. This way, if you happened to do a poor job of dividing your loads by color, you don't have to worry about anything getting too ruined. It may not actually get clean, either, but as long as your wife and kids can detect the lingering odor of detergent on their clothes, you can always blame the remaining stains and dirt streaks on the machine.

Third, take any clothes that would normally be ironed out of the dryer immediately and put them on hangers (this is one trick from college that still works). If, say, you're in the middle of your soap opera and don't get to the dryer quickly enough, just run that load for another 10 to 15 minutes, then take it out. This will keep the clothes from getting too wrinkled, so that they may not need to be ironed at all, especially if they are children's clothes. I've always thought ironing children's clothes is a waste of time, unless you plan to shellac the child, clothes and all.

Finally, take everything that's left — underwear, socks, jeans, T-shirts — and divide it into baskets by family member. (Don't bother to fold any of these. They're either *supposed* to be wrinkled or else not seen by anyone outside your family. You hope.) Then place each basket in that family member's closet, where with any luck it will already have been emptied before your wife gets home.

Child Care for Idiots (and I Don't Mean the Children)

I'll be dealing with the issue of child *rearing* in later chapters. What I want to talk about here is taking care of the kids when your wife is not home and when child care either is not available or else the occasion does not justify the cost, like when you just want to go play golf. That simply isn't a good enough reason to hire a baby sitter, regardless of the weather. Remember, though, that older children can caddy. For that matter, smaller children will probably fit in your locker.

The point is, no matter how you try to avoid it, there are going to be times when you find yourself stuck at home by yourself with the kids. This is due to the fact that your wife also has a full and busy life and that she doesn't like to be stuck at home alone with the kids any more than you do. And when outside childcare is not an option, both of you can't be away from home at the same time, as this is illegal. So it often comes down simply to who has the best excuse for being gone. My advice then is to work on your excuses, but also to hone your survival skills for those times when you will be the sole care provider.

Of course, in keeping with the theme of this chapter, you may occasionally even *offer* to stay with the kids just so your wife can have some time to herself. This is just a suggestion, mind you. But such an offer could have the dual advantages of putting your wife in your debt and allowing you to spend more time with your children. Then again, if your wife tends to be oblivious to feelings of indebtedness, or has no intention of repaying the debt in the, ah, currency you prefer, and extra time with your kids doesn't sound attractive, then you may want to disregard this suggestion. That's assuming you've gotten this far, and your eyes didn't glaze over as soon as you saw the words "child care" in the heading.

The trick to child care, as with any other chore, is to identify your objective and then accomplish it with as little effort as possible. In this case, your objective is for your children to be alive and your house relatively intact when your wife gets home. I suppose, from your wife's point of view, it would be nice if you were to teach the children conversational French while deep cleaning every room, but believe me when I say she will settle for alive and intact. In fact, this will actually be more than she secretly expects, and may even earn you the distinction of being "good with the kids."

All of this you can accomplish quite easily with a little help from that most versatile of household appliances, the television set. Yes, I know you've read all those articles in the parenting magazines decrying the use of television as a babysitter. Nonsense. Television makes a *great* babysitter, as your wife knows perfectly well. She can hardly blame you for doing that which she herself would do in your place, if she had been the one with the lamer excuse for getting out of the house.

The fact is, numerous scientific studies (conducted by me on my four children) have shown that even the most terrifyingly active of toddlers will sit slack-jawed for hours when confronted by an endless succession of Barney DVD's. Come to think of it, they make me slack-jawed, too.

Older children can be similarly tranquilized... er, entertained, by Disney movies, which they will watch and re-watch until you know the dialogue by heart just from being in the next room. (My daughter hasn't watched "The Little Mermaid" in at least ten years, yet I still sometimes find myself softly whistling "Under the Sea" in supermarket checkout lines.) And these movies always have such a great message, usually something like, "As long as you're at least sixteen, it's okay to defy the authority figure in your life and run away from home with the first person of the opposite sex who catches your eye."

As for teenagers, there's always MTV, the viewing of which, I'm relatively certain, probably won't cause permanent brain damage in some children.

With your charges properly stowed in front of the set — or sets, if age differences are a problem — you are free to go about your business. Heck, if the DVD is long enough and you live close enough to the course, you can probably get in a few holes. Chances are, you'll return 90 minutes later to find the children just as you left them, except perhaps marginally less intelligent. Your wife will never know you were gone. Your *children* will never know you were gone. You'll be happy, she'll be happy, they'll be happy.

And isn't that the point, after all, in being the kind of family man who works arm in arm, shoulder to shoulder with his wife to care for their home and nurture their children? Whether you're cooking, cleaning, or taking care of the kids, you're helping to build a strong foundation for a relationship that will last a lifetime. And the guys at work will probably never even find out.

Chapter 5

Marrying Your Wife's Family

Experts say that when you marry a woman, you marry her entire family. I'm not really sure what this means, except that it sounds like something illegal in this country but probably practiced regularly in emerging nations. Perhaps it means that what your wife brings to the marriage (in addition, if you're lucky, to a substantial savings account) is the sum total of all her experiences as a member of another family — a family that, in many cases, may be quite different from your own; a family whose habits, whose customs, whose traditions, whose very way of looking at the world might seem foreign to you. Heck, in this modern-day melting pot that is America, your wife's family may actually *be* foreign, or even from Wisconsin (a state noted for its sense of humor).

Remember when you used to wonder who actually eats liver and onions? Or what kind of tacky people celebrate Christmas by filling their yard with plywood Smurf cutouts? Then you met your wife, you met her family — and now you know.

And what about your wife? Remember that your family may seem just as foreign to her, especially if she is actually a foreigner. How do you think she felt the first time your father asked her to pull his finger, then broke wind so loudly the neighbors dialed 911? Or that first night she stayed at your parents' house, when your little brother barged into her room to ask if she'd seen his pet snake? Believe it or not, this may not have been considered normal behavior in her family. Then again, what do you expect from people who eat liver and onions?

Of course, the fact that the two of you got married, anyway, and that you've stayed married all these years means those issues really didn't bother you that much, after all. Or that you have since resolved them. Or that a deep and bitter pool of resentment festers within, just waiting to boil over. In any case, you're still married, your families are what they are, and you're going to have to learn to deal with them.

I certainly don't have all the answers where in-laws are concerned; in fact, I don't have any of the answers. Nevertheless, I do want to touch in this chapter upon three areas with which I *have* had some experience: visiting, doing business, and naming children.

Visiting and the Other Family

It's quite natural that you would rather visit your own family on holidays and other occasions. You feel more comfortable there. You are served the same dishes you learned to love, or at least tolerate, as a child. No one looks at you funny when you pass gas or asks you to sleep on the porch.

But as a family man, you have an obligation to your wife and children to visit her family at least as often as you visit your own. If mere love for your wife and respect for her feelings are not sufficient reasons, then remember that your wife's family members are your children's blood relatives. This explains why your children behave so strangely at times.

One of the best ways to achieve balance in your family visiting is to have some sort of prearranged schedule. This will prevent you and your wife from having to fight over, I mean *decide*, where you're going every time a holiday rolls around. A schedule can be as basic as a simple rotation system, alternating visits to her family and yours. Or, if you prefer, it can involve complicated formulae, the *Farmer's Almanac*, and calls to the Psychic Hotline.

The drawback to this method is that it is bound to be interrupted by some special event: while eating Thanksgiving dinner with your wife's family, for example, you learn that Aunt Marge from Wisconsin will be coming for Christmas. "Oh, honey, we just *have* to have Christmas at my family's this year! I haven't seen Aunt Marge since her face lift," your wife says, batting her eyes. You sit there wondering if her family serves Eggplant Parmesan instead of turkey for Christmas dinner, too.

This is nothing, however, that can't be settled through a little negotiation. One Christmas should be worth at least a Memorial Day, a Fourth of July, and a Labor Day, with perhaps a back rub thrown in.

Another possible schedule is to have set destinations for specific holidays: every Thanksgiving with your folks, every Christmas with hers, and so on. One of the advantages of this approach is that it allows for the development of family traditions, so that your children in particular will know exactly what to look forward to when spending Christmas at Grandma and Grandpa So-and-so's. (That would be your wife's parents, of course. Your parents may be many things, but they are definitely not so-and-sos).

The problem here is that, sooner or later, an individual on one side of the family or the other (probably someone's mother) is going to say something like, "It's such a shame you can't be here for Christmas this year." There are a number of possible responses to this kind of blatant manipulation, but here are two you should probably squelch: "We've been over this a hundred times, Mom" (if it's your mother speaking) and "Yes, but not as big a shame as the fact that we're here right now" (if it's your mother-in-law).

Instead, you should smile winningly and say, "Yes, it *is* a shame, but we'll be back for Easter [or whenever]. Meanwhile, you're welcome anytime to squeeze your fat, retired, lard butts into a car and come visit us." Okay, in the interests of family unity, you should probably leave out everything between "to" and "come." But that doesn't mean you can't think it, or that their butts aren't actually fat.

The truth is, many families nowadays are choosing not to travel at all, or to travel very little. Let's face it, whoever coined the phrase "Happy Holidays" wasn't thinking about loading presents for three kids into a minivan and driving six hours on Christmas Eve. So save yourself a post-season breakdown and let your family come visit you — especially those members of your family (including your in-laws) who are in fact retired and don't have small children at home. Who knows, maybe they'll even bring the Eggplant Parmesan.

Risky Business

Let me state, first of all, that what I am going to say in the next few paragraphs applies just as much to your own family as to your in-laws. After all, you probably have just as many deadbeats, weirdos, and incompetents in your family as your wife has in hers, give or take a few. Yes, I know they're *your* deadbeats, weirdos, and incompetents, as opposed to a bunch of deadbeats, weirdos, and incompetents you hardly know, but that really won't be much comfort in the long run.

One of the advantages to having a large extended family on both sides is that there is bound to be someone in that group who knows how to do just about anything — plumbing, automobile repair, braiding cornrows. Thus you can probably use your family ties to get a lot of free or very cheap labor. One caveat, however: such labor is usually worth exactly what you pay.

As a rule, then, I would advise against doing business with family members on a large scale, even if they offer you a discount. You're going to find it very difficult to maintain peace in the family while suing the pants off of that cousin or brother-in-law who installed your shower enclosure upside-down, or invested your company pension fund in Iraqi biomedical research, or lost his bubble gum while performing your wife's hysterectomy. For those kinds of major transactions, you should hire reputable, impersonal professionals unrelated to yourself by blood or marriage whom you can make to pay dearly for screwing up.

It is permissible, however, to ask family members for help with smaller, "do-it-yourself" type projects, such as painting, minor home repairs, or moving. In fact, if you get enough family members involved, you may actually be able to avoid doing-it-yourself. This is especially true if you have in the past rendered similar service to those very family members. Just make sure you're there to supervise; this way, if they start to destroy everything you've lived and worked for, you can always say something like, "Gee, you know, on second thought, I don't think I'll fix that hole in my roof after all. Bye. Thanks for your help. See you at Christmas."

The other type of business transaction that is common among family members is borrowing money. "Neither a borrower nor a lender be" is an excellent ideal, within families as well as in general, but the truth is we all need to borrow money occasionally, just as we all from time to time get hit up for loans. And I've found that family members are marginally more likely than mere acquaintances or even friends to pay you back when you lend and less likely to demand your car title or break your legs when you borrow. After all, they have to share Eggplant Parmesan with you at Thanksgiving.

Still, I believe you should borrow from or lend to only those family members with whom you share a strong bond of trust and friendship. That lets out all your wife's relatives, as well as most of your own. Just kidding, of course. I'm sure there are many people on your wife's side of the family for whom you would gladly give your life. Why, last Christmas at your in-laws, weren't you wishing you could just go ahead and die?

What's in a Name?

Nothing brings two families together like common grandchildren — and it's quite possible that nothing can drive a deeper wedge between them. Sometimes competition for the affection of the grandchild, along with attempts on the part of the child's parents to appease both sides of the family, can begin before the infant is even born. This is when the parents will be inundated with "suggestions" for naming the child.

After all, your wife's great aunt Gertrude was your mother-in-law's favorite relative, so why *shouldn't* you name the child after her if it's a girl? And your father may never forgive you if you decline to pass his name on to the third generation. What's wrong with Harold, anyway? It's a perfectly good, strong, masculine name. Then again, your father still hasn't forgiven you for deciding to go by your middle name, Scott, which was your mother's brother's name. And so it goes.

All these "suggestions," together with no small amount of pressure and the fact that you and your wife may be genuinely confused, can lead to some pretty poor naming decisions. For example, there are what I call "combination names," made by taking the names of two family members — usually one on the husband's side and one on the wife's — and putting them together to form the child's first and middle names. Often this is done without consideration for rhythm, alliteration, or ethnic origin. Thus there are children who go through life — or at least until marriage — with names like "Leigh Svetlana Morgenstern" or "Mortimer Christopher Higgins" or "Bill Runs-With-Wild-Horses Smith." And what about those children with two middle names instead of just one? Can anyone doubt that this is a transparent ploy on the part of the parents to be included in one more will?

Even worse are "hybrid names," formed by putting parts of two names together. I have no doubt your Aunt Matilda and your wife's second cousin Gwendolyn are two of the finest people who ever lived, but do you really think that will be of any comfort to your daughter, Gwentilda? And, call me crazy (yes, I know, you already have several times by now), but I'm convinced that, even though his two grandfathers *are* named

Ben and Mark, you probably want to think twice about calling your son Bark. Then he'd really be up a tree. (Hah!)

Finally, and worst of all, there are the "trans-gender" names. These usually result when parents make a firm decision on a name before even knowing the child's sex. There are two types of trans-gender names. The first occurs when parents choose a name — say, the name of the paternal grandfather, or of the mother's sister — and stick to their choice even when the baby turns out to be of the opposite sex. Thus we have girls with names like Charles and Michael and boys named Shirley and Lynn. The second type of trans-gender name is peculiar to girls and involves the feminizing (like that word? I just made it up) of the chosen masculine name; hence, "Rodericka," "Bobbette," and "Roscoline."

The best policy is for you and your wife to please yourselves, whether in the naming of your children or in anything else. You're never going to please everyone on both sides of the family, or even most of them, so why ruin your vacation or your child's entire life trying? Above all, never do anything just because of a little pressure from the family. Hold out for valuable heirlooms, or cash.

PART TWO:

The Associative Property of Multiplication

Next to your wife, your children are the most important people in your immediate family. Then again, other than your wife, your children are the *only* people in your immediate family. You, of course, don't count. If you doubt this, then you aren't spending nearly enough time at home.

It has been said that the best thing a man can do for society is to raise his children to be good citizens. I'm sure this is true in many cases. On the other hand, the best thing some of us could do for society would be to take our children to a remote wilderness and leave them there to be reared by wild animals. But then, that would bring the people from PETA down on our necks, and we don't want that.

Whenever young people who are contemplating matrimony ask me what kind of changes marriage brought about in my life, I always tell them the same thing: getting married wasn't a tremendously life-altering event for me. Since I had dated my wife-to-be for over a year at that point, it mostly meant we paid rent on one apartment instead of two and I didn't have to leave at night. And of course there were certain other fringe benefits.

No, the great change in my life, I tell them, came when our first child was born — as a result, incidentally, of those very fringe benefits. That's when my time began to be no longer my own. That's when I began to grow weak in the stomach worrying over everything from diaper rash to the rising cost of college tuition. That's when I began trying to get by on 42 minutes of sleep a night. I tell people this knowing full well it might cause them to think twice about having children. In some cases, that would probably be a good thing. They can have pets instead.

And by the way, as a family man, don't you just enjoy hearing, from couples who have made a conscious decision not to reproduce, how their pets are like children to them? Sure they are. We all make our children go to the bathroom outside, leave them in small cages to be cared for by strangers when we go on vacation, and neuter them as soon as they reach puberty (say, that's not a bad idea). It's amusing to observe one of these couples after they have an actual child. Sometimes you can even pick up a perfectly good dog, cheap.

For those of us who have chosen to raise children instead of animals, it can be the most rewarding and frustrating of life's endeavors. All family men know what a deeply spiritual experience it is to look into your infant's eyes, see him smiling up at you, and feel the warmth penetrate your very being as he urinates on your freshly laundered shirt. Such is the essence of parenthood.

(By the way, if you're raising both children *and* animals, I think all the same things apply, except you're roughly twice as likely to be peed upon. And if you're raising children who *are* animals — well, join the club.)

As a family man, your responsibility to your children is to be a father to them. This means more than merely contributing sperm, which apparently a dead man can do; more even than providing food, clothing, and a nice home for them to utterly destroy. It means being willing to discipline them when discipline is required, and when your wife can't be persuaded to do it instead of you. It means spending time with them, time you might rather spend playing golf or having a colonoscopy. Above all, it means teaching them to be good human beings, perhaps by showing them videotapes of good human beings you know.

Or maybe the best way to teach them is by your own example. So you might want to take a look at those good-human-being videos yourself, sometime.

Chapter 6

Where Would Rivalry Be Without Siblings?

They say that children are a gift from God — final and incontrovertible proof that God has quite the sense of humor. Perhaps, like many family men, you've been thus blessed two, three, even four or more times, as the trend these days seems to be moderately in that direction. I'm not sure if this is because people actually want more children, or if they just feel the need to justify their multi-passenger minivans and SUVs.

For my part, I've always thought that having only one child is a bit like having just one doughnut: it might be better for your health, but later on you'll probably wish you'd had more. I also believe that children raised without siblings are almost certain to grow up spoiled, obnoxious, and self-centered, as opposed to children raised *with* siblings, who are merely *likely* to grow up spoiled, obnoxious, and self-centered.

The real beauty of having more than one child, though, is that however your children turn out, you can place the blame — and the children themselves can place the blame, during expensive therapy sessions — at least partially on their brothers and sisters. Parents of an only child must be prepared to shoulder *all* the responsibility for screwing up that child's life. Best of all, if one of your children happens to turn out well, you and your wife may take all the credit, as this happy accident clearly occurred despite the child's conflicted relationships with his or her good-for-nothing siblings.

I mentioned that the trend seems to be toward having more than two children, and this is certainly the case, at least among couples I know. Even some of our friends who had steadfastly maintained for years that they would never have more than two children have recently had their third, either out of choice or by discovering that becoming intimate only once a month is not in and of itself a reliable form of birth control.

Occasionally one of these couples, upon learning they're expecting, will ask us what it's like to have a third child (my wife and I were among the first in our peer group to break the two-child barrier). It's like this, we tell them: when your first child is five or six months old, you put him in his high chair and give him a bowl of dry cereal to munch on. Soon, your floor is covered with dry cereal, which you dutifully sweep up. Later, when he finds one you missed and starts to put it in his mouth, you snatch it away from him in horror. "No, no. Yuckee, yuckee!" you say.

With your second child, you go through the same steps, except that when he begins to eat the cereal off the floor, you pretend you don't notice. (At this point both husband and wife begin to titter and nod knowingly.)

Your third child? You simply plop him on the floor, toss him a handful of cereal, and say, "Here, eat."

Of course, as I mentioned earlier, my wife and I have gone on even beyond three. I know four children is not a large family by pre-boomer standards, but for some people nowadays it seems to mark you as either ignorant of basic birth control methods or religious beyond all good sense.

When we were expecting our fourth, nearly everyone to whom I broke the news asked the same two questions: "Did you do this on purpose?" and "Which one of you is going to get fixed?" I always answered that not only had we done it on purpose, but that I had the date marked on my calendar for two months in advance; and that neither one of us needs to get anything fixed, thank you, as everything is obviously working just fine.

But I digress. You may not share with me the experience of having four kids, but if you're a family man, you probably have at least two. And that means you're going to have to deal with them not just as children but as siblings, with all that the term implies. What forces are really at work in sibling relationships? And what can you do to ensure that your children turn out to be well adjusted, or failing that, that they move out of state and change their names?

The most powerful motivator in any sibling relationship is competition. From infancy to adolescence, children spend their lives competing with one another for toys, for the last brownie, for who gets to sit up front in the family car — and for primacy in the eyes of their parents. No matter how much you try to assure your children that you love them all equally, each child will always suspect that you actually favor his or her brothers and sisters. Even if this is true, it isn't healthy for the child to believe it, and it can lead to a heightened sense of competition.

Of course, you can use this to your advantage and enjoy some really inexpensive entertainment by staging contests between your children for things like shoes and food. After all, it's a dog-eat-dog world out there, and a six-year-old who can't beat his eight-year-old sister at "HORSE" probably doesn't deserve to eat, anyway.

The dynamics of sibling relationships, however, are best understood in the context of the various brother-sister permutations, recognizing that some have mutated more variously than others.

Brothers in Arms

The first thing you should know about having boys is this: one boy will probably not be able to destroy your entire house by himself. At least, if you have some basic handyman skills and spend every free moment making repairs, you should just about be able to keep up with him. If you have more than one boy, however, there is no hope. Your only options are a) keep them chained to the wall in separate rooms; b) quit your job and devote all your time to damage control; c) hire a contractor full time; or, d) accept the fact that your home will be in shambles from the day the second boy is born until the day the last one moves out and begins venting his aggression on some unsuspecting college dormitory room.

Of course, there are things you can do to mitigate these destructive tendencies somewhat, such as encouraging your boys to play outside, preferably at a neighbor's house. If you live in the city, you can take them — better yet, persuade your wife to take them — to the park, where the cost of property damage is divided among all taxpayers and thus needn't come from your pocket alone. If you have a yard, you can erect sturdy play equipment, such as a metal swing set, which will last approximately six months with one boy, less with two or more. The wooden models, which are four times as expensive, may last a little longer, unless you have the incredibly poor judgment to buy your sons hatchets or allow them to take karate.

All of this destructiveness, however, though frustrating and expensive for you, has one singular advantage: it creates a powerful brotherly bonding experience.

There is no question that boys are competitive as well as aggressive. From the time the younger boy can walk, if not before, his older brother will begin teaching him to play rough games such as football and mixed martial arts, probably in your living room. You can deal with this by making strict rules, such as "any kick-off that breaks one of mom's irreplaceable collection of priceless Waterford crystal will automatically be brought back to midfield."

The older boy's motives here seem obvious: he knows he can dominate the little tyke and thus feed his own self-esteem on his brother's bloated carcass, figuratively speaking (or perhaps not). But there is also another force at work, the age-old law of the jungle, in which the older male says to the younger one, "let me show you what it takes to survive!" If only he would share that information with you.

Thus, as your boys grow, you will see them more and more often teaming up against outsiders, when they are not fighting each other, which is to say every third Tuesday.

Included among these "outsiders" are you and your wife, as well as their sisters. This may be difficult for you to accept, but it's a necessary step in their psychosocial development. (I picked up that term in college. Impressive, huh?) Don't despair, though: you can probably worm your way into their confidence and become at least a temporary member of the club by helping them conspire against their mother and sisters.

The Feminine Mistake

Girls relate to each other — and to their parents — in much more subtle ways. When boys would throw punches, girls merely stop speaking to one another. When boys would try to drown you out with loud voices, girls beseech with long imploring looks. And, in play, while boys strive to outdo one another in feats of bravado, girls are almost coldly analytical in their observations of peers.

It has been noted that pre-adolescent girls tend to favor games like "house" and "hospital," in which all participants have roughly equal roles, as opposed to highly competitive boys' games like "kill the man with the ball." There is at least one very good reason for this, if I may say so without sounding too sexist (although why I should worry about that at this point, I don't know): most girls attempting to play kill the man with the ball would be, well, killed. And besides, in a few years they won't need to carry a ball to be chased by boys. On the other hand, the only socially acceptable reason for a boy to be chased by other boys is that he is, in fact, carrying a ball.

Girls do other things as well that might seem foreign to you. For example, as a boy growing up, would you even have considered allowing your brother to borrow your clothes? Your new clothes, I mean. The hand-me-downs he should be thankful for. Or how about sharing each other's personal hygiene products? If you're like me, you'd much rather stink than have to pick another guy's underarm hair off your deodorant stick.

But none of this seems to bother sisters. In fact, they appear to thrive on it, rummaging blissfully through each other's closets and drawers even when not on speaking terms. Plus, by the time they start to use deodorant, they've begun shaving their underarms, anyway. Thus, some might conclude that sisters are naturally kinder to each other, more loving of one another, less prone to the fits of rage and near hatred that stem from open competition.

Don't bet on it.

In some ways, I believe girls are even more competitive than boys, or perhaps it would be more accurate to say they're competitive on a deeper level. I know I could be crucified for saying this — so let's just keep it between us family men — but with girls, competition seems to take on almost Darwinian overtones. I'm not saying your eight- and ten-year-old daughters are competing for male sexual attention; if they are, you have bigger problems than mere sibling rivalry. It's just that, whereas boys make up games to *simulate* aggression and competition, but in which no one actually gets hurt (unless you're foolish enough to join in, in which case *you* will get hurt), girls seem to understand early on that it is life itself which is the real game, no holds barred and winner take all.

So my advice to the family man as the father of daughters is this: don't mess with them. Be kind, gentle, and considerate with your daughters. Discipline them when necessary, which is to say when you can't persuade your wife to take care of it or think of a good excuse to get out of it. Model for them the kind of man you would want them to marry. (Remember, if your daughter marries a jerk, it's your fault. And, by the way, feel free to use this line of reasoning in your next argument with your father-in-law.) But don't put yourself in a position where you might be a permanent object of a daughter's wrath.

Above all, don't ever come between two sisters. I know when you were a kid, you and your brother could be trading blows one minute and defending the earth against hordes of alien invaders the next. Girls need more time to work things out. They'll either forgive each other eventually, or else they won't speak to each other for the next 74 years. Either way, there's nothing you can do about it.

Boys and Girls Together

Perhaps the most complex sibling relationships are those between brothers and sisters. What makes these so interesting is that they sometimes take on the aspects of same-sex relationships. In other words, sometimes a brother and sister will act like brothers, while at other times they'll act like sisters. This is especially true if your children have gender-identity problems to begin with.

If a boy and girl are the only two children in a home, or the only two old enough to play, you may notice that each will occasionally co-opt the other into his or her games. For example, if there are no other boys around, your son may from time to time persuade his sister to play football with him in the yard. If he comes in bloody after these sessions, I suggest you steer him into art classes. Likewise, your daughter may attempt to engage her brother in her favorite pastimes: house, dolls, etc. Despite your natural aversion to your son's playing with dolls, most psychologists warn that you shouldn't discourage him from doing so, unless the dolls in question are life-size and inflatable.

Brother-sister relationships are also strongly influenced by the siblings' respective ages. An older sister, for example, will usually attempt to "mother" her little brother, even if the age difference is only a year or two, while an older brother will almost always tend to be overly protective of his sister, to the point of driving off or even disabling potential dates. (There is something vaguely Freudian in that, but I can't quite put my finger on it. Maybe I'm just dreaming it up.) In either case, the younger brother or sister may well come to resent his or her older sibling, but that is the eternal price he or she will have to pay for being born second.

The dynamics of brother-sister relationships can be even more pronounced when there are more than two children involved. A girl with more than one younger brother will, by the time she is seven, come to sound more like their mother than, well, their mother. And if you have several attractive young daughters, you may come home from work one day to find your elder son digging a moat.

Conversely, a girl raised with several older brothers is likely to become either a hardened tomboy (these girls often grow up to be pro athletes or college professors) or the kind of little princess who wears lace dresses to play kickball; while a boy raised with older sisters will either be very, shall we say, "sensitive," or begin lifting weights at age six.

Competition between brothers and sisters often manifests itself — more so than in other sibling relationships — through jealousy, especially where their parents' attention is concerned. The boys will be convinced that you are easier on the girls, while a girl who isn't interested in some of the same things you are, like sports, may complain that you spend more time with her brothers. There are things you can do to balance out these perceived inequities, which I will touch on in subsequent chapters. For now, you simply need to understand that such feelings are a natural result of sibling rivalry, and that the only way for you not to be your children's chief enemy is to pit them against one another. As I've already indicated, this can be fun but may have negative side effects.

These, then, are just a few of the things you'll need to keep in mind as you attempt to referee your children's sibling rivalries. Like all referees, you can expect at times to be berated and subjected to abusive language — and that's just from your wife. But you must at all costs maintain your composure. After all, you may not be able to prevent your kids from competing with one another, but you can keep your self-respect from being the prize.

Chapter 7

Of Spare Rods and Spoiled Children

When we hear the word "discipline," most of us think immediately of *punishment.* We must always bear in mind, however, that discipline is much more than mere punishment. That's just the fun part. The word itself is derived from the Latin word for "student," so discipline is actually the process of teaching and training our children as they grow. And we all know some of the best ways to do this include severe beatings, sensory deprivation, and withholding of basic necessities.

Just kidding. The truth, of course, is that most of us don't enjoy disciplining our children at all, which is why we don't do it as much as we should. But as a family man and a parent, you have a responsibility to the community to see that your children are properly trained. Otherwise, they might pee on the carpet.

The first key to effective discipline, according to the experts, is setting appropriate limits. This means that the rules and guidelines you make for your children are reasonable and calculated to be in their best interests. Personally, I think this concept is somewhat overrated. It certainly fails to take into account the psychological advantage parents can gain by making rules that are arbitrary and ridiculous (see Chapter 1), not to mention the practical value of such arbitrary and ridiculous rules. After all, how can we claim to be preparing our children for the real world if our homes are bastions of reason and fairness?

A more important aspect of good discipline, and one on which the experts also agree, is consistency. This means, first of all, that whatever rules you make and whatever punishments you proscribe will be rigidly and uniformly enforced. I think this is basically a good idea, especially in the case of younger children, who in order to feel secure must be able to anticipate the consequences of various behaviors. However, it may be confusing to older children, who have probably already noted the apparent randomness of such events as having blond hair or getting hit by a truck.

Being consistent also means that you and your wife have agreed beforehand on your approach to discipline, and that you are both equally involved in enforcing the rules and meting out punishments. This is a great thing for you as a father, because it means your children will resent your wife just as much as they resent you. And, of course, as I have stated repeatedly, it is vital that you and your wife appear to be united in all things, *especially* discipline, even if in this case it just means that the two of you seem equally petty and sadistic.

Choose Your Weapon

Speaking of sadism, there has been much debate over the years concerning what methods of punishment are acceptable in society and which are most effective. For centuries, *corporal punishment* — the common spanking — was considered the *sine qua non* of parental guidance, but lately it has fallen out of favor. Its supporters point to the famous warning in the Bible about the dangers of "sparing the rod." Detractors argue that the reference here is to the shepherd's crook, which generally was used in ancient times to guide wayward sheep gently back onto the path, not to bludgeon the crap out of them.

Spanking is thus considered by many to be too violent, a throwback to a more barbaric era. And indeed, those times were known for their particularly brutal forms of punishment, such as burning, hanging, and beheading, not to mention ear pulling, pinching, and having one's knuckles smacked with a wooden ruler.

A more modern form of punishment is what we might refer to as *incarceration*, meaning to remove the offender from the company of non-offenders and place him in a restrictive environment. Some refer to this as “jail” or “prison,” while others call it “dinner at the in-laws.” As a tool for disciplining children, incarceration takes on a variety of forms, from the five-minute “time-out” to four years of military boarding school. Most experts agree that incarceration is a much more effective form of punishment than spanking; after all, what ten-year-old wouldn’t rather get four licks with a hardwood paddle the size of a cutting board than spend fifteen minutes playing Nintendo in his room?

Another common form of punishment involves *loss of privileges*, which in this context has nothing to do with the demise of your love life. A common example of this in society is when a judge revokes the license of a convicted drunk driver, thus effectively taking away his privilege to drive. Of course, it is sometimes difficult to translate this sort of thing into family life, since, to their way of thinking, our children have no privileges, only *rights*. Nevertheless, you can always get a child’s attention by taking away something he or she values: a favorite toy, television time, drinking water, basic human dignity.

Those who view discipline as a true learning process, and not just an excuse to administer punishment, might argue that *gentle persuasion* is preferable to force or duress. In fact, we have a term for such people. We call them “parents of juvenile delinquents.” Their basic philosophy is that children respond better to reason than to force, and that they will be motivated more by love than by fear. This sounds perfectly plausible, as long as you’re speaking abstractly about someone else’s children. As for yours, the only reason they need is BECAUSE YOU SAID SO!

Finally, there is my favorite way of imposing discipline, which is by using *psychological dirty tricks*, or what your teenager might call “head games.” One common variety of dirty trick involves the white lies, half-truths, exaggerations, and fairy stories we tell our children in order to manipulate them into doing what we want. These are particularly effective with younger children, but if you’re creative enough, and a good enough liar, you should be able to influence even the older ones this way — or, failing that, at least severely tick them off.

Another widely used dirty trick actually comes in the guise of a beneficial and highly recommended approach. The textbooks call it "positive reinforcement," but it is better known as "bribery." There is no question that children react favorably to bribery; indeed, it often works when all threats fail. But I call it a dirty trick because, from the child's point of view, the desired behavior is seldom worth the reward offered.

A dollar for cleaning up one's room? Really? A brownie for eating an entire plate full of dead green food? Come on. We may be able to pull this on younger children, who still think two pennies are worth more than one dime (I picked up a lot of extra change that way when my kids were small), but it gets harder as they grow. Ultimately, we must either up the ante — how about a new car for dumping the tattooed boyfriend? — or revert to other forms of persuasion, such as begging. In the case of the tattooed boyfriend, it might be worth it.

The Personality Test

In any case, the method and severity of the discipline you choose in any given instance will depend on a number of factors, including the nature of the infraction, the child's age and personality, your own stress level, and the alignment of Venus with Mercury. The experts will tell you it's best to make the punishment fit the crime, and I agree in most cases. However, you should never underestimate the psychological advantage to be gained from the occasional outrageous discrepancy between the seriousness of the infraction and the punishment assigned.

Don't you think if we summarily shot every hundredth speeder, for example, our highways would be a little safer? So it is with our children: the seven-year-old who is grounded for two months for picking his nose in public will think twice before inserting *that* finger again.

You must also take into account the personality of the child. I mean, there probably *are* some children who will respond to gentle persuasion, especially if they are first properly sedated and restrained. And even within the same family, there will be children for whom a spanking is the worst possible punishment and others whom it won't even phase; kids who are always on the make for a bribe (who's manipulating whom?) and others who will simply stare at you like the scumbag you are. As a father, you will eventually get a feel for what works best with your own children, mostly through the kind of trial and error that they'll be explaining to therapists for decades to come.

By far the most important factor in choosing a punishment, however, is the age of the child. It is simply a fact that some forms are more effective with certain age groups. Moreover, your approach to using each form will be different when you deal with children of different ages. You may not accomplish much by sending your fifteen-year-old to time-out, for example, or by rescinding your infant's cell phone privileges. But that doesn't mean those *types* of punishments can't be effective when adjusted for the five basic age groups.

Pavlov's Babies

It is a common misconception that infants are too young to be disciplined. If we recognize discipline for what it really is, a form of teaching or training, we see that this is manifestly not true. After all, we all know the story of Pavlov's dogs, which were trained to salivate at the sound of a bell. Most infants are at least as smart as dogs. Heck, they salivate all the time, whether they hear a bell or not.

Of course, with infants, you're very limited in your methods. You can't exactly slap a two-month-old around; your wife might leave you, you might be arrested, and it might even affect how that child feels about you. Nor can you deprive him of very much, other than food (again, you're looking at jail time), attention, and sensory stimulation. The child, on the other hand, can deprive you of a great deal, and often will.

What you're left with, then, is essentially a hybrid form of incarceration and loss of privilege. I believe a child has the capacity to learn, at three or four months of age, that if she exhibits certain undesirable behaviors — loud crying, for example, or excessive drooling — then she may be placed into a small, barred enclosure in a dark, quiet room and left to scream for hours. Well, okay, maybe minutes, but it will seem like hours to the child.

Thus, as long as you and your wife are consistent in your reaction to a particular behavior, the child will begin to make the connection, through a kind of Pavlovian thought process: "If I cry, Mommy and Daddy will put me away in a dark room and leave me for many baby-hours. Therefore, I will not cry. I will grow to resent Mommy and Daddy bitterly and may join a street gang at age twelve to get back at them, but in the meantime, I will not cry." As a parent, this is all you can hope for.

Suffer the Children

With toddlers, on the other hand, the possibilities are endless. We're talking here about ages one through three, which according to Piaget is the time of life when children learn to recognize the separateness of their own bodies, to identify activities they particularly enjoy, and to form attachments to objects and individuals. All of these wonderful psychosocial developments can be easily manipulated for the purpose of exacting punishment.

Spanking, for example, is very effective with toddlers, who are generally old enough not to bruise easily and have a very low tolerance for pain. (Their own pain, I mean; their capacity for inflicting pain on others is endless). You should be careful, though, not to apply too much force and to use only the palm side of your open hand, unless a hairbrush or wooden mixing spoon is readily available. Personally, I believe spanking is particularly called for when the behavior is something that might ultimately endanger the child, such as playing in the street or attempting to drink from the toilet.

If you don't have the stomach for swatting the little tyke, you may be able to achieve the same result through a form or incarceration known as the "time out," which basically involves putting the child aside in a quiet room or even in a separate chair for a short period of time. Why exactly this works so well with toddlers, I don't know. But a child who might choose on his own to sit in a certain chair for a quarter of an hour will act as though he has been dipped in lye if *forced* to sit there for thirty seconds.

Toddlers also hate to have their toys taken away from them — even those toys they haven't played with since discarding them in favor of the box last Christmas. This type of punishment (essentially, loss of privilege) works best when the toy in question was actually involved in the infraction — for example, braining a younger sibling with a steel dump truck. (Sample parental response: "No, no Tyler! If you open another gash requiring 20 stitches in little sister's forehead, Daddy will take the truck away from you!")

Some would argue that toddlers can be reasoned with, gently persuaded to see the error of their ways. These are, no doubt, the same people who take their dogs to psychiatrists and believe chimps can learn to sign Virgil's *Aeneid.*

It's not that I'm opposed to taking a mental approach to disciplining toddlers. I just believe that this approach should consist mostly of psychological dirty tricks, like the stories we tell our children of the bogeymen, witches, and monsters who will do unspeakable things to them if they misbehave. (As opposed to their older brothers and sisters, who will do unspeakable things to them whether they behave or not.)

Or you can combine mind games with other forms of punishment. For example, instead of merely taking your child's favorite toy away from him, tell him you're going to give it to another little boy, perhaps even adopt that little boy and give him your child's room. You may wonder, years later, why he still wets his bed at age seventeen, but at least you won't have let the little bugger get away with anything.

The Wonder Years

The next age group is roughly four through eight or nine, depending on the child. Actually, I could say, "depending on the sex of the child," because I've learned that girls really do mature faster than boys and thus can enter the "pre-teen" years as early as age eight (age four, if regularly entered in beauty pageants). This is something I did not want to accept when I was a nine-year-old boy, despite ample visual evidence, which I admit I spent a great deal of time observing. Approaching middle age, however, I've decided there is some justice in the universe, after all. Those snooty girls who reached puberty years ahead of me? They still look years older — unfortunately for them.

In any case, it is with the four-to-nine age group that discipline really begins to be fun, because these kids respond to so many different types of punishment. Please understand that when I say "respond," I don't mean they learn to behave. Far from it. But their reactions are much more animated than, say, an infant's, and they are more susceptible than toddlers or pre-teens to combinations of conventional punishments and psychological dirty tricks.

Take spanking, for instance. With a toddler, you might just give his or her little bottom a swat. But with older children, there are all kinds of cool mind games you can play. One that my mother used regularly was the "wait till your father gets home" game. (I suppose, in our liberated society, a father could just as easily play "wait till your mother gets home.") A toddler may not have the imagination necessary to make this game worthwhile, but a five- or six-year-old can and will spend an entire day obsessing about the punishment to come, to the point where the fear and anxiety become far more excruciating than the spanking itself would ever be. This, of course, is exactly what you have in mind.

Then there is the "cut your own switch" game. Forcing a child to select and prepare the instrument of his own punishment has got to be one of the more diabolical forms of torture humankind has ever conceived. But it's fun. To prolong the pleasure, you can even reject the child's first selection or two. This will reduce him/her to a quivering mass long before the first blow is delivered, making the spanking itself almost an afterthought.

Children in this age group can also be manipulated through incarceration and loss of privilege. I should warn you, though, that simply sending an eight- or nine-year-old to his or her room probably won't have much effect on the child's behavior, since the room of a typical eight- or nine-year-old nowadays is equipped with enough electronic equipment to outfit a small air force. Sitting for thirty minutes in front of a computer game called "Misanthropic Mass Murderers from Mars" may seem like punishment to you, but it probably won't to your son.

You can, however, use other forms of incarceration with this age group: making the child stay inside on a nice day when everyone else is playing outside, keeping the child home from an outing or activity, locking the child in a medium-sized storage trunk and shoving it under the stairwell. This last one works especially well if you plan on having company over, or if you want to borrow the child's laptop.

Ultimately, though, the most effective form of punishment for these children is loss of privilege. Because, unlike toddlers, they actually *have* privileges, such as getting to stay up late on certain nights, going over to friends' houses, and abusing their younger siblings. They also have some pretty neat stuff, like bikes, roller blades, firearms, and recreational vehicles. Confiscating any of these items can be an excellent form of punishment, especially if you get to play with it. I mean, you probably never had stuff like that when *you* were a kid. Now you can be a conscientious father, appropriately disciplining your child, while at the same time getting to spend the entire afternoon riding a four-wheeler. What could be better?

They Grow Up Too Fast

Knowing how to discipline children in the middle age group — nine to twelve — can be difficult, since they exhibit almost a kind of schizophrenia. Sometimes they act like children, sometimes like teenagers. I've found that the best response is to treat them like teenagers but expect them to act like children, unless of course you *want* them to act like children, in which case they're certain to act like teenagers.

Pre-teens are a little too big — and frankly, not much fun — to spank. They've long since become inured to both the "wait till your father gets home" and the "cut your own switch" games, and you might actually hurt yourself hitting one of them. They do respond, however, to forms of incarceration and loss of privilege.

Pre-teens are at an age when they value their freedom highly, even if that only means getting to ride their bikes around the neighborhood whenever they want or going to the mall with their friends. In fact, if the key to having a good disciplinary strategy is understanding what an individual values — and I believe it is — then it's important for parents to recognize that, for the average suburban pre-teen, the weekly or bi-weekly trip to the mall is the most important event on the social calendar, or any other calendar.

You know what I'm talking about. You've seen them at the local mall, running in small packs, the Alpha male or female surrounded by four or five other gangly, pimply, Beta wannabes. You've wondered, as you've craned your neck and cursed them for standing in front of the Victoria's Secret poster, "where in the world are these kids' parents?" Their parents are at home, of course, enjoying a quiet Saturday, thrilled beyond belief that their pre-teens are at the mall annoying *you*, instead of at home annoying *them*, just as you would be.

Now, as one of those parents, you must recognize the power this knowledge gives you. Loathe as you may be to do it (no doubt, you've planned your weekends for months in advance on the assumption that your pre-teen would be at the mall annoying someone else), if your twelve- or thirteen-year-old disobeys house rules or otherwise misbehaves, then for the sake of discipline you may have to make the mall off limits for a week or two. This is known as *grounding*.

Even the threat of such a grounding is likely to be effective, because there are few things a child in this age group fears more. After one week away from the mall, the pre-teen's position in the pack begins to erode. In two weeks, the styles can change completely, and your unwitting son or daughter may show up at the end of his or her sentence in an outfit that has been *passé* for days.

Which brings me to the other concern that dominates the pre-teen's life: his or her appearance. Now, you may be tempted to think you can punish your pre-teen by making him or her wear clothes that are out-of-style — in other words, the ones you bought at the beginning of the school year. Unfortunately, this won't work; the child will simply go naked (as opposed to the teenager, who is alarmingly liable to go naked regardless). What you can do, however, is use the pre-teen's sensitivity about his or her appearance to subtly manipulate the child using psychological dirty tricks.

For example, it's always a good idea to suggest connections between undesirable behaviors and outbreaks of horrible acne. An older teenager may know from health class (the only class in which most teenagers listen, since the teacher occasionally mentions sex) that lying does not cause pimples.

But a pre-teen will probably believe you implicitly, especially if you talk knowingly about stress-induced acne and later allow the child to overhear you discussing casually with your wife an article you recently read on the subject. To reinforce this, wait until he shows up at the breakfast table with a brand-new, shiny red eruption, then lean over and ask softly, "Is there anything you'd like to tell me, son?"

Teen Angles

I don't intend to say too much about teenagers at this point, as I plan to devote an entire chapter to the species a little later. Let me just say, for our purposes here, that teenagers are by far the most difficult group to discipline — even more so than infants, with whom they have a lot in common: they sleep all the time, rising only to eat and complain; they are utterly egocentric; and they're liable to dump on you just when you're trying to make their life a little more pleasant.

Teenagers for the most part are far too big to be physically intimidated, too smart to be reasoned with, and too sophisticated to fall for your psychological dirty tricks, unless you have a truly devious mind. Indeed, the typical teenager thinks *you* are the stupid one, and that he or she can therefore manipulate *you*, a belief confirmed in the child's mind by those glen plaid golf slacks you like to wear on your day off. Thus, only the most devious of parents can play mind games with a teenager, usually by carefully turning the teen's attempted manipulations against him or her.

For example, say your seventeen-year-old son tells you he's planning to reserve a hotel room with his girlfriend after the prom. He assures you that this is only so the two of them can attend a post-prom party, sponsored by several parents, to be held at the hotel. No one can get in without a room reservation, he says without a trace of guile.

Now, there are several ways you might react. The permissive parent (also known as "the grandparent-to-be") will say, "Fine, go ahead, just be careful." (Ha!) The strict parent will say, "No way. Be home at 11:30," thus dooming the couple to hurried groping in the car, probably ruining their nice clothes, not to mention your upholstery.

The truly devious parent, however, will simply say, "Okay," then begin to lay his own plans, possibly involving a bribe to the concierge, a carefully constructed smoke bomb attached to the bed and designed to be triggered by pressure on the springs, and a strategically placed smoke detector. That's just one idea, but you see how much fun it could be, especially if you're outside with a water hose and a video camera. (Please note that, to play mind games with your teenager and win, it helps to have advanced CIA training.)

If you don't feel comfortable playing these kinds of games with your teenager (and most of us who haven't been under deep cover behind the iron curtain for five or six years don't), then you're left with only one bit of leverage: the fact that no self-respecting teenager will by choice spend even one waking minute at home. This makes grounding an ideal punishment for kids in this age group, provided you have bars on your windows, trained attack dogs, and hourly manned patrols. What isn't so bad for a younger child, or even a pre-teen — sitting at home watching TV or playing video games — is excruciating torture for a teenager, who would much rather be at *someone else's* house watching TV and playing video games. Please remember, though, before you pass sentence, that all in all you'd rather your teen were at someone else's house, too.

Finally, you can discipline your teens by taking things away from them, such as cell phones and car keys. The latter are especially important to older kids, as they symbolize mobility, the means to escape the suffocating environment you've worked all your life to provide. The fact that the keys are to *your* car is irrelevant to the teen; with the keys in his pocket, he is theoretically able to get in the vehicle and drive anyplace in the continental United States — as long as you give him money for gas.

I'll conclude this chapter with a few brief words of advice: don't hesitate to discipline your children, unless you can hire someone to do it for you, and ex-CIA agents don't work cheap. Set limits that are, if not reasonable and appropriate, at least arbitrary and ridiculous, and then stand firmly by those limits whenever you're not making exceptions or granting full immunity. Above all, make sure you and your wife are in complete agreement that she is totally responsible for enforcing the rules, as your doctor has told you that such a strain is likely to exacerbate your hemorrhoids. If you follow these simple guidelines, you will be virtually assured of having children that are no less well-adjusted than anyone else's. And that's saying something.

Chapter 8

Tempus Fugit or The Joy of Cursing in Latin

One of the great pleasures in life is spending time with your children. In fact, about the only thing more enjoyable is spending time away from them. It's not that you don't love your children, I know. It's just that they're... well, loud. And destructive. And obnoxious. Which isn't necessarily all bad. At least no one questions their paternity.

As a family man, you're going to find yourself spending a lot of time with your kids, whether you want to or not. In fact, all "dad-time" can be divided into two types: **elective** (time you *choose* to spend with your children) and **non-elective** (time you *have* to spend with them even though you'd rather be someplace else, such as Afghanistan). Elective time usually involves playing with your children at home or taking them on outings. Non-elective time, as the term implies, results from your inability to get out of it, either because your wife has the better excuse for being gone, or because some circumstance (e.g., bad weather, your neighbor's backed-up septic tank) has thrown you and the kids together in the house and there's nothing any of you can do about it.

Both types of time are crucial to a child's development. Children need to know first of all that their fathers value them enough to want to spend time with them. This builds self-esteem and leads to healthy gender role identification, a term which might mean almost anything but certainly sounds good in this context.

But children also need to understand that one cannot always do as one pleases, unless of course one has pictures of one's superiors in embarrassing situations or compromising positions (which is why it's always a bad idea to buy your child a camera). Thus, when you show your children you're there for them even when you don't want to be, being sure to let them know just how badly you don't want to be, you exemplify for them the kind of character and commitment to duty that made this country the late-night talk-show punch-line it is today.

Being with your children is also important for *your* physical health and psychological well-being. On a practical level, there are few better ways for you as a busy family man to stay in shape than by playing games with your kids in the front yard, games such as "keep the two-year-old out of the street" and "catch the ball before it shatters the neighbor's window."

Moreover, if you're physically and intellectually inferior to most of the adults you know, playing with children can actually boost *your* self-esteem. You may be the last one chosen for basketball at the Y, but with a little practice you can easily learn to back a five-year-old down under his six-foot goal and dunk in his face. Don't like losing all the time at poker or gin rummy? Toddlers are notoriously poor card players, and often have several dollars' worth of coins in their little piggy banks.

So it is definitely to your advantage to make the most of the time you spend with your children, whether you want to or not. What follows in this chapter, then, is a guide for doing just that.

Sex, Dinosaurs, and Video Tape

The most common reason for spending non-elective time with your children is that your wife is away for the evening and you're stuck at home with the kids. Chapter Four includes a lengthy discussion of babysitting as a household chore, and I don't intend to rehash those points here. My focus is rather on ways you can use this situation actually to spend time with your kids, as opposed to merely parking them in front of the TV (though I'm not backing away from my assertion that that's a good idea).

There are a number of fun things you and your kids can do when Mom is out for the evening. One is to rent a family video and watch it together. Now, you may think this sounds suspiciously like parking them in front of the TV, but what I have in mind here is something much more family-oriented and interactive, with all of you together in one room, the kids snuggled up on the couch or floor and you asleep in your recliner. If you keep the volume up, they probably won't even hear you snoring.

Even such a simple activity as this, however, is not without its inherent difficulties. First, there is the problem of *finding* a decent family movie, even if we define "decent" in the broadest possible terms as "not containing graphic depictions of human copulation." You may be shocked at some of the movies your pre-teenage and even younger children pick out, the so-called "PG-13" films which they will assure you their friends have watched repeatedly and which those friends' parents reportedly have not found offensive. This tells you more than you wanted to know about their friends' parents. On the bright side, if you do manage to stay awake through one of these films, you may learn something that will prove useful later, when Mom returns.

Your best bet for family entertainment is probably an animated film, preferably one that has not been secretly doctored by some perverted cartoonist. The message of some of these animated "classics," as I've noted elsewhere, may not be exactly what you would like, unless you want your daughter to run away from home at age sixteen and move in with some guy who looks like Chewbacca in drag. But at least they don't contain sexually explicit scenes, or none that you can see, anyway, as long as you play the tape at normal speed.

Animal films are also a good choice, especially for younger children. They may in fact contain explicit scenes, but watching animals copulate can at least be considered educational. The worst thing about animal movies is that they're often sad. I don't know about you, but I can watch any number of people, good or bad, being gunned down, eaten by crocodiles, or decapitated in car crashes without a trace of emotion, while "Old Yeller" never fails to reduce me to tears. So I guess the moral of the story is this: if you don't want your sons to be wimps, leave "Where the Red Fern Grows" on the shelf. Show them "Godfather, Part II" instead.

Once you have narrowed your choices, out of the 10,000 movies available, to the two or three you find acceptable, you still have the problem of *agreeing* on which one to rent. The girls will want the one featuring a princess, while the boys will hold out for more violence. Or you might get all your kids to agree on dinosaurs, but the younger ones will be thinking "Barney" while the older ones have something more like "Jurassic Park" or "Godzilla" in mind. One solution is to opt for multiple selections, thus pleasing everyone — but only if you want to spend more money renting movies each month than you do on food. A better plan is to pick the film *you* like best, even if it means sending the kids to bed early so you can watch it.

Games of Chance

Another fun activity for you and your children is playing games. I have a couple of suggestions here. First, always choose games at which you can win. This will help build self-esteem (yours) while reminding the children of their place. I've already mentioned the typical toddler's ineptitude at cards, so Old Maid, Uno, and Rook, not to mention poker and blackjack, are all fair game for that age group. You might even consider teaching a particularly advanced older child — say, up to age ten or twelve — to play chess. Unless the child is exceptionally precocious, or unless you're practically a moron, you will almost certainly win, especially if you make up arcane and impossible-to-remember rules as you go: "Yes, Matthew, the Bishop does move diagonally, but it can only move more than two spaces every fifth turn."

Secondly, never choose a game that takes too long to play. After all, togetherness is fine, but you've got to get the kids in bed in time for you to watch "Dancing with the Stars." This effectively rules out Monopoly and Risk for younger kids — and that's a shame, because you'd annihilate them — though with older children you may be able to get in a game in under two hours, especially if you cheat.

Finally, you can spend time with your children in simple conversation, just sitting around talking. I know this doesn't sound like much fun. It probably won't do anything for your ego, and you won't be able to sleep through it. I can't even say I recommend it, as you may be alarmed to find that your children have ideas, opinions, and personalities different from your own (thank goodness). Worst of all, you may be tricked into telling embarrassing stories about your childhood. Even so, talking with your children can be a wonderful way to spend time together, especially during a power outage.

How to Become a Sports Legend

There will, of course, be occasions when you actually *choose* to spend time with your children, perhaps by playing with them outside, even though your wife is at home and you could be doing something else. (I don't intend to deal here with possible ulterior motives, such as the fact that playing badminton is marginally more enjoyable than painting the laundry room. Your children will have to take that issue up with their therapists.)

If you do choose to play outdoor games and sports with your kids, either for the sheer fun of it or in the hope that they will one day become ludicrously wealthy professional athletes, able to support you in style in your old age, consider these few words of advice:

The most important thing, once again, is to play only games you're good at — preferably games at which your (to them) god-like skills inspire reverential awe. This will become more difficult as your kids get older. If, for example, when you are playing baseball with your pre-teen son and his friends, they at any point ask you to lie down and be home plate, this may indicate that they have lost respect for your athletic abilities. About the only thing you can do then is remind them you're not over the hill yet, that in fact you're still quite capable of being — I mean *playing* — first base.

Second, always be the one to choose teams. Just because you're trying to be a good father doesn't mean you have to lose. Besides, you have the children to think about. They don't want a loser for a father. If this means pitting yourself, your twelve-year old son, and your ten-year-old daughter against the toddler, the baby, and the family cat in three-on-three tackle football, then so be it. The little tykes are going to have to toughen up sometime.

Finally, be sure to lay out the rules of the game in advance, except for those you make up as you go. This is similar to my suggestion regarding indoor board games, only potentially more violent. Remember that, as far as your children are concerned, you are the ultimate sports authority, at least until they learn that you are actually an aging geek who couldn't make the junior varsity handball team. That realization usually comes at about age six. Until then, if you tell them they can execute a triple play by using the ball to strike the base runner in the left buttock, they'll have no reason not to believe you. Just be sure to wear thick pants.

In the Dark or at the Park?

At other times, you may choose to spend time with your children by taking them away from home, often for the very good purpose of taking *yourself* away from home. This is really a good strategy when you need one-on-one time with a particular child, or when there is some activity or attraction that one or more of your children would enjoy, or anytime your wife mentions the word "plumbing." In these instances, you may take all the children or just one, on a "father-son outing" or "daddy-daughter date."

If you're going to take all the kids, you'll need to pick someplace they'll all enjoy, such as the circus, the zoo, the park, or a movie. You may have some of the same problems I described above, but once again the best solution is simply to do what *you* would like to do.

For example, if you're going to a movie, and your kids can't decide between "Bertha the Overweight Fairy Princess" and "Foul-Mouthed Pubescent Little Leaguers go to Europe," you're well within your rights to step in and declare the film of choice to be "Rocky XII: Clone of Balboa." So what if it's something the kids probably shouldn't see? You can always put dark glasses on them and tell them it's 3-D. Ply them with enough candy and soft drinks and they'll never even notice they can barely see the screen.

In the worst-case scenario — the kids agree on a movie and it's not one you want to see — you still have options. You can seat them in the theater, supply them with $50.00 worth of snacks — which is to say, one bag of popcorn and one small soda apiece — then excuse yourself to go to the bathroom. Once out in the hall of the modern multiplex cinema, you are free to choose any film you like, as long as it's over about the same time as the children's movie. On the surface, this may seem to defeat the idea of spending time together, but with any luck the kids will never know you were gone. You may even be fortunate enough to learn there wasn't a pervert sitting next to them in the dark theater.

Anyway, going to a movie probably isn't the best way to spend quality time with your kids: it's dark, you're not allowed to talk, and you're surrounded by strangers — kind of like your first visit to your in-laws. Of the other options mentioned above, I find that the zoo requires too much walking and the circus is too expensive — and besides, those flying trapeze women don't look nearly as good in tights as they did when you were ten, possibly because they're the same women.

My favorite place for an outing with the kids is the park. It's cheap, it's fun, and it has benches where you can sit and read, sleep, or just people-watch. Sure, you may have to spend a few minutes getting a small child started on the swing set, unless you have older children to do that for you. But it sure beats walking ten miles or paying 50 bucks to observe the same kinds of animal behavior you get to see every day at home.

A Little Male Bonding

There will be other times when you want or need just to spend time with a particular child. If that child happens to be a boy, you're in luck. One of the great things about father-son outings — at least, once your son gets beyond the age of four — is that you can do most of the same things you would do if you were by yourself or with your buddies. I recognize that occasionally a father who was an all-county high-school linebacker will have a son who is more interested in ballet, but this sort of thing is so rare they make Lifetime Channel movies about it. In most cases, your son will grow up liking what you like, primarily because you're the one who taught him to like it.

What this means in practical terms is that you can justify going off to do just about anything as long as you take your son with you. Whereas your wife might look askance at your plans to catch a ball game with your buddies, she won't bat an eye when you announce you're going to take your *son* to the game. Rather go camping this weekend than clean out the garage? Fine — just take your *son*. Your wife won't merely approve, she'll actually think you're being a good father.

Of course, like anything else, this approach has its potential problems. One arises when your son isn't quite old enough to do what you want to do. Teaching your eight-year-old to hunt small game with a pellet rifle is one thing, and may very well get you out of the house on many a Saturday, but I don't think the boy is up for a week in the Colorado high country looking for bighorn. Don't worry, though. That problem will be solved in time, and if you're willing to put off your bighorn vacation for a few more years, you may very well be able to make it an annual event thereafter.

The other problem is one I alluded to above: what if your son *doesn't like* to do the same things you like to do? Or what if he enjoys those things, but likes to do other things, too, things you have no interest in? At this point in his life, adoption is probably out of the question, and your wife may well be offended if you insist on a blood test. My advice is to recognize that, however much you'd like him to be a chip off the old block, your son is an individual, with his own tastes and preferences. So what if he'd rather see "Soap Stars on Ice" than a hockey game? At least you'll be getting out of the house, and who knows — you might get lucky and see a halfway decent fight.

Don't Expect a Goodnight Kiss

It's just as important for a father to spend one-on-one time with his daughters, but it isn't always as easy to know what to do. Your daughter may enjoy the occasional sporting event or camping trip, but chances are she'll have other interests that have nothing to do with balls or trees. This doesn't mean you can't enjoy spending time with your daughter. It just means you'll have to expand your horizons, sort of like when you began dating. Remember, it's the time together that's most important — that and reassuring your daughter you don't wish that she were a boy. Even if you do.

One thing your daughter may enjoy, especially as a preteen or younger, is going out to dinner and a movie, just like a "real date." You can use this as an opportunity to model for her the way a young man should act on a date — holding her car door open, pulling her chair out at the restaurant, maintaining a distance of at least three feet at all times — and you may even get a good meal out of the bargain.

Obviously, you should let her choose the movie, so it most likely won't be anything you care to see — probably either singing animals or young teenagers in comic situations (what other situations do young teenagers find themselves in?) At this point you may either enact the bathroom contingency plan described above or just gut it out and make the most of the time with your not-so-little girl.

One word of caution here: never take your daughter to a movie containing nudity. The embarrassment will be too much for you to deal with. Yours, I mean. She's probably seen worse in health class.

Another activity that may appeal to your daughter is going shopping. At least, she'll enjoy having you take her shopping until she's about thirteen. After that, she'll simply ask for your wallet, and maybe your keys, too. But up to that point she'll be more than happy to have you follow her around the mall, as long as you keep a respectful distance, so that any friends she chances to meet won't know she's with her dad. They'll doubtless assume she drove herself, or came with her rich Austrian boyfriend. It also helps if you're willing to come across with a hundred bucks or so for a pair of jeans and a "top" (what men refer to as a "shirt").

Finally, there may be times when you'll want to take your daughter someplace really special, such as to a Broadway show, a play, or a concert. I don't mean a rock concert. I mean something that requires dressing up and at which her friends wouldn't be caught dead. This will help teach her about the finer things in life and also give her a sense of being worldly and sophisticated, at least for the evening (hopefully, *just* for the evening). Best of all, even if you don't particularly enjoy the show, you'll have the comfort of knowing that neither did she.

Quality Assurance

In closing this chapter, let me address briefly the concept of "quality time." I have tried very hard in this book not to offend anyone, other than women, attorneys, Iraqis, interior designers, citizens of emerging nations, and my entire extended family. But it strikes me that the term "quality time" was probably coined by parents who don't actually spend a large *quantity* of time with their children. The theory, as I understand it, is that spending an hour doing something really interesting with your child, like putting together a puzzle or reading the *Sports Illustrated* swimsuit issue, is better than spending an entire day doing routine and boring things, such as talking.

I have to say I don't agree. If you want your children to learn your values, you're going to have to spend considerable time with them, even more time than you spend playing golf or working in your yard. If they don't learn your values, whose will they learn? (Answer: those of some television sitcom personality whose moral fiber can be seen only with an electron microscope.) And if your values aren't worth learning, then why do you have them?

Don't get me wrong. I think you should make every minute with your children count, which is basically what this whole chapter has been about. Okay, it's actually been about goofing off while making yourself look good by pretending to spend time with your kids. But, seriously, you must understand that not all time together has to be "quality" time. Most of it won't be. Trust me. I know many of you personally, and any time spent with you will be less than quality time. But if you want your children to know you, you're going to have to be around a lot. Ultimately, that may be the only way they have to distinguish you from the meter reader.

Chapter 9

Teach Your Children? Well . . .

One of a father's primary duties, as I suggested at the end of the previous chapter, is to teach his children. Among the things we are responsible for teaching are the difference between right and wrong, the value of hard work, the importance of being a good citizen, and how to suppress a fart in mixed company. There are a number of methods by which we teach our children, but the most important of these is example. If you make a habit of farting loudly in public, how can you expect your children not to do the same?

Another very effective method of teaching children is often overlooked, perhaps because many parents find it frightening. This method is known as "talking." I never cease to be amazed at the things children do simply because they have never specifically been told not to. I can't guarantee your five-year-old *won't* write his name in magic marker on your new white sofa just because you sat him down and had a little talk about the evils of home graffiti. But it might work, especially if you're prepared to back up your remarks with some serious disciplinary measures, such as revoking his Internet privileges.

I also recognize that no parent can anticipate *all* behaviors, and some children are masters at exploiting this particular disciplinary loophole. ("But you never *told* me not to take off my shoes and juggle them in church.")

But the truth is that you *can* anticipate many of the more dangerous behaviors, such as using drugs or alcohol, engaging in sexual activity, and taunting professional wrestlers. And you can address those behaviors directly with your children, explaining why they're dangerous and setting appropriate limits. This will make it much easier for you to punish the kids later, after they go ahead and do them anyway.

But enough about punishment. I've already had my fun with that — beaten it to death, so to speak. My purpose in this chapter is to encourage you to take an active part in teaching your children. After all, they're going to learn from someone. Considering the alternatives, it might as well be you.

Walk This Way

Children learn at least as much from what we *do* as from what we *say* — probably more. We've all heard the clichés, "What you do speaks so loudly I can't hear what you say" and the more subtle "monkey see, monkey do." One you may not have heard is, "If you want your kids to be healthy, law-abiding, and honest, then stop smoking, speeding, and cheating on your income tax." Okay, you haven't heard that one before because I just made it up. And technically it isn't a cliché, since no one else is saying it. But I predict they will be. Soon.

Again, I must admit I'm amazed at the things parents do while expecting their children not to do them. I'm going to resist the temptation to mention specific behaviors here, because I don't want to offend anyone I haven't already offended (having recently added smokers, speeders, and tax evaders to the list). Instead, let me tell you a little story, one that may in fact sound familiar.

A few years ago I was driving through town with my middle son — age three at the time — in his car seat behind me. Suddenly, a car ahead of us swerved without warning into our lane, cutting us off and forcing me to hit the brakes hard. Stunned and slightly shaken, I wasn't even able to form a coherent thought before my son piped up: "You *idiot*!" He was talking, of course, to the other driver. Or so I assume.

I tell this story in part to show how smart my son is, to be able to recognize an idiot when he sees one. It's a shame he isn't allowed to vote. But the main point I'm trying to illustrate is this: where did that little boy learn to talk that way? From his mother, of course. Okay, okay, he learned it from me. Not that I ever consciously taught him to use the word "idiot." I believe my original suggestion was "moron." But he called that driver a name because he had heard me call other drivers names in similar situations; and if he had waited a few seconds longer, he would have heard me do it again.

Do I want my children to go through life cursing people and calling them names? Only if they intend to be college football coaches. Otherwise, I pray they'll be more circumspect in their judgments and more refined in their language. But I can't really expect that of them unless I exemplify the same qualities. And even then — even if I continue to be the paragon of civilized behavior I am today — they still may not turn out just as I would like. But at least then it won't be my fault. It will be their mother's.

The Moral of the Story

Another responsibility we have to our children is to make sure they know the difference between right and wrong. This is not nearly as difficult as it sounds, despite all the hemming and hawing we so often hear about "gray areas." The fact is, right and wrong are nearly always readily distinguishable, especially for young people, as long as they remember a few simple guidelines. You'll probably recognize these. They've been the same for every generation since Cain and Able:

Wrong	**Right**
Everything you want to do	Everything you ought to do
Everything you like to do	Everything your parents would like you to do
Anything that's fun	Anything that's boring

Anything that keeps you out late	Anything that gets you up early in the morning
Things that appeal to the senses	Things that require an act of will
Your own ideas	Your father's ideas
The way people do it now	The way they used to do it

In addition to emphasizing these rules, you can also teach right and wrong by using others as examples, or "role models." For instance, you can have your children note the way certain well-known actors or politicians or athletes conduct themselves. Then, to teach *acceptable* behavior, you can... well, you get the point.

Your World and Welcome to It

If you're like most parents, you probably think teaching children about the world around them is the school's job. I'm not surprised you think that, since you're most likely a product of the public school system yourself. But let me say this: if you rely on the schools to do all the teaching, you're liable to wind up with kids who know less about the world than you do, and that's pretty scary.

Don't get me wrong. Our schools for the most part do a good job of teaching kids a lot of what they need to know. The problem is that most schools seem bent on teaching the same things in the same way year after year. Innovative, they're not. Remember when you figured out how to memorize the periodic table by converting the letter symbols for the elements into a dirty limerick? You just can't learn that in school. That's the sort of thing your children need you to teach them. Or maybe not.

Another problem with the subject matter taught in most schools is that it tends to be very limited in scope: reading, writing, arithmetic, yada, yada, yada. Your own experiences, on the other hand, can be an unlimited source of useful information your kids will never get in school. I mean, Columbus was a great explorer and all, but chances are you've done lots of things he never did, like fly fishing, or outhouse tipping, or disco dancing. Did Columbus know all the words to "Stayin' Alive"? I think not.

You've also been places and seen things your kids won't learn about in school, places even Columbus never saw, such as — well, Columbus. You may have built more forts than Daniel Boone, memorized poems that don't appear in any literature book, concocted theories that would make Newton's head spin. You really should share these things with your children, insofar as they're suitable for young ears, which I realize may severely limit you. School presents one rather narrow view of the world. Your kids need to know how *you* see the world, so that they may then conclude — as their friends have long since concluded about their parents — that you are a complete loser.

Citizen Pain

Citizenship is one of the most demanding yet most important requirements of modern life. If we expect our country to prosper and remain strong, we must all do our part, which for some might entail leaving. But if you believe, perhaps mistakenly, that the country will not be harmed by your presence, then you must strive continually to meet the fundamental requirements of citizenship: staying current on the issues, exercising your right to vote, and working to improve your community. Moreover, you must teach these concepts to your children, both by example and by other means, such as showing them home videos of the 1987 "Save the Whales" rally where you met their mother.

For instance, you can begin teaching a child early in life to be well informed simply by leaving the television on MSNBC instead of *Sesame Street,* or by turning on Rush

Limbaugh at nap time. I know of one parent who, when his child was small, each day left the morning newspaper within easy reach of the toddler's crib. We may never know just how much of that information the child actually ingested, but I bet the ink dyes made for some interesting patterns in his diapers.

As for teaching your children to vote, you can do this first of all by voting yourself (not to be confused with voting *for* yourself, which you should do only if you're running). When the kids are young, you can make election day an "event," perhaps by passing out those little straw boater hats, or by making colorful signs, or by painting yourself red, white, and blue. You should also make sure — and this goes back to point one, above — that your children understand, as much as they are capable of understanding, the relevant issues. To this end you should explain to them in simple, straightforward terms why you have chosen to vote for a certain candidate and why his opponent is a worthless scumbag.

Another way you can teach children about voting is by holding mock elections. These are usually conducted in elementary and junior high classrooms, but if you have at least two or three kids, you can give it a try at home. I vaguely remember my father doing this during the presidential campaign of 1964. (Okay, I was only three, but I have a very good memory.) He, my mother, and my brother all voted for Goldwater. I thought he said "who wants *cold water*," and as it was nearly bath time I went with the other option. I was grounded for four months, but I think it may have been my vote that pushed Johnson over the top. Hey, I know I was just a kid, but at least I had a pulse.

The final element of citizenship is community awareness, which we can teach by creating opportunities for our children to serve others (besides us, I mean). Some families, for example, like to work together in community cleanup efforts aimed at beautifying the cities and towns in which they live. Others take their kids with them to work in soup kitchens, feeding the homeless. And others still might undertake to paint large bullseyes on area fire hydrants, as a service to visually impaired dogs.

Whether or not any of these activities in particular appeals to you, I'm sure you can find some project that will be both educational and useful to the community. The point is to get your kids involved at an early age, so that service will become a way of life. In fact, if you have enough kids, and get them involved in enough projects, you can claim civic consciousness without actually lifting a finger yourself. Maybe you'll even win an award.

The Ultimate in Time Saving Technology

Perhaps the most important thing we can teach our children is the value of hard work. Once they master this principle, they can become the kind of responsible, successful, self-fulfilled, high achievers who will one day be able to support us in luxury. The problem, in a nutshell, is this: *no one likes to work.* (Contrary to the popular myth, a "workaholic" is not someone who loves to work, but someone who can't stand to be around his family.) Children, in particular, hate to work. They would much rather play, or have chicken pox.

Another problem is that parents themselves are often lazy. I don't just mean they refuse to work and thus set a poor example for their kids, although that does happen. What I'm really talking about is the fact that parents, though resigned to certain tasks, don't want to do any more work than necessary. And we all know that teaching a child to do anything requires twice as much time and effort as simply doing it ourselves. Thus we too often succumb to frustration, sending the child back to the den to watch "Mutant Biker Rodents" and finishing the job ourselves. This creates children who are lazy as well as culturally deprived.

In this, we as parents are both irresponsible and short-sighted — irresponsible because we are developing children who neither know how to do anything nor understand the importance of completing a task. These are the kids who will one day be building our cars, wiring our houses, and investing our mutual funds, not to mention marrying our sons and daughters.

More to the point, though, we are being terribly shortsighted in failing to realize that, if we just spend a few extra minutes now, we can save ourselves hours in the future. Because once a child has learned to perform a certain task, that task then becomes his or hers *forever*. I know it may take weeks of running over the shrubbery before your young son finally learns to handle the riding mower, just to use one example. You may even have to spend extra time at first going back over the areas he's missed, not to mention re-planting.

But once he learns how, he will then be able to mow the lawn from that point on. Don't you see the implications? You will never, ever have to mow the lawn again — at least, not until your last child leaves home, at which point you can retire to a condominium in Florida, like everyone else.

The same holds true for any other task, such as doing the dishes, cleaning out the garage, and overhauling the transmission. By passing on to your children your considerable expertise in these areas, you will have fulfilled your obligation as a parent and made your life that much easier, all in one fell swoop. And, ultimately, about the only thing more satisfying than knowing you have taught your child to perform some useful task is the knowledge that you yourself will never have to spend another minute on that kind of tedious, backbreaking labor. You can spend all your time reading my books, instead.

You cannot, however, simply wait until a child is eight or ten and then begin assigning difficult and complex tasks. You must begin teaching children to work at an early age. One of the best ways to do this, as I've stated all along, is by modeling the desired behavior — that is, by letting your young children see you constantly at work around the house. While other fathers are watching football, you'll be scrubbing mold from under the eaves with a toothbrush. While others are fishing, you'll be trimming the hedges into miniature replicas of the Tower of London. While others nap, you'll be organizing your spare nuts and bolts by size and thread count.

Okay, I said that's *one* way to teach your young children to work, not the only way. Now that you've totally rejected this first suggestion, perhaps you'll be more interested in my second one: *assign chores.*

The basic principal here is that no child who can walk is too young to have chores. A one-year-old may not be legally able to operate heavy machinery in some states, but he *can* learn to pick up after himself. And if all you teach that child is to pick up his toys without throwing them at you, or at least *after* he's thrown them at you, you've accomplished something.

You can even teach older children to work *together* by assigning joint chores. For example, the two-year-old can empty the wastebaskets, while the four-year-old follows behind with a garbage bag, picking up the piles of newly-emptied waste.

Some other examples of age-appropriate chores are as follows:

Age	Job(s)
Zero to one	Fill diaper basket, prevent parents from oversleeping
One to two	Clean toilet with hands, remove stale Cheerios from under kitchen table
Two to three	Clean own room, reorganize shoes in parents' closet
Three to four	Set table, sweep up broken dishes

Four to five	Separate laundry, fold socks, keep neighbors informed as to intimate family matters
Five to six	Babysit younger siblings, give directions to 911 operator

Once a child reaches the age of six or seven, he or she can be assigned to do just about any simple task around the house that you no longer care to do yourself. In other words, nearly everything. Heavy yard work, automobile repair, and major household renovations may have to wait a few years, but those too will come in time. And in the end, your reward will be the knowledge that, in teaching your children to work, you have performed a valuable service for them, for the community, and — most importantly — for yourself. Isn't that what parenting is all about?

Chapter 10

Why Must It Be a Teenager I Love?

Before you read this chapter, I need to tell you, in the interests of full disclosure, that I'm brand new to parenting a teenager, my oldest daughter having just turned 13 as I write this chapter. That fact might lead some people to think that I don't know anything about raising teens.

I have a couple of responses to that. First, not knowing what I'm talking about has not to this point deterred me from writing about it anyway, nor (allow me to point out) has it kept you from reading. And, besides, it would be inaccurate to say I don't know *anything* about teenagers, since I've been one myself. Quite recently, in fact. Okay, so it wasn't very recent, but I still remember it. Sort of.

I've also done quite a bit of work with teenagers, both in the course of my profession and as a volunteer. I admit this freely, despite the results of a recent study conducted by two sociologists from the University of Winnipeg, which concluded that anyone who volunteers to work with teenagers is either a lunatic or a pervert. I assure you that I am not a pervert and have not been one since my own teenage years. (First rule of parenting a teenage daughter: **ALL** teenage boys are perverts.)

So I do know something about teenagers, though not much, which puts me in a category with an awful lot of other people, including those who have been parents of teenagers for some time. In this chapter, then, I have no intention of trying to cover every aspect of raising teenagers. Instead, I'll limit my discussion to four main topics: Independence, Driving, Dating, and Discipline (known as the "One I and Three D's"). My comments will be based on my own observations, extensive reading on the subject, conversations with other parents, and things I've heard on television talk shows.

Just Another Word for Nothing Left to Lose

What all teenagers want more than anything else is to be independent of their parents. This means that they do not wish to depend on their parents for anything, other than food and shelter. And clean clothing. And transportation. And gas. And spending money. But other than that, they want to be left completely alone. Teenagers also don't want anybody telling them what to do, except for the other 473 teenagers they're friends with on Facebook.

The essential problem is that teenagers see themselves as adults, whereas their parents still see them as children. It's basically a question of perspective. A sixteen-year-old feels that he or she has been alive for quite a long time. As adults, most of us have *socks* older than that. Teenagers also believe that, as a result of their advanced age, they know a pretty good bit about the world, such as, for instance, everything. As parents, we see that they have barely begun to scratch the surface, and we know from experience how dangerous a little knowledge can be, since most of us have very little ourselves.

Another problem is that teenagers want all of the *freedoms* associated with adulthood without any of the accompanying *responsibilities*. This actually puts them in the same category as about two thirds of the adults I know. The rest of us, however, understand exactly what adult freedom is all about: the freedom to stay up until 2:00 am working on a project, the freedom to get up at 6:00 the next morning regardless, the freedom to work ten hours a day, the freedom to call the bank and ask for an extension on a loan. If a teenager really wants that kind of freedom, I know I'd be happy to take a little acne and a minor identity crisis in trade.

But teenagers can't see this. In their own way, they're not unlike the toddler who wants to "be big" before his time. And, just as the toddler can be badly hurt by climbing up on the dinner table, so teenagers can be hurt — and much worse — by many of the so-called "adult" behaviors they long to emulate, such as drinking, indiscriminate sexual intercourse, and karaoke.

On the other hand, we can't treat teenagers like children forever. If they're not adults now, they're going to be adults much sooner than we want to admit, and we might as well begin preparing them. Thus, the trick to raising a responsible teenager (and it *is* a trick, I'm convinced, like making an elephant disappear) — the trick lies in knowing just how much freedom to give a child at a particular point in his or her life.

How can you know this? A better question would be, how can you make an elephant disappear? The answer to both is the same: you can't. When it comes to figuring out how much freedom to allow your teenager, you're simply left having to guess. But there are a couple of strategies that can help you in your guesswork.

The first and most obvious — and most widely used — strategy is trial and error. It works something like this: You give your fifteen-year-old son the freedom to drive the family car, even though he doesn't have a license. He has an accident. You get sued for 7.5 million dollars. You lose your home, your business, and all prospects of a future. At this point, you conclude that you have made an error.

Or perhaps you allow your daughter to have boys over when you and your wife aren't home. Three years pass, and she miraculously does not become pregnant. You may conclude that either your wife's missing birth control pills were not eaten by rodents, or that all your daughter's male friends are gay.

The obvious problem with trial and error is that the consequences of error can be catastrophic. And even when you believe in retrospect that you've made the right decision, you have no way of knowing it wasn't just dumb luck, or perhaps the wonders of modern medicine.

A better approach is to find *role models*, other parents in your church or community whose teenagers seem to have turned out well. (Definition of “turned out well”: not in jail, in rehab, or working as White House interns.) You will discover, once you get to know them, that most of these parents are guessing just like you and have simply been lucky. But occasionally you will come across a couple who really seem to know what they’re doing. They won’t be all that hard to recognize: theirs is the house where all the other teenagers in the neighborhood, including yours, hang out. It’s as if they’re drawn there by something in the air — wisdom, decisiveness, order. Fresh-baked apple pie. All those things that are as absent from the atmosphere in your home as uranium ions.

And you always thought it was because they had a pool.

Once you’ve found these parents, study them diligently. Observe closely their interaction with their teenagers. See what they allow their children to do, and at what ages. Emulate them shamelessly, down to wearing the same brand of loafers (hey, you never know what little details might be significant). Finagle every opportunity for your children to spend time with their children. If you do all this and your teenager *still* turns out to be a White House intern — well, I don’t know what to tell you. It must be genetic.

You Drive Them Wild. They'll Drive You Crazy

An important difference between younger children and teenagers is that, with younger children, the term "driving me crazy" is merely a figure of speech. With teenagers, it's a daily reality.

First comes what we'll call the "pre-driving" stage, which occupies ages 13 and 14 (or, in some rural parts of the country, ages eight through ten). At this stage, young teens exhibit a growing fascination with driving, which may manifest itself in repeated requests (okay, *begging*) to drive the car "just in the driveway." Some parents even begin allowing their young teens to drive short distances, such as down the street to a friend's house and back. I think this is incredibly foolish. You might as well go ahead and send them to the grocery store and the dry cleaner.

Next is the "learning to drive" stage, when the teen reaches the age of fifteen and obtains a learner's permit. It now becomes the responsibility of the parent to teach the child how to drive safely, without eliciting obscene gestures or gunfire from other motorists. Some parents, of course, try to foist this responsibility off on the schools, most of which offer driver education courses. I have only my own experience from which to judge, but I think it's a mistake for parents totally to entrust this important duty to an assistant football coach who knows primarily two things about teaching driving: how to thread a projector and how to apply the auxiliary brake.

I also remember my embarrassment upon getting behind the wheel of the driver's ed car for the first time and discovering I was the only one in my class who had never been in that situation before. Heck, in the rural area where I grew up, some of my classmates had been making moonshine runs in the family GTO for years. Needless to say, I was the worst driver by far in that class. I would never even have gotten the weekly shipment out of Catoosa County.

It's not that I'm against driver's ed classes. I think they're a good thing, and that all students should take them. If nothing else, these classes can lower your insurance rates and allow your school to employ more assistant football coaches. But I think there is a bonding that occurs when a parent — especially a father — takes it upon himself to teach his son or daughter to drive. It may only be a bonding of your brand new Buick and the neighbor's mailbox, but it is nevertheless an important touchstone in your relationship.

After that first-day driver's ed fiasco, my father began taking me to an empty church parking lot on Sunday afternoons. There he could teach me to drive with a minimum of fear, which is to say his anxiety level was about the same as if he'd been locked in a cage with an adult lion. This was a special time for us as father and son. My dad said things to me during those sessions he had never said before, such as "Left! Left! I said LEFT, @#%&#!"

I'm certainly looking forward to teaching each of my children to drive. Unless, of course, I can afford to hire somebody else to do it for me. Hey, bonding has its limits.

The final stage is that of actually driving. It begins with the anxiety-filled day on which your just-turned-sixteen-year-old takes the driver's test for the first time. Amazingly, most pass in one try, which probably tells us more about the difficulty of the exam and the nerves of the testing officers than about anyone's driving ability. You may also conclude at this point that if your teen had shown as much concern for his algebra final, he might not be repeating tenth grade. But passing algebra never made anyone more popular with the girls. Even Einstein couldn't get a date until he could drive.

And so one day your baby, whom you so recently bounced upon your knee (that explains the cartilage damage), is driving around by himself or herself in a two-ton lethal projectile. After a few moments spent dabbing your eyes at the thought, you may then begin planning the little twerp's itinerary: Drop off brother at T-ball practice. Pick up dry cleaning.

Do week's grocery shopping. Take cat to be neutered. The possibilities are endless. All your anxiety over the prospect notwithstanding, the fact of the matter is that once your teen can drive, you need never leave the house again, except to go to work or to the golf course.

At first your teenager will not mind this at all. For several weeks, at least, she will jump at any excuse to drive any vehicle to any place for any reason. After the newness wears off, though, the child will begin to feel you're taking advantage of her, but only because you're taking advantage of her. At about this same time, the teen will also begin wanting her *own car*, if she doesn't have one already.

Here's what I recommend, and what I plan to do. I have this on the best authority — friends of mine whose eight children all appear, amazingly, to have turned out quite well. First, never buy your child his or her own car. This gives the child a degree of autonomy you don't even want to contemplate and opens you up, when attempting to exercise discipline, to the vile, offensive, and politically incorrect accusation of "Indian giver." ("What do you mean you're taking away my keys? It's *my* car! Indian giver!")

Instead, if you can afford another vehicle at all, purchase one — *used, not new* — to be designated for that child's *use* but to remain in your name. That way, the teen will always need your permission to take the vehicle, and you can use car privileges as incentive (i.e., a bribe) for the child to obey curfew and other rules and to continue to run your errands.

Another advantage to this approach is that it will foster in your home a sense of nearly puritanical frugality, which your child may well resent at the time but will come to regard with pride later in life. "Yeah," your son will say to his own teenagers one day, "when I was your age *I didn't even have my own car*! All the other kids had new Mustangs and Camaros and four-wheel-drive Toyota trucks, but I had to drive my mom's '94 *Escort!*"

The guidelines for purchasing an additional car are fairly straightforward. Of course you want the vehicle to be safe and reliable, inexpensive to operate, and in reasonably good shape. It should also be — and this is a really good piece of advice, so pay attention — the vehicle itself should also be inexpensive enough not to warrant full insurance coverage. This alone can save you thousands of dollars, as any parent with driving teenagers will tell you that the main expense is not the car but the insurance. If the car is cheap enough, you can get by with just purchasing liability insurance. Then, if the child totals the car, as long as he or she can walk away, you have no worries. The child can just keep on walking — to school, to the mall, to work to pay for a new car.

One more thing: make sure your extra car, though inexpensive, is nice enough that you would not mind driving it yourself. This is not because you are concerned about your teenager's fragile ego and fears about status, but because you *will* end up driving it yourself about half the time, while your teen takes the new Explorer. You can solve this problem, however, by driving a minivan. There is no teen in the world who wouldn't rather drive a '72 Gremlin than be caught dead in a minivan.

And what about those teenagers who want to get a job just so they can buy a car? As a parent, I would never discourage a teenager from working, unless it interfered with school or other important activities, such as picking up my dry cleaning. Indeed, I think teenagers *should* do something — maybe get a part-time job during the summer — to help pay for the additional insurance and gas. But one of the advantages of the extra-car approach is that it relieves them of the adult burden of having to meet loan payments. There'll be time enough for that later. Meanwhile, as teenagers, they can focus on more important things: school, extracurricular activities, and getting dates.

Some Things Are Better in Groups

Which brings us to our next topic, one that all parents approach with fear and trembling: dating. I want to make it clear, once again, that I mean *dating* here in the old-fashioned sense of the word, not in the modern euphemistic sense. I actually don't believe teenagers should be "dating" at all, euphemistically speaking. This, apparently, is a view I share with approximately five dozen other people scattered across the country, mostly in remote compounds. Certainly none of them works in the movie or television industries.

But it is not my purpose here to impose my moral values upon you. I must also admit that there was an important period in my life when I myself did not have the same high ideals — namely, when I was a teenager. But that's only because, like all teenage boys, I was a pervert. It certainly doesn't mean I was right. Heck, if we're going to let the perverts make the rules, we might as well start electing them to Congress. Oh, wait.

In any case, you may notice that I put dating, as a topic, after driving. This is because I firmly believe that the one should come before the other — in other words, that a teen should be old enough to drive before being allowed to date. It would be nice, too, if teens were required to take a course or pass a test before dating, but I don't think I can arrange that, except for those teenage boys who will be coming to pick up *my* daughter.

For guys, this is in part a very practical consideration: no teenage boy wants to arrive at his date's house with his mom or dad driving. At the very least, this would put a tremendous damper on the end-of-date make-out session. So you may not have many problems getting your son to wait until sixteen before dating, unless he has older girls wanting to pick him up, in which case you probably ought to be reading Magic Johnson's book, not mine.

Where girls are concerned, however, the dilemma is much greater. Since guys traditionally do the picking up and driving, a girl can theoretically date long before she turns sixteen. And, most likely, she will be dating much older boys — boys who can drive. This is not something I would recommend.

Bear in mind the first principle: that all teenage boys are perverts. I know this may not be true of every single teenage boy in the world; a recent survey showed that 0.0003 per cent are considering studying for the priesthood. But, as a father, can you afford to assume the best?

So why *does* this sixteen- or seventeen-year-old boy want to go out with your fourteen-year-old daughter? Because he is *attracted* to her, which is a polite way of saying he would like to sample her goodies. Perhaps he is even under the impression that, being young and immature, she will be more susceptible to his charms. In this impression, he may well be correct.

And how about your daughter? Why does she want to go out with *him*? Either because she is attracted to him (you don't even want to think about his goodies), or because she values the prestige associated with dating an older guy, or both. And what is she likely to *do* as a result of that attraction, or in order to maintain that prestige? From a father's perspective, such questions are as valid as "what kind of ammunition does the most damage to soft tissue?"

Face it: a fourteen-year-old is immature. It's only been three years since she got her last *Barbie*, for crying out loud. She isn't ready to make such difficult decisions under what may, for her, constitute considerable duress. Fortunately, you can make the decision for her, simply by not allowing her to be in a car — or anywhere else, but especially in a car — alone with a boy until she is at least sixteen. This will make you extremely unpopular as a father, but you might prefer that to being an extremely popular grandfather.

I don't mean to imply that sixteen is a magical age at which all teenagers suddenly gain wisdom and maturity. That's only in Disney movies. *Your* sixteen-year-old will still be subject to peer pressure and hormonal urges and may as a result make bad decisions. The same could be said for members of Congress. But you can't keep her locked in her room until she's 21 (can you?) and those extra couple of years might make all the difference in the world.

If you're still not comfortable with one-on-one dating even when your teen turns sixteen, let me suggest that, for the first few months or longer, you allow only *group dating*. Now, I realize that if you interpret the word "dating" euphemistically, then this sounds sick. But what I'm talking about is a group of teenagers — that is, more than one couple — going out together to a movie, restaurant, or sporting event. You've probably heard the old saying, "there's safety in numbers." I'm not sure to what extent that's true, but I do think most teenagers will be less anxious to take off their clothes when in groups of more than two.

The most common type of group date is the double date, which involves two couples (hence the term). Double dates are popular because four is the maximum number of people that can fit comfortably into most cars ("comfortably" being defined as "with room to lie down"). Larger groups may be formed with couples traveling in separate vehicles. For your purposes, you may wish to insist, regardless of the ultimate size of the group, that your teen and his or her date ride with at least one other couple. This may not prevent them from lying down, but it should ensure that a minimum of clothing is removed.

Sooner or later, though, you're going to have to let your teen go on a single-couple car date and just have confidence — make that *pray* — that he or she will make good decisions. If you don't see much chance of that, then hope for dumb luck. When it comes to parenting, luck counts.

I have a few other suggestions regarding dating, and then I'll drop the subject (and not a moment too soon).

First, be sure you know or at least meet the other teenager (let's hope it's a teenager). This is relatively easy when a young man comes to pick up your daughter, assuming he's polite enough to come to the door instead of just pulling up in the driveway and honking. If not, I suggest you go out and invite him in, with a tire iron, if necessary. Then, since your daughter will be taking another half hour to fix her hair anyway, the two of you can get to know one another. One brief note: this process will be greatly enhanced if you are a body builder wearing a tight T-shirt. If you're not a body builder, but have a pre-teen daughter, then I recommend that you become one.

If your dating teenager is a boy, it will be difficult for you to meet his date unless he brings her over expressly for that purpose, or unless you hide in his backseat. The latter is probably not a good idea, as you may at some point in the evening be squashed, but you should insist that he do the former. If he is serious about the girl (definition of "serious": he wears a shirt with a collar when he goes to pick her up), then perhaps you can arrange to have her over for dinner one evening. This should give you every opportunity to observe all the many ways in which she falls short of being good enough for your son.

Of course, simply knowing whom your children are dating will not always allow you to avert disaster. But you may be able to sense potential problems before they occur, which if nothing else will give you the satisfaction later of being able to say, "I told you so" — perhaps for the next forty years.

Second, know where your child is going. Your primary purpose here is not so much to monitor the child's activities, though you may of course nix any idea you find particularly objectionable, such as an R-rated movie or a body-piercing convention. But you have a right to know where to find the child in case of emergency. And yes, as a father, having second thoughts about that boy *does* constitute an emergency.

Third, give the teen a firm curfew, or, if you don't like that term, a set time to be home from the date. I think you can be reasonable and flexible here without being too lenient. Just remember that the longer teenagers are alone together with nothing constructive to do, the more likely they are to spend that time in each other's pants. (Excuse my bluntness here, but am I, or am I not, telling the truth?)

Thus, for an early movie followed by a late dinner, it is reasonable to expect your daughter to be home by 11:00. (You may give your son an extra fifteen minutes, since he has to drop off his date.) For something special like the prom, however, you may decide to extend the child's curfew to 12:00 — as long as you know where he's going to be during that time (at the prom itself, at a party sponsored by parents, etc.). Just make sure he knows you meant 12:00 *am*.

Fourth, you may want to consider allowing your daughter and her date to park in your driveway or in front of your house for ten or fifteen minutes beyond curfew. I know this idea will stir controversy among parents who expect their teenage children to abstain from all physical contact with the opposite sex. For those parents I suggest psychological help, as they are clearly divorced from reality. The rest of us may recognize that our teenagers are less likely to rebel completely if we give them just a little bit of closely-monitored freedom, especially if they're right where we can see them with our new infrared binoculars.

When I first began dating my wife-to-be, she insisted that we park only in her driveway. I found this disappointing, but as it was better than not parking at all, I went along. My future father-in-law would give us about fifteen minutes, then begin turning the porch light off and on as a signal to her that it was time to come in. It actually took me a while to catch on. I just thought her kisses were making my head spin.

Finally, before your teenage daughter goes out on a date, be sure to give her enough money to get home if she has to ditch the bum. (I have heard this referred to as "mad money." I prefer to think of it as "get your hand off my breast" money.) In addition, you will certainly want to make sure that she has her own cell phone. And a sharp object. And a can of mace disguised as hand cream. Whatever you do, just make sure that if a date ever tells her to "put out or get out," she'll have no fear of taking the latter option, preferably after inflicting severe injury.

If you follow these simple guidelines, your years as the father of a dating teenager are likely to be somewhat less stressful than, say, waiting for the results of your colon polyp biopsy. But only somewhat. Once it's all over with, though, and your children have turned out reasonably well, you'll be able to look back on these years and think to yourself, "How in the heck did *that* happen?"

It's Your Car, Anyway

I know I've already touched on the subject of discipline in Chapter Seven, but I do want to reiterate a few points in light of some of the topics discussed here.

You need to recognize that the best way to get teenagers to do what you want, short of offering them large sums of money (and that's not an approach to be overlooked), is to understand what they value most and then use that against them. In other words, the form of discipline to which teenagers respond best is what I call in Chapter Seven "loss of privileges."

So your teenager wants to be left alone? There certainly are times when you can grant the child some degree of freedom in exchange for a promise to exercise the appropriate responsibility. A simple example of this would be agreeing not to go in your son's room as long as he agrees to keep it reasonably clean. Of course, if you don't go into the room you may not know just how clean he's keeping it, but strong odors or the sight of vermin escaping from under the door may be important clues. You would then have every excuse to go into the child's room and clean it thoroughly, including all the drawers and under the mattress. After that, he'll keep his room at the rehab center spotless.

And how about driving? As long as you follow my advice and make sure *you own the car*, you can use driving privileges to get the child to do just about anything, including not wearing his nose ring to church. You might even want to devise a system of reward and punishment based on use of the car. For example: if your teenager keeps his or her grades at a certain level, is always in by curfew, doesn't become pregnant/ impregnate anyone, then he or she can have unlimited use of the car. If, on the other hand, the teenager fails to live up to expectations, he or she will be grounded for a specified period of time. I recommend six years.

Be warned that your teenagers will think this grossly unfair. And in all honesty they probably have a point. I mean, all they want is for you to buy them a car (preferably a late model sports car), pay for the insurance, furnish the gas, give them money for beer and condoms, and otherwise leave them alone. What could be more reasonable? That is, after all, exactly what their friends' parents are doing.

If you decide to buck the trend, I can't guarantee your kids will turn out all right. But I do think the odds become slightly skewed in your favor. And who knows? You may eventually find that *yours* is the house where all the neighborhood teenagers hang out — even if you don't have a pool.

PART THREE:

It's Not an Adventure
It's Just a Job

One thing that distinguishes the true family man from the ordinary male of the species is that he is not defined solely by his occupation; that is, he does not confuse the question, "who are you?" with the question, "what do you do for a living?" Regardless of whether he is a doctor, a teacher, a construction worker, a loan shark, or a telephone psychic, he is first and foremost a family man, and thinks of himself as such. If he occasionally fails to think that way, he is quickly reminded by his wife.

Not that the family man doesn't take his work seriously — as you can see, I take mine very seriously indeed — or that he doesn't vigorously pursue success in his chosen field. If he has much of a family at all, he had certainly better. In fact, some of the most successful men I know are also devoted husbands with several children. Whether this springs from some sort of Darwinian survival instinct, or merely indicates a connection between being prolific at home and prolific at work, is a question better left for someone with more expertise, which is to say just about anyone.

The point is that a man can enjoy professional success without having to sacrifice his family life, and vice versa. He will only have to sacrifice sleep, his friends, all forms of recreation, and every last vestige of self-determination.

Nor do I mean to imply that the family man cannot find satisfaction and fulfillment in his work. It is certainly no sin for him to do so, unless of course the job itself is something reprehensible, like being a male prostitute or an IRS auditor. Otherwise, the family man is free to pursue any challenging and rewarding career he chooses, so long as it does not interfere with his wife's schedule, his children's little league games and dance recitals, church activities, or his own household obligations. Some careers that fit this description are out-of-work actor, industrial fortune heir, and best-selling author.

If you're not lucky enough to find work in one of those fields, then like the rest of us you'll just have to learn how to balance your job and your family life, which is one of the main topics I want to cover in Part Three. Other topics include moving up the career ladder, changes in your job and how they affect your family, the "after-work letdown," and taking your kids to work with you.

A final note before I move on: this section is intended to be not so much a humorous look at the modern workplace — I'll leave that to the capable hands of others — as an examination of the role that career plays in the life of today's family man. I certainly don't want to step on anyone's toes, encroach upon anyone else's territory, or be the defendant in an expensive copyright lawsuit. But, since most family men *do* have jobs, I feel the subject is well within the purview of this book. I also feel a bit giddy at the thought that this book *has* a purview.

So if you have a family and a job, and you've been pulling your hair out for years wondering how to make those two things compatible — well, hunker down in your cubicle, swivel your back to the opening, and read on.

Chapter 11

The Greatest Show on Earth

What has only in the last two or three decades become a major issue for women — how to balance home life with a career — has been a concern for men since the dawn of time. Well, okay, maybe not since the actual dawn of time, since early man did not technically speaking have a career, unless you count hunter-gatherer. He probably didn't have much of a family life either, as he lived solely to impregnate as many females as possible during his short lifetime, much like the modern NFL star. But it's been an issue for us for a long time, or at least it ought to have been.

True, we haven't always treated the concept of balance with the importance it deserves. But bear in mind that, for centuries, most families survived by subsistence farming. Men spent quality time with their wives and children by hitching them to a plow. Only in recent years, as women have relinquished their traditional role as primary nurturer to move into the workforce, and men have had to take on more of the responsibility for child rearing, have we slowly begun to recognize that, like women, we must address certain conflicts. Sometimes, like women, we must even address Christmas cards.

As true twenty-first century family men, we now recognize the need to be productive at home as well as on the job. We realize that the work we do with our children is more important and more satisfying than the work we do at the office, if not as lucrative. And we accept, along with our wives, though somewhat more reluctantly, the challenge of finding ways to balance all the many things we must do throughout the day in order to be good husbands, good fathers, and good employees. This provides a nice contrast to our misspent youth, when we were merely good for nothing.

If this all begins to sound like a circus act, rest assured you're not the first to comment on the resemblance. Note, for instance, the implied metaphor in such terms as "balance" and "juggle." Just don't make the mistake of thinking you're the ringmaster. You're more like the trained poodle, jumping through hoops that, alarmingly often, are on fire.

First Things First

It is easy to assert that, for the family man, work should always come before pleasure and family before work. This, however, is an oversimplification of what is actually a very complex problem. The fact is, few of us would hesitate to put our families first when the situation warrants, such as in a medical emergency. (Example: your son is rushed to hospital for an appendectomy. If you leave the office immediately, you can get in nine holes and still be there when he wakes up in the recovery room.)

At other times, though, work *has* to come first, if you wish to remain employed. Sure, we'd all like to leave work early to attend a child's soccer game or band concert. Shoot, most of us would leave work early to watch an autopsy. But many times that just isn't possible. For obvious reasons, most autopsies are scheduled before lunch.

Then there are the truly gray areas — those dance recitals or PTA meetings that take place outside regular business hours but at times when you really need to be in the office or out with a client. What do you do? Reschedule? The PTA might not be able to get the auditorium any other night.

There are also times when pleasure or relaxation is a priority — when you just need to play golf or whatever to sharpen the old saw. Some of these times include early evenings right after work, Sunday afternoons, and all day Saturdays.

That's why you need to have clearly established priorities, a written or at least mental checklist of what is more important in a given situation. By identifying your priorities beforehand — and doing so in close consultation with your wife — you can save a great deal of time and hand-wringing later and also give yourself some degree of deniability when it comes to making tough decisions. For example, once you get your wife to agree in principle that your job is more important than your social life — and you can probably make a case for this that sounds deceptively self-sacrificing — you can then use that "priority" to get out of any number of unwelcome receptions, recitals, bar mitzvahs, dinner parties, and family get-togethers.

To identify your priorities, first consider all the many demands of home life, family, work, community, and personal interests. Then ask yourself three questions about each:

1) Is it a matter of life and death?
2) Who will benefit or suffer, and to what degree, from my attention or inattention to this demand?
3) What will be the immediate outcome of my response to this demand? The long-term outcome? (Okay, that's four questions.)

Any sort of physical emergency will obviously take precedence over something that is not a physical emergency. Any action that will benefit someone who is important to you, such as yourself, is a higher priority than an action that will benefit someone who is not as important, such as a co-worker. And any option that promises a positive long-term outcome (immense wealth, a happy marriage, well-adjusted children) will be preferable to those options that offer only quick fixes (an extra fifty bucks, immediate gratification, children who aren't whining at that precise moment).

Thus, your son's emergency appendectomy is more important than your meeting because he theoretically could die, whereas no one at the meeting will die without you there. (At least, you hope not. You'd hate to miss that.) On the other hand, your meeting is more important than your wife's cousin's wedding reception, because you and your entire immediate family will benefit from your attendance at the meeting through your continued employment and possible advancement, while the only person who stands to benefit from your going to the reception is your wife's cousin, who can probably get by with one less set of Ginsu knives. Then again, the reception is more important than your golf date, since the long-term benefits of the former (your wife's happiness and gratitude) outweigh the short-term gains of the latter (a 53 on the front-nine, seven lost balls, and a hangover).

See how easy it is to set priorities? All you really have to do is decide what's important to you, then discard that in favor of what's important to your wife, your kids, and your boss, in that order. Your own wants, desires, and needs come near the bottom of the list, just after those of the cat but before the house plants.

Can We Talk?

Once you've established your priorities, the next step is to make sure you've communicated them clearly to all concerned — foremost among those, of course, being your wife.

As I said, you can probably save a lot of trouble and difficult decision-making in your marriage by including your wife in the priority-setting stage. Never assume, however, that just because she's been in on the process, you and she will always be on the same page. You may need to articulate to her clearly, and perhaps often, that certain times and functions related to your job are inviolate except in the case of emergency, and that the dog's unexpected pregnancy does not qualify. (Her own, however, may.)

The same thing applies to your kids. There will be days when you can leave work at lunch to read a book to your daughter's first grade class and evenings when you can help coach your son's little league team. But there will also be lots of times when you can't, and your children need to understand that beforehand. You will still be guilt-ridden, and they will still wish you were more like Bobby and Cindy's dad, who apparently gets paid to hang out at the ballpark, but at least you will have communicated.

One thing I've found useful in this regard is a family calendar. Start with one of those large calendars banks give away, the ones with big spaces for writing on each date. Then take time regularly as a family to fill in events and activities as they come up. When your daughter gets her softball schedule, take a few moments to write it on the calendar. When your son brings home a field trip notice, write it in. When you or your wife has an important business meeting or client dinner, write it in. When you're entered in a golf tournament, write it in. Then, as conflicts occur, you and your wife can decide who will be going where and what activities will take precedence. Just make sure that *your* important dates are not written in pencil, while everyone else's are in pen.

Keeping a calendar like this can prevent a great deal of confusion, misunderstanding, and hurt feelings. Your son will know in advance that you won't be able to come to his ball game because you're going to be out of town on business. Your daughter will know you won't be able to make her dance recital because you have a late meeting. Your wife will know you won't be taking her to the theater because you have a foursome. And your divorce attorney will know you're free for lunch on Friday.

The other key person to whom you must communicate your priorities is your boss. This can be a bit more complicated. He probably *doesn't* have a large calendar in his office on which you can pencil in the times you need off for family functions. He — or she — may even be so insensitive as to expect you to put in a full forty hours each week, despite the demands of your wife and kids.

There are several ways to deal with such a boss. One is to exaggerate the importance of every event. For example, he may not let you off for just any ball game, but what if it were for the *district championship*? (He probably won't be aware that your son's team is 1-9.) A Cub Scout meeting is one thing, but what if *Clarence Thomas* is going to be there to present your child's good citizenship award? And you can assure your boss you wouldn't ask off for just *any* family get-together, but since your Aunt Marge was recently diagnosed with cancer of the septum and has only six weeks to live...

Okay, so this is a form of lying, and it's morally wrong. Even worse, it won't work for very long, unless your boss is a complete moron, and I'm not discounting that possibility. The good news, though, is that you'll soon be able to try all these lines on a new employer.

A better way to deal with this situation is to be totally up front. Let your boss know you're a family man — if he can't already tell from the strained peaches on your tie — and that, though you value your job and wish to do it well, your home life is also very important to you. Once he stops laughing and realizes you're serious, he may very well be willing to work with you, perhaps by allowing you to trade off with other employees or work overtime in exchange for comp time. Who knows? He may even be a family man himself. At least that would explain the "Looney Tunes" neckties.

The Hobgoblin of Small Minds

The last step in balancing your home and family life is to be consistent. Once you've established your priorities and communicated them to everyone involved, make sure you stick by them. As a matter of fact, I think this concept is somehow implied in the term "priority."

Consistency, in this case, has to do with both people and events. It would be inconsistent, for example, for you to take off work for your son's district championship football game but not for your daughter's year-end orchestra concert, however much you may prefer violence to violins. In the lives of your children, the two events are roughly analogous; from your standpoint, both children are equally precious. Your system of priorities must take these factors into account and make the necessary adjustments.

Consistency also means that your relationships with certain people, such as your wife, must *always* take precedence over your relationships with others, such as your neighbor's wife. If you say or imply to your wife that she is the most important person in the world to you, yet you actually spend far more time alone with your boss, she may well have reason to doubt you. She may also have reason to insist you get a blood test.

This does not mean, finally, that you will be completely inflexible. A rational system of priorities recognizes that there will be times when you are able to devote your attention to certain events or people, and other times when you may have to forego similar events or neglect those same people. In the latter instance, just make sure you're not actually wearing your golf clothes when you break the news. You can change later at the clubhouse.

Chapter 12

Ascending the Career Ladder (Emphasis on the First Syllable)

Because family men are less likely than other men to live solely for their careers, they generally tend not to be what I would call "climbers" — the kind of employee who will do *whatever* it takes to advance his career, from working 80-hour weeks to stabbing co-workers in the back, figuratively speaking (or maybe not). With a little thought and practice, the family man can learn to stab his co-workers in the back quite efficiently and still be home in plenty of time for dinner.

Nevertheless, and ironically, it is the family man who has the greatest *need* to move steadily up the career ladder. As his family grows, he finds that he must advance in order for his income merely to keep pace with the interest generated by his various credit accounts. Thus, he is forced to be, if not a climber, then at least a competitor in the workplace environment. In other words, the family man may not be a lion, but he can be a hyena — and the hyena usually has the last laugh.

It's also true that many family men manage to do well simply because they love their work and are good at it. A significant number of these are even able to love their work and succeed at it without loving their families any less or failing as husbands and fathers. In fact, the rest of us have a name for such men, but I can't print it here. You'll have to go to my website, or to the third-floor men's room, second stall from the left.

For the rest of us, this chapter is intended to serve as a kind of battle plan or survival guide. I don't necessarily recommend any of these approaches, but, hey, the chapter has to be about something.

Kissing Up Isn't As Bad As It Sounds

You probably learned long ago to despise "kiss ups" or "brown nosers," those who seek to ingratiate themselves with authority figures through lies and manipulations. You may have sworn, in your youthful days of purity and idealism, that you would never "kiss butt" just to get ahead. Your personal road to success, you vowed, would be paved with hard work, ability, and integrity.

Well, that was then and this is now. As you look around your stark and meager work space, you realize that hard work, ability, and integrity can only take you so far, and this is it. The coveted corner office down the hall — the one with a window — is occupied by a kiss-up, even though he has much less ability than you. (At least, you're convinced he has less ability, and your wife agrees. You hope.)

It's time you learned to play the game.

The most common variety of kiss-up is the so-called "yes man," who simply echoes the boss's opinions and tells him what he wants to hear. This is actually a pretty good policy. Because no matter how much your boss protests that he want employees who think for themselves, who are not afraid to disagree with him, rest assured that he probably doesn't.

This isn't necessarily to his discredit. (See how circumspect I'm being here? I have a boss, too, you know.) He — or she — got to be the boss by believing in himself and his ideas, by having strong opinions, which he wisely kept to himself when he wasn't the boss, but which he held nevertheless. This great self-confidence naturally leads him to believe that he is right about just about everything; ergo, if you disagree, you are wrong. No one wants people working for him who are always wrong.

So it definitely pays to be on the same wavelength as the boss — in other words, *right*. This makes you a *team player*, a *part of the family*, *someone who can be trusted*, not to mention *brilliant*, *insightful*, even *visionary*, if you happen to articulate his precise position before he does. (I wouldn't recommend you try this too often, as you run the risk of being wrong most of the time. But occasionally, if you have some inside information — maybe you've glanced over his shoulder at his notes, or put two and two together from previous conversations — it's worth the risk.) And everyone wants to be a team player, since the alternative is usually being cut from the squad.

Another common form of kissing up is flattery. Now, you might suppose that any but the most subtle forms of flattery would appear ridiculously transparent to someone intelligent enough to be the boss. Not so. The trick is simply to sound *sincere*. Your boss will accept just about any compliment as merely his or her due, so long as there is a clearly detectable note of sincerity in your voice.

This quasi-sincerity is something that can be cultivated. You can practice by making the most outrageous assertions in a tone calculated to suggest that any rational person would find them perfectly plausible. Try these, for starters (remember, sound convincing): "I really do believe that most politicians are basically honest." "You know, I think professional athletes deserve every penny they get." "This is the best book I've ever read."

Once you've developed your technique, you can test it at home on your wife. For example, when she comes in one evening after working in the garden for three hours, you might say something to her like, "You know, you're one of those rare women who looks just as good in old jeans and a T-shirt as you do in a cocktail dress." (Note to my wife: you really *are* one of those women, I swear.) Or how about this, at dinner one night: "Sweetheart, I don't know what you did to this macaroni and cheese, but it sure doesn't taste like it came out of a box." If she buys either one of those lines, you're ready for the boss.

Of course, you don't want to be *too* obvious. Don't, for instance, compliment your boss's outfit every day; just once or twice a week, especially when it's obvious that he's put a bit of extra effort into his appearance. (He's trimmed his nose hair, for example, or re-varnished his comb-over.) What doesn't matter is whether or not he *actually* looks good. It doesn't matter if he's color blind, or has a penchant for wearing stripes with plaids. If it's obvious from your boss's body language that *he* thinks he looks good, then it behooves you to reinforce that notion.

It's even more important for you to compliment your boss's *ideas*. This *is* something that you should do regularly, at least as often as you go to the bathroom, though not necessarily at the same time. Here again, it doesn't matter if the idea is actually a good one, only that *he* thinks it is. And it isn't enough merely to be a yes-man, repeating the boss's ideas and pretending they're also your own. You must periodically come right out and say, "That's a great idea." Try it with me now: "That's a great idea." A little more sincerity: "That's a *great* idea!" Well, work on it.

Since the sincerest form of flattery is imitation, you can carry things a bit further by trying to look and act like your boss. Here you must be careful; you don't want to be seen as trying to *mock* the guy. It's okay if you *are* mocking him, as long it's not apparent to anyone other than yourself or perhaps another trusted co-worker, of which there is actually no such thing. So enjoy your little joke, but keep it to yourself.

You wouldn't want to wear identical clothes, for example, even if you could find the same Goodwill store. But if your boss favors dark suits, white shirts, and conservative ties, you might want to consider moth balling the tweed jackets and mock turtlenecks. And if the boss keeps his hair cut short, you should probably think about trimming your own locks. (Yes, I know you've worn your hair that way since college. Maybe it's time it went the way of your AC/DC T-shirt. Oh. Still got that? Never mind.) Above all, if your boss's hair is thinning, do *not* wear yours in a style that flaunts its luxurious fullness. That is career suicide.

You can also imitate the way your boss speaks and the things he says. I warn you that the risk of apparent mockery is at its highest here. But as long as you maintain your tone of sincerity, along with a kind of simple-minded innocence, no one is likely to notice, least of all your boss. He'll be too busy congratulating himself on hiring such a bright, attractive, well-spoken employee.

Another way you can kiss up to your boss is to allow him to take credit for your accomplishments. Now, I say this knowing full well that he is *going* to take credit for your accomplishments whether you *allow* him to or not. I'm simply suggesting that you can either fight it and feel resentful, or you can accept the fact as a necessary element of work-place survival.

Once you have reached a state of acceptance, you can begin handing over your accomplishments to your boss on a silver platter, as it were, along with thinly-veiled hints that he may openly take credit without fear of resentment or outright protest from you. ("I couldn't have done this without your support," or "This was all based on an idea you gave me, anyway.") If you do this often enough, your boss may soon realize that a fair number of his supposed "accomplishments" are actually yours. Then you will have entered that Nirvana of workers everywhere, *indispensability*, which is another term for "perpetual employment."

Finally — and this is very subtle, so don't miss it — you can kiss up to your boss by defending him to co-workers. This may be very difficult to arrange, since to have any effect your boss must *hear* you do it, and none of your co-workers is likely to say anything insulting in his hearing. So you must always be alert for opportunities that present themselves.

Consider the following scenario: You're in a department meeting, and your boss has just announced another one of his hair-brained schemes. As your colleagues sit in stunned silence, you rise and say something like this: "I know what most of you are thinking, because you've discussed it with me in relation to past proposals. You think that this idea is totally impractical. Well, I think that's just because we don't see the big picture. We're not the visionaries (your boss's name here) is. I think we need to stop asking 'why?' and start asking 'how?'" Then sit down. Your boss may not actually kiss you on the lips, but he will want to.

If such an opportunity does not readily present itself, you can try manufacturing one. At a similar meeting, for example, you could offer an opinion that you know to be your boss's. One of your unwitting co-workers will inevitably walk right into the trap and say something profound and incisive, like, "That's crap." To which you may reply, sweetly yet with conviction, "Well, it was actually Mr. So-and-so's idea to begin with, and I think it's a good one." Cha-ching! Up you go on the Scale of the Boss's Caprice. Your co-worker-slash-competitor, meanwhile, is toast. Office Darwinism at its finest.

Back-Stabbing: It Worked for Brutus

Speaking of office Darwinism, another good way to get ahead is to undermine your co-workers. The basic theory at work here is that the worse they look, the better you'll look in comparison. You might not be exceptionally bright or talented, but if all of your co-workers are complete buffoons, you may appear to your superiors to be the firm's only hope of survival, and they will lavish you with promotions, raises, and bonuses. (This explains, by the way, how your current boss got where he is.) If your co-workers are *not* complete buffoons, then it's your job to make them *look* that way.

There are any number of strategies for accomplishing this objective. You can log onto their computers when they're at lunch and make changes in their reports. When a co-worker is a few minutes late — or has just gone to the bathroom — you can stick your head in the boss's office and say something like, "Have you seen Bill? He was supposed to meet me here first thing this morning to work on the McPherson project. No?

Guess I'll go call him at home." Or you can ask a colleague, when leaving the office on Friday, if he got the memo about "dress-down Monday." I'm really just brainstorming here. The possibilities are endless.

If your co-workers are genuinely capable, as opposed to yourself, you can still make yourself look superior by taking credit for their work. It is a truism in most office settings that the first person to present an idea generally gets credit for it. Thus, if your talents run less to creativity, originality, and self motivation and more to eavesdropping, snooping, and outright thievery, you're probably in a good position to earn the boss's approbation by stealing your co-workers ideas — only the good ones, of course, and only those you know he'll like — and presenting them to your boss before they do. This strategy has the added benefit of making your co-workers look like plagiarists or johnny-come-lately's once they do make their presentations. The boss will think they stole those ideas from *you*.

Another method of undermining your co-workers is to help spread vicious rumors about them. There is usually no shortage of rumors in an office, so for the most part you'll merely be a conduit, whose job it is to see that these rumors ultimately reach the boss's ears (unless of course they *involve* the boss — or yourself). The best kinds are those that deal with embarrassing situations or imply an underlying instability, such as rumors of sexual misconduct, drug use, binge drinking, or religious affiliation. You might say that, as a conscientious employee, it's your *duty* to make sure your boss knows of such allegations. After all, they might be true.

If rumors are in scarce supply, you can always take it upon to yourself to create some. You'll have to be very careful here, as you do not want these stories traced back to you. It's always best to begin with "I heard" or "Somebody told me." You can even put yourself on the side of the angels by claiming disbelief, as in, "You know, I've heard that Marvin is an alcoholic, but I just find it hard to believe. I mean, he shows up on time for work most days, he seems to be pretty lucid most of the time, and you rarely see him leave his desk more than 20 or 30 times a day. It's obviously just a vicious rumor."

Finally, you can undermine your co-workers by using the age-old strategy of pitting them against each other while you stand above the fray. Try something like this, for example: Take a report you're working on with a colleague to another co-worker who is not involved in the project and ask him to go over the figures as a favor. Then go back to your colleague, say, "I'll get that report to you a little bit later. Bill wanted to check your figures," and watch them go at it. Or you can stir up the entire office by telling each of your co-workers what "you heard" the others are making in salary — exaggerated for effect, of course.

Be assured that, as you put these strategies into effect, your co-workers will certainly come to hate you. But what better way of showing upper management what excellent boss material you are than to be despised by everyone around you? Besides, one day, when you *are* the boss, they're going to hate you anyway, so you might as well get a head start.

A Last Resort

If all else fails — if you can't bring yourself to kiss up, you don't have the stomach to step on a few fingers on your way up the corporate ladder, or you're just one of those guys who is far too nice for his own good — then you can try to improve your lot by actually doing a good job. I don't really recommend this, though, for a number of reasons.

First, if you always do excellent work, then your boss will come to expect it, and will be disappointed when you are only, say, above average. This is why you see so many of your colleagues doing mediocre work, even though they have slightly above-average capability. They understand that the first rule of work-place survival is to lower expectations. Thus the public is not surprised when banks close at four, when a two-mile stretch of highway takes a year to complete, when our high school graduates read at an eighth-grade level: we don't expect anything more. Just imagine how frustrated we'd be if we thought that everyone was actually trying to do a good job.

Secondly, unless you have FBI counter-espionage training, doing good work will only allow your less scrupulous colleagues to advance their own careers by stealing your ideas and claiming them as their own. When this happens, you can't go complaining to the boss all the time without being seen as a whiner. You can combat the problem, however, by doing most of your important work at home. Bring it in only when you are ready to show the boss. If this means that you aren't doing anything worthwhile at your desk all day, then you should fit in well with the rest of the office staff.

Thirdly, suppose you do manage to do a good job, despite all the obstacles. Suppose your boss even recognizes you for it, on his way to the meeting where he will take credit. The only result will be that your co-workers will hate you far more than if you simply sought to undermine them like everyone else. You are raising expectations, not only for yourself but for them as well, and they will deeply resent it.

Your boss may even come to resent it. He won't necessarily mind your good ideas, as long as he can take credit for them and thereby ensure his own high performance evaluations, and as long as you don't make him look bad by flaunting those good ideas in front of the other employees — or in front of *his* bosses. But he certainly doesn't want to be shown up. (Please note that, depending on your boss, it may take considerable effort on your part *not* to show him up.)

Which brings me to my last point: if you think the keys to success are hard work, imagination, and achievement, then you're in for a rude awakening, not to mention a lot of brush-offs, lost promotions, and downsizings. Again, all you have to do is take a look at those above *you*. Do you think they got there by being good at what they do? Then how do you explain the fact that they aren't good at it *now*?

No, you're much better off spending your time kissing up to the boss and plotting against your colleagues than actually working. But you'll have to excuse me. I need to close this chapter now. My co-worker down the hall has just gone to lunch, and there's something I wanted to look at on his computer...

Chapter 13

The More Things Change, the More They Stay Insane

Despite what I said in Chapter 12 about "perpetual employment," these days there's really no such thing as job security, except perhaps for license plate makers and former White House interns. Very few people stay in one job their entire career, what with all the layoffs, downsizings, reorganizations, and sexual harassment lawsuits that seem to be the order of the day. And that's just in the federal government.

It's also true that people sometimes make changes of their own choosing, accepting promotions within their companies, moving from one job to another, or even changing careers altogether. They do this for a variety of reasons, the most important being more money. Other reasons include increased autonomy, more money, better working conditions, more money, and more money.

For the family man, the concern is that these kinds of perfectly normal life changes can cause tremendous stress for those he cares about most: the other three members of his foursome. When things happen that are beyond his control, a man's entire life can be thrown into turmoil, much as if some distant set of relatives had shown up on his doorstep with luggage. It is at such times that the family man must show his strength of character by dealing with those situations in a way that does not involve firearms.

Even positive changes, involving a higher salary, more prestige, and a better quality of life, can cause serious problems at home. Often, as a result of his new responsibilities, a man finds himself spending less time with his family, driving greater distances to work, or bringing his work home with him more frequently. He may even have to move his entire household, if he has taken a job in another city or if his new status requires a Jeffersonian move to a better neighborhood. (I'm talking about *George* Jefferson, not Thomas.)

Thus, it is incumbent upon you as a family man to be prepared for sudden and unexpected job changes, and to weigh carefully the impact on your family before choosing to make any change. Above all, remember that change is good, whether of your choosing or not. It enables you to grow, to develop new skills and abilities, and with any luck, to sell your house before the dry rot is visible from the outside.

Up the Down Elevator

The dynamics of the modern workplace are often quite volatile. In most organizations of any size at all, employees are constantly coming in, going out, moving up, moving down, so that the company phone list has to be updated almost weekly. (Hey, talk about job security. If your current position is downsized, maybe you can get on as phone-list updater.)

Obviously, the best kind of internal career move is a promotion. Simply put, this means that you are given a better job within the same organization — "better" being defined as carrying more prestige and probably involving more responsibility. You might also get an increase in salary, but don't assume that will necessarily be the case. Sometimes, you just have to settle for other coveted perks, such as an impressive title, a new office, use of the executive washroom, and an additional twenty working hours per week.

I've already discussed at length how you can *get* a promotion (see Chapter 12). Now let's talk about the impact it might have on your family.

First of all, if your promotion does come with a pay raise, this will probably be the most significant change as far as your family is concerned. Oh, I'm sure your wife will be impressed with your new title — remember guys, power is the ultimate aphrodisiac — and the kids may enjoy the occasional surreptitious weekend visit to the executive washroom (I hear they have genuine, two-ply, facial-quality toilet paper in there), but it's the money that will mean the most to them. Don't worry, though. The excitement will soon pass. After a few weeks of feeling almost decadently affluent, you will buy something new — a house, a car, bedroom furniture — and you'll be just as broke as ever.

A more lasting result of your promotion is likely to be the stress induced by its new responsibilities. You see, the problem with being given a promotion is that you are then expected to *perform*. Quite the little bait-and-switch, isn't it? If you fail to perform at the expected level, you may very well lose your promotion, even your job, which you can hardly afford to do, having just bought that new house/car/furniture. So you have no choice but to perform, whatever that takes. (And you think this is not a conscious manipulation on the part of your "superiors"?)

Which leads us to the next problem associated with getting a promotion: increased working hours. *Hugely* increase-ed working hours. Working hours increased to the point that, even after your raise, your hourly rate is still 20 per cent less than it was before. Such is the essence of the modern work-place: just when you thought you were beating the system, the system wins again, and it is your employer — not you — who profits from the exchange by getting more work at a cheaper rate.

This can cause tremendous problems at home, since you'll hardly ever be there. Want to go out with your wife? Sorry, gotta work. Spend time with the kids? Nope. Take a vacation? Hah! (Ever notice the only time your boss can't seem to get by without you is when you're scheduled to be on vacation? The rest of the time it's the "No One is Indis-pensable" speech.) You've gotten your promotion, received your raise, *spent it*, and now you're stuck working seventy hours a week for the foreseeable future. Welcome to Middle America.

About the only thing you can do is keep trying to work your way up the ladder until you reach the level of those-who-no-longer-need-to-be-productive-because-everyone-under-them-is-doing-all-the-work: a vice-presidency, a partnership, a demi-godhood, however it's defined in your organization. Then all you'll have to do is show up at the office a few hours a week, play golf with clients, and manipulate the pathetic careers of those beneath you. Where's the stress in that?

Of course, as far as your family is concerned, none of that will matter. By the time you reach that point, your wife will have left you long ago for the furniture delivery man and your children will be grown and billing you for therapy. These are just a few things for you to take into consideration before you start putting into action my excellent advice in Chapter 12.

On the other hand, there are certainly worse things than getting a promotion. One of them is getting a *demotion*, which usually involves a drop in prestige *and* a drop in salary, but with no corresponding reduction in workload. In this case, you probably won't be buying anything new, but maybe giving up something instead. The good news is that you won't have to spend any less time with your family. In fact, if you're the kind of father who likes to get down on the floor and play with your children, you may come home one day to discover a lot more play area where the living room furniture used to be.

Then there's the worst career move of all: getting fired. Occasionally employees are still dismissed for old-fashioned reasons — incompetence, dishonesty, knocking up the boss's daughter. But more and more, workers are being let go due to no fault of their own, for reasons only euphemistically alluded to in the jargon of modern business. For instance, you can be "laid off," meaning, "You were a good employee, but now we have a machine to do your job." Or you can be "downsized," which means, "You were a good employee, but we've recently discovered that we never really needed you." In either case, your only recourse is to try to find another job, perhaps with a company that is "laying on" or "upsizing."

What this all means is that, nowadays, pretty much anybody can be fired. Yes, I know that's a depressing thought. The upside is that you'll experience a sharp reduction in both job-related responsibilities and working hours. Of course, you won't have any income, either. So you can spend all the time you want with your family, but it will probably be at your wife's parents' house.

Take This Job and Shove It

Now, when was the last time you read a book that cited Aristophanes, Freud, *and* Johnny Paycheck? Talk about eclectic.

Anyhow, the time may come when it will be necessary or advantageous for you to take an entirely new job, with a different company. Once again, this turn of events can be the product of choice (you've found a better job with a better salary, better working conditions, etc.), or not (you've been fired, laid off, downsized, whatever). In either case, your new job is bound to present some issues that need to be resolved within your family.

There are basically three types of new jobs: those that are a step (or more) down, those that supposedly represent what we call a "lateral move," and those that entail a definite move up. The only people who take a step down are 1) those who have been fired and are therefore happy to have any job at all and 2) complete lunatics, such as those who leave prestigious and lucrative positions in law or business to accept government appointments. On the other hand, anyone can make a lateral move, though most of these aren't what they seem. And, of course, all of us are looking for that great move up, that perfect job which will deliver us from our current hell and put us on the fast track to demi-godhood — uh, I mean a vice presidency.

If you have been fired from your previous job and are therefore forced to take a lesser and lower paying one, you will probably want to sit down and talk with your family about a corresponding lowering of their expectations. This won't necessarily be all bad. After all, your wife's liposuction can wait a few years, and the fact that you'll only be able to afford two meals a day in the meantime will surely help. And, you know, your son might really have struggled at Harvard, whereas he should do quite well at the community college, provided he can get a job in the snack bar. Your daughter's braces? She didn't really need those, anyway. Just teach her how to smile with her lips closed.

You may actually be amazed, if you find yourself in such a situation, at how your family pulls together through the whole ordeal. It may even be *good* for them, in some ways. They will probably learn a number of new and useful skills, such as how to garden and can vegetables, how to budget, how to prepare low cost, nutritious meals, how to make a prom dress out of discarded pillow cases. And your kids will discover that there *is* in fact a free lunch, after all, at least for a family of five making less than $35,000 a year.

Most of all, you shouldn't worry about how your wife and kids will view you now that you're no longer Mr. High-Powered Executive. They'll eventually warm to your new career path, especially when your new boss begins letting you take home all those loaves of bread and gallons of milk that have passed their expiration dates. Hey, every job has its perks.

If you're making a "lateral move," you may also want to discuss with your family the reasons for your decision. I say this because everyone knows there's really no such thing as a lateral move, unless, after being fired from one job, you are fortunate enough to be hired by another company in a similar capacity and at the same salary. Apart from that, any move is actually a move up or a move down.

For example, if you are somehow being forced out of a job you like — not fired, just made to feel uncomfortable or unwanted by those more adept than you at manipulation — then any other job, even at the same salary, will probably seem like a step down. Conversely, if you leave for another, and apparently similar, position because it just seems more attractive — perhaps you perceive that the boss is not a sadistic moron, or that the cubicles are large enough to hold actual desks, or that the health plan really does cover most illnesses and injuries — then that is in truth a move up. Remember, not all compensation is in the form of money. If your job is like mine, most of it isn't.

Moving Experiences

Then, of course, there's the third kind of job change — the obvious move up. For the most part, this is very similar to a promotion, with basically the same advantages and disadvantages, except that you are going to a different company. However, there is one other variable involved in this type of move: the possibility of *relocation*.

Now, I realize these days just about any change in your employment can cause you to have to move your family. If you work for a large company, you can be transferred to another city on a whim, or if you're lucky, on a moving van. In either case, though, whether you accept a transfer or take another job altogether, it's generally a choice you make. You don't *have* to move, but for whatever reason (more money? continued employment?) you want to.

Consider the impact this is likely to have on your family. Will their lives be completely disrupted? Will the upheaval cause permanent psychological damage? Will your wife leave you? Will your children hate you for the rest of their lives? The answers are yes, yes, possibly, and probably.

For these reasons, this is not a decision you should make alone, unless you plan to live with the consequences — alone. Before accepting any job that requires a move, you need to sit down with your family and discuss all the pros and cons. From your children's point of view, the main disadvantage will be leaving everything familiar to them. They like their house, they like their neighborhood, they like their friends, they like their school, blah, blah, blah. I don't suppose it ever occurred to you that your children's happiness could be such a nuisance.

You wife's objections are likely to be more complex. She, too, may like all those same things — house, school, etc. — but there may also be something even more important at stake: her own job. Never forget that if you are one half of a two-career couple, you must always demonstrate as much concern for your wife's career as for your own, whether you actually care about it or not. This is true even if you're convinced your career is far more important and that she ought to be willing to sacrifice for the good of the family, meaning for your own personal benefit. (Word to the wise: whatever you do, don't use the word "sacrifice" in your negotiations, unless you're prepared for a lengthy diatribe on pregnancy, labor and delivery, breast feeding, etc. Hey, it's not your fault you can't bear children.)

In any case, please note my use of the word *negotiation.* Because that's really what it comes down to. You want to take a new job in a different city, and the rest of your family doesn't want to move. Fine. You now have several options. You can go without them and either get a divorce or maintain a long-distance relationship — neither of which is advisable, as both involve sleeping alone (presumably) and supporting, or helping to support, two households. You can insist they come anyway and steel yourself to deal with their bitter resentment for the rest of your natural life, which may not be very long. Or — and this is what I suggest — you can *negotiate.*

The first significant issue in these negotiations will be money. I don't mean to imply that your family can be bought, but, hey, let's face it: your family can be bought. If your new job is going to pay enough to dramatically improve your lifestyle, you can probably persuade the rest of your family that the move will be worth a few inconveniences. Once the money issue is resolved, everything else will fall into place. So your wife and kids are going to miss your house? Buy them a bigger one. Neighborhood? How about one with a pool and tennis courts. Friends? The best money can buy. And so on.

You can probably even persuade your wife to leave her job using the same basic argument, essentially promising to help her find a new and better paying job in your new city. The fact that you may eventually have to live up to that promise can be a bit of a sticking point, but by then you will be safely ensconced in your big new executive home in the suburbs. If your wife gets bored, she can always play tennis with the other wives.

On the other hand, if your new job *won't* pay enough to ensure a dramatically improved lifestyle, then you would be wise never to broach the subject. Maybe your family can be bought, but if they're like mine, they're not cheap. No one — not your wife, not your kids — is going to follow you around the country just to indulge your sense of adventure, pander to some sophomoric, "grass is always greener" need for change, or help improve your grasp of American geography. Nor should you ask them to, unless of course they're just as flaky as you are (and I've known families like that).

The Seven Year Itch

Some guys go through a phase, in their mid-thirties to early forties, when they want not just a new job but a whole new *career*, just as some men supposedly go through a phase when they want to leave their wives. Not that this has ever happened to me personally — the wanting to leave my wife part, that is (note to my wife: I mean that in all sincerity). But I have thought many times about changing my career, to something like shoe model, white water rafting guide, or nuclear engineer.

And tell the truth: haven't you always admired the guy with the guts to go ahead and take the plunge? I've known a few, including one who left a prestigious and promising position in banking to go into the ministry, and another who gave up a lucrative sales job to become an artist. I have great admiration for both these men, mingled with sincere doubts as to their sanity. There's something in me that wants to say, "If they can do it, I can do it." Then my wife talks to their wives, and I have the good sense to tell that something in me to shut up.

Because, as romantic as it sounds, the harsh reality is that someone who wants to completely change his career must have or acquire at least one of the following: 1) a great deal of money; 2) additional formal training; and/or 3) a willingness to start over at the bottom.

The problem is that, for most guys, change means *change*. Thus, the accountant doesn't want to become an investment banker, the latter profession being at least somewhat related to the former. Oh, no. He wants to raise sheep in Australia. Which is perfectly fine, as long as he has *a great deal of money*. If he expects to actually make a living at his new occupation, he's going to find himself in deep sheep-dip.

Likewise, the ambulance driver isn't content merely to dream of escaping his dead-end job for a position in management. No, he wants to be a lawyer, of all things. This means acquiring a tremendous amount of *additional formal training*, probably in the form of years of night school (unless he drives at night, in which case it would be day school). By the time he finally gets to the point where he could legally chase himself, he's missed hours of overtime in which he could have made a killing. (Please forgive the awful puns. They were irresistible.)

The biggest problem I have with changing careers, though, is the idea of *starting over at the bottom*. I've been in my current profession all my adult life, and I've reached, shall we say, a certain point. It's not much of a point, but it's mine. More importantly, it is considerably higher than "entry level." Okay, it's a little higher than entry level. But as I look at the advertisements for other professions — even those more glamorous than mine, which is to say all of them — I see that most are hiring only at the entry level. And I am keenly aware that there is no way I can afford to take one of those jobs, not if I want my family to continue to enjoy its current lifestyle. Do you have any idea what they pay entry-level shoe models these days?

So we're back to square one. Unless you have large amounts of money, or unless your family is willing to suffer through years of deprivation just so you can feel fulfilled (hah!), you're probably stuck with the career you have. You can either wallow in self-pity or make the most of it.

Okay, so while you're wallowing, could you pass me the want ads?

Chapter 14

The After-Work Letdown

If you're like most guys, you spend a good part of your workday wishing you were at home. Then, when you get home, you spend the first thirty minutes to an hour wishing you were back at work. This is what we call the "after-work letdown."

I think the problem is rooted in unrealistic expectations. Your time at work can be tedious, boring, and stressful. You naturally assume that, once you get home, your time there will be invigorating, entertaining, and relaxing. In truth, your home life is seldom any of those things. Instead, it is often tedious, boring, and stressful. And you don't even get paid for it.

Shall I recount the ways in which home life can be tedious, boring, and stressful? Let's see: crying babies, grocery shopping, dirty dishes, financial statements, driving teenagers, unfolded laundry, leaky faucets, waist high grass, dented fenders, little league practices, math homework, mortgage payments, meal preparation, notes from the teacher, toddlers and swing sets, annoying neighbors, daughters' boyfriends, telemarketers, stopped-up toilets, boys and footballs, credit card offers, book reports, oil changes, broken Barbies... and that's just for starters. I'm sure your wife could supply a more complete list.

It's not so much that you *mind* helping your wife in the kitchen — make that *working with* your wife in the kitchen — or paying the bills, or doing odd jobs around the house. Having read and re-read the first section of this book, you duly accept those responsibilities as part and parcel of your calling as a family man. And you certainly don't mind spending time with your kids — *just not right when you walk in the door*. And there lies the rub.

Just as you have expectations of what your time at home will be like, so your wife and kids have expectations of you, beginning, unfortunately, right when you walk in the door. Some of their expectations, like your own, may be unrealistic, but many of them are quite reasonable. You *do* have certain responsibilities, and some of them must be attended to right away. On the other hand, are your own expectations so entirely out of line?

Of course they are. But if you insist on believing otherwise, then you must at least learn to balance your expectations against those of other family members. This means, first, finding a way to take some time for yourself — a kind of buffer between job and home. Secondly, you might have to change your own attitude. If, upon walking in the door and being immediately overrun, you display your annoyance too openly, your family might think you're annoyed with *them*. You are, of course, but you don't want to hurt their feelings. Their bodies, maybe, but not their feelings.

Ultimately, you must work with your wife and kids to reach compromises that address the needs of everyone involved — or, failing that, at least address the needs of everyone other than yourself. For the family man, that's generally what "compromise" means.

It Isn't Miller Time

The image of the weary office worker stopping by his cozy, cheerful neighborhood pub for a drink or two on his way home from work has become something of a cliché in modern society. I suspect this is not because it's really all that common, but because the beer companies sponsor so much of our television programming.

It's not my purpose here to preach to you about what you should and shouldn't do. However, the after-work happy hour isn't something I recommend for the family man. First of all, I'm not sure having a couple of beers on the way home is the best way to make your life easier once you *get* home — though, admittedly, you may not notice the stress quite as much. Moreover, your wife is likely to resent this particular diversion, and your only defense will be, “That’s *my* time.” With that attitude, you’re likely to have *a lot* of time to yourself — in a motel down by the freeway.

Instead, do something constructive, or at least something you can defend to your wife as constructive. Like exercise. If you want to stop off somewhere for an hour or so on your way home from work, why not make it a gym instead of a bar? You can lift weights, run, play a little racquetball or basketball, belch loudly without having to say “excuse me,” catch a whopping dose of athlete’s foot — all those things you enjoyed so much when you were younger. This will be a great stress reducer, and it will also make you look and feel better in the long term, which I’m not sure can be said of happy hour. Best of all, how can your wife object? Doesn’t she want you to be healthier and live longer? Even if she doesn’t, she can hardly say so.

If you’re not into lifting weights, contact sports, or skin rashes, you can still get some exercise and create a little stress-free breathing space simply by *walking*. For those who live close enough, this could mean walking to and from the office — or *cycling*, though that requires more equipment and is more demanding on the leg muscles, not to mention the prostate. But even if you have to drive to work like most people, I’m sure you can find a small park, not too far out of the way, where you can stop several evenings per week and enjoy a quiet, relaxing walk before heading on home. This may prevent you from taking a hike once you do get home.

On the other hand, you don’t necessarily have to wait until after work to exercise. If your schedule at the end of the day is tight, or if stopping by the gym or the park will put you home so late that the health benefits will be more than offset by the potential threat to life and limb, then consider exercising at another time, such as during your lunch break, or better yet, during the boss's lunch break. You'll still look and feel better, and you'll still be reducing your stress level, which is bound to help when you confront the wife and kids at the end of the day. (Note: you may find that looking better leads to more satisfactory confrontations, as well.)

For the athletically disinclined, another ostensibly constructive way to catch a breather between work and home is to stop by the public library. Here you can spend anything from ten minutes to an hour, browsing through the stacks or just relaxing in peaceful solitude. (Spend much more than an hour relaxing in peaceful solitude and some guy with a pushcart may come by and ask you to swap shoes.) If your wife wants to know why you weren't home sooner, just tell her you've been improving your mind. How can she object to that? She's suggested it often enough.

Seriously, though, I think you can tell your wife the truth about your library visits, at least once a week. The other evenings you can tell her you're doing research for work, or looking up hot new job prospects. Surely she won't have a problem with one purely self-indulgent visit to the library per week, especially if you check out a book for her, too — maybe a popular novel, or better yet a self-help book like *1001 Ways to Make Your Man Happy*. She'll be far too touched by your thoughtfulness to be upset just because you're a little late getting home.

Weird Al in Traffic

If you live so far from work, or you commute is so demanding, that you can't take time to stop *anywhere* on your way home — except maybe in the middle of the interstate — I have a few other suggestions.

Most people are conditioned to hate commuting, especially the sitting in traffic part. Some, however, have learned to use this time wisely. So it takes you 90 minutes to get home in rush hour traffic? *Then there's your built-in buffer*

— provided you learn to use it as such, instead of using it to honk and swear and fume and raise your blood pressure, and perhaps bring yourself to the attention of the lethally armed.

My suggestion is that you make use of what your automobile has to offer, and I don't mean reclining seats. I'm talking about the sound system. If you're going to be stuck in traffic for 45 minutes to an hour anyway, and since you can't very well exercise, read, or watch TV during that time, you might as well listen to something you enjoy.

You can try the radio, of course, but it may not help much. At that time of day, you're unlikely to find anything on the dial but inane deejay chatter, depressing news stories, and "up-to-the-minute" reports on the traffic jam you've already been sitting in for twenty minutes. You need something more soothing and uplifting. Treat yourself to tapes or CD's by some of the world's great composers, like Beethoven, Mozart, Barry Manilow, and Weird Al Yankovic. Or, if you feel intimidated by that level of sophistication, just bring out some of your old favorite recordings, the ones that pick up your spirits and make you feel young again: Fleetwood Mac, Steely Dan, the Archies. Leave Ozzie Osborne for another time.

When you tire of music, try self-help cassettes, or books-on-tape. Personally, I like comedy, like Monty Python, Steve Martin's old albums, and anything by Al Gore. The objective is to lighten your mood, to make you feel better than you did when you left the office, so that when you do walk in your front door, you won't be tempted to kick the first person you see in the solar plexus. This is bound to improve both your commute and its aftermath.

One more point about taking time for yourself: if you aren't able to do it right after work, then find some other time. If the only time you can exercise, or read, or listen to vice-presidential humor is late in the evening after the kids have gone to bed, do it then. This will give you something to look forward to, which may help alleviate some of the after-work letdown, and will certainly reduce your overall stress level.

You may even find there are things you and your wife can do *together* to help ease stress — other than that, I mean. Then the time won't be entirely your own, but, hey, if you wanted to do everything alone, you wouldn't have gotten married, would you?

Attitude Adjustment

Whether or not you find time to unwind after work, you must try to develop a more positive attitude toward that first hour or so at home. I say this knowing full well how difficult that can be. When you were young, "attitude adjustment" usually meant being struck repeatedly in the buttocks with a large, flat object. Now you're going to have to do it on your own — change your attitude, I mean, not strike yourself in the buttocks. That requires a degree of coordination most of us no longer possess.

I think there are several keys here. First, you must always bear in mind that all of this — job, home, wife, kids — is *your choice*. No one is *making* you be a family man. If you wanted to badly enough, you could turn that car right around and head for... wherever. Of course, you wouldn't get far before your wife canceled the credit cards and changed the ATM password. But, hey, you're a resourceful guy. You could get by.

Doesn't sound too attractive, does it? If you had wanted to live in a motel down by the freeway or a cabin in the woods, you'd already be doing that. If you had wanted to live the swinging single life, you could have done that, too. The fact is, you *chose* the life you have now over the other possibilities that were open to you. (Which is not to say you would have chosen it over possibilities that *weren't* open to you, such as being a professional athlete or an international playboy — but you probably would have. At least, that's the story I'd go with.) You *wanted* to be married, you *wanted* to have kids, you *wanted* a challenging career and a house in the suburbs. Now you have them, and there's no one to blame but yourself.

Stressed out after a tough day? Don't blame your wife. Just look at her. She's stressed out, too, as the force with which she's wielding that paring knife might suggest. If her day had been any worse, there'd be nothing left of that poor cucumber.

Want to sit down and put your feet up? Then you shouldn't have had children, especially boys who like to play ball. Tell the truth: didn't you swear, after hearing Harry Chapin's "Cat's in the Cradle" for the fiftieth time, that when *you* had a son, you would never tell him, "not today"?

Acknowledging all this may not actually reduce the very real stress you feel, but it can strengthen your resolve to *behave* better. I've always admired the philosophies of the early twentieth-century psychologist William James, who taught that, if you want to *be* something, you should *act* as if you already are. Of course this idea forms the basis for transvestitism, among other things; but for our purposes what it suggests is that, even if you don't *feel* patient, you can *act* patient. And even when you don't *feel* like helping get dinner on the table, or playing ball in the front yard, or reading a book to a child, you can make yourself do it anyway — if not with a smile, then at least without muttering obscenities.

The Win-Win Situation

Finally, you can do a great deal to address the after-work letdown and remain in your family's good graces simply by being willing to compromise. For example, your wife and kids want you to come directly home after work, so you can do whatever it is they want you to do. You want to stop by the gym. An acceptable compromise, from their point of view, would be for you to come directly home after work, in return for which they agree not to leave you or sue for alimony and child support. Remember, the term "win-win" contains only two "wins." Your wife wins. Your children win. You lose.

If this is not your idea of a compromise, then you haven't been married very long. Strike that. What I meant to say was, if this isn't your idea of a compromise, then you need to sit down and have a talk with your wife. Let her know you love her, you love the kids, you love to spend as much time with them as possible — lie if you have to — but you just need a few minutes to unwind after work. I'm sure she'll understand. If not, just show her the results of your most recent physical exam (available at www.bogusdoc.med).

Faced with this new evidence, she may agree to your stopping by the gym, or the library, a couple of times a week — provided you come directly home on the other days. Or she may agree to give you a brief, twenty- or thirty-minute respite after you walk in the door, provided that you then attend to your household duties. I'll bet she can even be persuaded to let you to go wherever you want, whenever you want — as long as you take the kids with you and bring home take-out. Compromise doesn't get any better than that.

Those who become expert negotiators can use this method to obtain other concessions, such as sex. Okay, that's unlikely, but how about weekend outings? Essentially, you say to your wife, "I agree to come straight home from work every evening to help you with the housework and tend to the children. But Saturday mornings are mine. That's when I'm going to play golf with my buddies." To which your wife replies: "Ha!" Hey, it was worth a try.

Actually, I'm sure your wife would be willing to trade a little Saturday morning golf for a week's worth of help in the evenings. She'll be relieved you didn't ask for sex.

In conclusion, it's worth bearing in mind that if your wife also works full time, she is probably battling after-work letdown, too. In that case, compromise may well involve taking turns being the one to get home later. Perhaps you could work out an arrangement whereby she goes to the gym on Mondays and Wednesdays, and you go on Tuesdays and Thursdays. Or maybe, two or three nights a week, *you* can be the one to give *her* a thirty minute break after she gets home — provided she pitches right in afterward to help with the kids and the evening chores. Excuse me: to *work with you* on those things.

Chapter 15

From Day Care to Sweat Shop

The idea of taking your kids to visit your work place has only recently begun to gain acceptability, with the advent of such nationally recognized programs as "Take Your Daughter to Work Day" and "Help Your Good-for-Nothing Teenage Son Find a Job Day." However, people have been doing it for years, usually because the babysitter is sick.

I can think of plenty of other good reasons for taking your kids to work, though. First of all, it's good for your kids to see you at work, to gain a better understanding of just what it is you do when you're not at home, or on the golf course, or fishing, or at the racetrack. Once they see how hard you work during a typical day, they're much more likely to appreciate you and all the things your job provides: food, shelter, clothing, dental floss. (Note: If you don't normally work all that hard, you might want to fake it when your children are there — unless, of course, your entire purpose for bringing them is to get them to do your work for you, which I'll touch on shortly.)

Taking your children to work can also help them learn how a business operates. Unless you keep them hidden in your cubicle — i.e., you only brought them because you didn't have a sitter — they will probably come into contact with many of your co-workers and thus be able to observe a variety of different job-related activities. They'll see clerical workers doing *their* thing, technical support people doing *their* thing, middle managers doing *no*thing. Best of all, they'll have front row seats as upper management does *its* thing, in the form of your boss's ten-minute tirade on the impropriety of bringing children to the office. Hey, it's good to be humiliated in front of your kids every once in a while. Keeps them from putting you on a pedestal.

Your boss really shouldn't be upset, though. Because having young people visit is good for business, too, which is why companies like Wal-Mart, Coca-Cola, General Motors, and McDonald's actively encourage schools to visit their plants and stores. These field trips are great for public relations, and they allow the companies to market their products to new generations of consumers. They also help perpetuate the work force by exposing impressionable children to glamorous careers such as fry cook and rear-window installer.

So if your boss gives you any trouble about having your children at work, just tell him you're supervising a small field trip. If it helps, get the kids little hats, badges, coffee mugs, laptop computers — whatever your company uses as giveaways. And be sure and stick some of those "HI, I'm_" labels to their little shirtfronts.

Most importantly, taking your kids to work can be good for *you,* provided it doesn't get you fired. If the children are there for a legitimate reason, such as one of the programs mentioned above, then you can probably get away with doing nothing all day, other than showing them around. And the two places I recommend you spend the most time showing them are the break room and the inside of your office, with the door shut. Be sure to bring lots of comic books, or hand-held video games. Bring something for the kids, too.

Beasts of Burden

If you have especially bright or gullible children, you may even be able to con them into doing some of your work for you. How many of us, for example, have a ten- or eleven-year-old child who is already more technologically advanced than we ever aspire to be? The guys who don't have their hands up are the techno-geeks. The rest of us could use some help — and we shouldn't be embarrassed to ask our children. After all, we're the ones who helped them with their math homework, all the way through second grade.

Arranging for your son or daughter to help you at work may require a certain amount of subterfuge on your part. First, you have to get the child out of school, which in some parts of the country might require plastic explosives and a get-away helicopter. However, you can usually arrange for a day away from classes by convincing the child's teacher it's some sort of special occasion. Remember that your children have only so many grandparents, so the "death-in-the-family" excuse should be used sparingly. It's better to claim that it's "Take Your Daughter to Work Day." (After all, how many people know the actual date?) Or invent some similar program sponsored exclusively by your company, like "Technological Morons Take Their Genius Children to Work Day." Your child's teacher shouldn't have much trouble believing at least the first part.

Once you get the child to work, you may have to hide him or her from the boss. This too can be difficult, especially if the child is sitting at your desk, using your computer. You can try dressing the child up to look like you and placing him on a stack of phone books. This way, if your boss just happens to walk by and glance into your cubicle, he may not notice the difference, unless the fact that the person seated at your desk is actually hard at work gives the whole thing away. Or you can stow the child under your desk, to give you verbal instructions while watching your computer screen through one those little cardboard periscopes.

Even if your children are not geniuses — in other words, they take after you — you can still find ways to put them to work. You can always bring them by the office after school to help with some of your more menial tasks, like collating and stapling pages for a report. This is especially handy if you aren't able to time your report to coincide with the one day of the month when the office's $250,000 copier is actually working.

If your job involves manual labor, like some sort of construction, you can lighten your own workload and include your kids by having them carry lumber, stack bricks, or operate the jackhammer. Boys especially love this sort of thing. You can even get them their own little hard hats and butt-crack-revealing jeans.

The point is to spend some relationship-building time with your children while blatantly shirking your own work duties. If you handle it just right your kids won't even realize what you're doing. They'll think collating a 200-page report or hauling four tons of bricks is great fun.

A Better World for Women: Your Contribution to Gender Equity

I've already mentioned the national "Take Your Daughter to Work" program a couple of times in passing, so I thought I'd take a few paragraphs to deal with it more fully. First of all let me say I think it's an excellent program. About the only thing better would be a "Send Your Daughter to Work in Your Place" day.

I suppose this program was first conceived as a way of introducing young girls to careers that in the past have been closed to them. Nowadays, of course, women can be anything men can be, including close-minded, pig-headed, and chauvinistic. That's the beauty of a truly egalitarian society.

For this reason, it is especially important that fathers in fields where women have been traditionally under-represented — such as engineering, law enforcement, and public sanitation, to name a few — be among the first to participate. This is not to say that if you are a teacher or a nurse, you *shouldn't* take your daughter to work with you. Those are perfectly honorable professions, for women as well as men, regardless of what extreme elements in the women's movement might say. Even so, you may want to consider steering your daughter into law or international finance, unless, of course, you think you can actually live on your pension.

A word of caution is also in order here. There are some fathers who, due to the nature of their jobs, should never take their daughters to work with them. I mean, some environments are simply unsuitable for young girls, even in the interests of gender equity. Included on this list would be prison guards, pimps, politicians, and male prostitutes (excuse the redundancy).

If you *are* able to take your daughter to work with you, I strongly urge you to do so at least once, in part for the reasons stated above: you can get out of most of your own work for the day, and you may even be able to get your daughter to do some of it for you (remember how her mother did your homework in college?). More importantly, though, you should do it for your daughter's sake. She is preparing to enter the work force one day and thus needs to be exposed to a positive professional role model. With any luck, you may have a colleague who fits that description.

Once you have arranged for your daughter to visit your work place, take time to plan the special day in advance. You want everything to be just right. You especially want to convey to her what an important person you are in the company. To this end, I suggest you bribe co-workers to call you "Sir" and "Mr." and bring "reports" to your desk throughout the day. If one of your superiors is on vacation that week, see if you can finagle to use his office. You can always tell his secretary you're there to fix his computer. If you discover it actually does need to be fixed, get your daughter to do it.

You should also plan activities to keep your daughter busy and interested during her day: touring the facilities, talking with various employees, viewing demonstrations, editing your quarterly report. While she is thus engaged, you can simply follow her around with your tie loosened and your hands in your pocket, smiling benignly. Though you are in reality doing nothing useful, people will think you're being a good father *and* a good representative of the company. This isn't quite as much fun as playing golf, but it sure beats working.

Be prepared, though, for some head-shaking and quizzical looks from your fellow employees. They will be thoroughly charmed by your daughter, and thus will secretly suspect she's adopted.

In closing this section, I'd like to say a few words about taking your young *son* to work: don't do it. He'll only destroy a piece of expensive equipment, draw characters from "World of Warcraft" on your financial statements, and leave a foul odor in the men's room — almost as foul as yours. Moreover, he probably *won't* charm your co-workers, much less your boss. In other words, they'll look at him and see a miniature you. I don't think you can afford that kind of validation of your less endearing qualities.

Of course, none of this applies if your son is especially well behaved — i.e., a catatonic schizophrenic — or if he possesses certain skills that can help you stay one step ahead of being downsized. In that case, all the same things discussed above apply, except that you either need to invent your own special "day" or disguise him as a girl. If you've walked by any display window at the mall lately, you'll know the latter option shouldn't be too difficult. Just have him wear a pair of skinny jeans and a nondescript T-shirt — in other words, what he would normally wear — and call him "Michelle."

The Best in Free Child Care

Perhaps the most common reason for taking your children to work — and in this case, it really can be child*ren* — is that you simply have nothing else to do with them. Maybe the sitter is sick, or school is out for the day, or they've been suspended for routing Internet pornography to the principal's PC. Fortunately, such events are rare — and, frankly, many principals wouldn't look a gift horse in the mouth.

And even when something like this does happen, it should be your problem only half the time, assuming your wife works outside the home. If not, then it's her problem *all* the time, unless she can find a way to get out of it, like faking major surgery. Never underestimate her resourcefulness in that regard.

So you shouldn't have to take your kids to work with you under adverse circumstances very often. But inevitably you might at some point, so you should probably know how to deal with it.

One approach is to be completely open with your boss. Explain the circumstances, and promise that the children will be quiet and non-disruptive. If necessary, produce the Valium tablets you brought from home and demonstrate how quickly one dissolves in Kool-Aid. (After the demonstration, when your boss isn't looking, quickly drink the Kool-Aid. This will help prepare you for the day ahead.) If this is the first time you have had to bring your kids to the office, and if your boss is good-natured and understanding, and if the Valium has the desired effect (on both the kids and yourself), you should be able to survive the day with your job intact. The other 99.3 per cent of the time, I'm afraid you're going to have to be more devious.

When openness is not an option, here are a couple of other strategies you may find useful. First, as I've already mentioned above, you can claim that it's some sort of special day. This is easy if you have only girls. Just go with "Take Your Daughter to Work Day" and leave it at that. After all, your boss is no more likely than the child's teacher to know the correct date. Months later, when he happens to hear or read about the real thing and asks you about it, just look at him funny and say, "That was last year." He'll merely nod and walk away, mumbling to himself. (Note: If, on the other hand, he happens to hear about it the next *week*, you're dead. So be sure to check the dates yourself.)

Having boys presents more of a problem. (It always does.) You might want to try a variation on my suggestion for getting your kids out of class: tell your boss you're participating in some sort of special program sponsored by the children's school or pre-school. He'll probably buy "Take Your Juvenile Delinquent to Work Day" or "I'm Sick and Tired of Watching Your Brat Day." Or you can always go with the disguise idea, provided you're secure enough in your son's masculinity not to worry about the occasional bit of cross-dressing.

The problem with these suggestions is that they work only once each year. If you find yourself having to take the kids to the office more often than that, you'll need to develop a more comprehensive game plan. This will require, first of all, a place to stash the little (or not-so-little) tykes. The best place is your own work area, as long as you have an office with a door that closes, or at least a large, mostly empty filing cabinet. Failing that, look for a little-used room elsewhere in the building — perhaps an oversized storage closet or the company fitness center.

Next, you'll need to provide something for the kids to do all day, assuming they don't already have a full schedule completing your work assignments. If you're able to keep them in your office, you can let them play on your PC while you do what you would normally do: catnap and daydream about being someplace else. A word of warning, though: many companies nowadays monitor their employees' computers. Unless you normally visit Dora the Explorer's website on a regular basis, they may notice something is wrong.

You can also bring items from home to occupy your children's time — items such as books, toys, and hand-held video games. That should occupy them until at least 8:30. But what you really need is a TV and DVD player. Maybe you'll get lucky and discover that the company keeps a portable unit in the very closet where you've hidden the kids (or maybe that's why you chose that particular closet). As long as no one needs it that day, you're in the clear. Otherwise, you may have to bring the necessary equipment from home. If your boss observes you trying to sneak it in the back door, just tell him you're working on a video presentation. Explain that the *Dumbo* DVD is for your special effects collage.

And don't forget the groceries. Your children are going to need a mid-morning snack, a late-morning snack, lunch, a mid-afternoon snack, and a late-afternoon snack. You may be able to smuggle all this in under the pretense of collecting food for Balkan refugees. If not, the kids will just have to get by on a box of Wheat Thins and a can of Cheese Whiz.

Finally, bear in mind that, unless they are right there in the office with you, you're going to have to check on the children periodically throughout the day. For this task, you can elicit the help of one or two trusted co-workers. Okay, so having read Chapter 12, you realize you *have* no trusted co-workers. That's all right. Just pick one or two who, if all the people in your office were taking turns stabbing you in the back, would probably be among the last in line.

Because the truth is you may be able to hide the kids from your boss, but you can't hide them from everyone. After all, isn't there at least one guy in every office who can smell Cheese Whiz from a distance of four city blocks? Don't worry, though. Given the typical worker's dislike of management and the resulting "us against them" mentality, your colleagues probably won't use this information against you — at least, not until you're competing for a promotion.

For this reason, you should be careful about how *many* people you tell. You need a couple of confederates who can help you smuggle in food and take turns with you checking on the kids, so that no one person's repeated forays attract unwanted attention. But you certainly don't want *everyone* to know. Otherwise, the boss may come out of his office to see what all the commotion is about, only to find his entire staff stuffed into a storage closet, watching *Dumbo*.

PART FOUR:

The Family That Spends Time Together Could Probably Think of a Better Rhyme Together

I've already established how important it is for you as a husband and father to spend one-on-one time with your wife and with each of your children (see chapters two and eight). However, it's also important for you to plan and lead activities that bring the whole family together. If you don't, your wife will, and all in all you'd probably prefer your planned activities to hers.

This doesn't mean you shouldn't include your wife in the planning. Of course you should, unless you want to try having a family activity by yourself. (You've tried that before, remember? It's called "being single.") There will even be times — in this area as in all others — when you may have to go along with something *she* wants in order to be able to do what *you* want another time. This is acceptable, as long as you do occasionally get your way. For the family man, "occasionally" means about once every four or five years, on average.

One problem with this sort of trade-off, though, is that it can lead to activities that more than half the people in your family don't enjoy. Not that this is always a bad thing. I mean, your wife is probably right in believing the children ought to be exposed to the ballet at least once, though preferably not right after a big meal. And, from your point of view, how can your wife and daughters say they don't like drag racing until they've spent an evening at the strip?

(Once again you'll have to forgive my shameless stereotyping. Maybe your wife is the racing buff, and you're the one who's into ballet. Then again, for all I know, each of you could have a secret life the other knows nothing about. Maybe when you hear words like "drag" and "strip," cars are not the first things that come to mind. But, hey, that's your business.)

Most of the time, though, compromise is a better approach than trading off. This way, you can ensure family unity and solidarity by settling on activities absolutely *no one* likes.

On rare occasions, compromise can be simple and relatively pain-free for everyone involved. For example, if you want to take the kids fishing (mostly because *you* want to go fishing but don't have the guts to tell your wife you're going by yourself), and your wife wants to go on a family picnic, you can easily arrive at the perfect solution: find a park with a nice place for you and the kids to fish while your wife lays out the picnic items. You can even plan to eat your catch as part of the adventure. Be sure to have a "Plan B," though — bologna sandwiches — to allow for your three-year-old's version of fishing, which consists of throwing rocks in the lake.

Unfortunately, most compromises aren't this obvious. When the gap between what you want to do and what your wife wants to do is considerable, you may have to be a bit more creative in your approach. Take our above example, for instance. How do you reach a compromise between two activities as disparate as ballet and drag racing? This is where creativity is really important. Think about the excitement of racing. Think about men in tights. Suddenly, the answer is clear: You can take the family to a professional wrestling match! Okay, so it's not Swan Lake, but then no one is likely to be decapitated by a flying tire, either.

To complicate matters further, when your children are old enough, they too need to be included in the planning. "Old enough," for our purposes, may be defined as when you need their full cooperation in order to make the activity work. When your children are small, they'll tag along with you just about any place you want to go — especially, I've found, if you administer a moderate dose of children's pain-reliever beforehand. A little older and they'll still go willingly, as long as the activity isn't too blatantly "middle aged" (an art exhibit, a Rolling Stones concert). However, once they reach the pre-teen years, their favorite activity becomes anything that doesn't involve you. That's when compromise is again essential to the process.

The difficulty in trying to compromise with older children is that you can often agree on the *type* of activity yet not on the details. Take something as simple as eating out, for example. You agree that you're hungry, but you want steak while the kids want fast food. Movies? You want romance, they want violence (note: an S&M flick is *not* an acceptable compromise). Or suppose you all agree — parents and children — that you're up for a day in the great outdoors. But what they have in mind is a twenty-mile trek over something called "The Devil's Sidewalk," whereas you were thinking more along the lines of a two-hour jaunt through gentle hills, with six ten-minute rest stops.

I'm not sure I have much advice for you here. Maybe you'll just have to get back in shape and remember what it was like to be young. (I suggest hypnotic regression therapy.) Or maybe you can pipe "Honky-Tonk Woman" into your children's rooms at night while they sleep, until at last they are assimilated. But the fact is that, at some point, you're going to have to compromise. If you believe it's important for your family to do things together — and it is — then you're going to have to do some of their stuff, and they're going to have to do some of your stuff. Just be thankful. A lot of families don't have any stuff.

Finally, there are those activities you don't plan at all, but which are planned for you by a higher power, such as the school board or the Little League scheduling committee. I mention these here at the end of the introduction to Part Four not because they are the least common, but merely to provide another neat segue into Chapter 16. Actually, these types of activities are probably the most common and can also cause the most frustration. Because no matter how difficult it can be to choose a family activity, it's even more difficult when the activity chooses *you*.

Chapter 16

Wagging the Dog

If you have two or more kids, ages six and up, you already know how their activities can dominate not only your calendar, but your life. If your kids are not that old yet, then you'd better prepare yourself — preferably by becoming independently wealthy, so you'll no longer have to work and can therefore devote *that* time to their activities as well as every other waking moment, including some when you shouldn't be. Awake, I mean. When your children are small, you may complain that you never get out of the house. Once they reach school age, you don't have that problem anymore. The problem becomes remembering what your house looks like.

I think this is somewhat of a recent phenomenon. I don't remember my parents being at every single Cub Scout honor ceremony or Little League game. I certainly don't remember my Mom there wearing a button with my picture on it, or a T-shirt with the inscription, "Rob's Mom." As far as I could tell, she spent most of her time trying to hide the fact.

But then again, my parents spent a lot of time watching me do other things, like mow the lawn and detail their cars. I don't think they felt the need to prove their love by "being there" at every supposedly significant event in my life. They took in the occasional ball game or choral concert and came to all the true "biggies": graduation, wedding, arraignment. That was enough to show they really did love me. At least, I think they did.

Today's parents, though, are very different. My parents had a life of their own — not just one lived vicariously through me or my brothers. It wasn't a particularly exciting life, but it was theirs. (Maybe they should have tried the vicarious thing.) I'm not sure the same can be said for many parents nowadays. They seem to subjugate their own lives to those of their children, so that little remains of the parent as an individual. You look around the ball park and wonder just when that cute little Pam Jones, whom you used to go out with in high school, turned into "Ryan's Mom." If the answer is "long after you stopped dating her," then you're in the clear.

Perhaps this trend began in the seventies, when mothers went back to work in droves (or in banks, or stores, or hospitals, or wherever) and children were sent to day care and after-school programs. Soon, neither parent was around for all the normal, everyday events like first steps and diarrhea. So all the emphasis was shifted onto "special" events — in other words, activities, most of which are held after work hours and thus can be attended by one or both parents.

And the parents do attend, because they'll feel guilty if they don't. Let's be perfectly honest here: how many of us really *enjoy* watching a T-ball game, or a bunch of twelve-year-olds doing the aria from *La Boheme*? Exactly. We go out of guilt. After all, we may not have been there for the child's first steps, but at least we can be there for his first base hit, or her first big role, as a radish in the school health fair. Even when we do enjoy the event itself, guilt still plays a big part. It's what organizers count on when they set ticket prices.

Don't get me wrong. I'm not knocking any of this, nor do I claim to be above it. I think it's good to be supportive of your kids, and I have to admit that my wife and I are right there at the fifty-yard-line, figuratively speaking (and, for ten weeks every fall, quite literally), video camera in hand, with all the other guilt-ridden parents. But sometimes I wonder what happened to my life. But at least my children will never have to wonder about that. We have it all on video tape.

In any case, I wrote in the introduction to Part Four about activities that choose you, instead of the other way around. I think the kinds of children's activities I'm going to talk about in this chapter — related to sports, school, church, and community — are all in this category. Oh, I don't mean to imply that you don't have any choice in the matter. Of course you choose to sign your kids up for baseball, or allow them to participate in Girl Scouts, or whatever. But at the time you're making those choices, you don't fully realize — even when you think you do realize — just what you're getting yourself into.

It's a bit like going into a pool with what you think is a trained seal, and then discovering it's really an octopus. All these activities have tentacles that can drag you down and hold you under, until your lungs feel as though they are about to burst. Or maybe that's just your small intestine, after too many ballpark hot dogs.

One more brief note before I move on. I will not be dealing, in this chapter, with the issue of the family man as *leader* in these activities — coach, pack leader, etc. I'll save that topic for later. Here I mainly want to bring attention to the father's *other* roles in relation to his children's activities: enabler, spectator, and volunteer. After all, not all fathers can coach a team, but every one of them can yell at the man who does.

The Sporting Life

Among the most popular activities for children of all ages are team sports. A few years ago I might have been accused of being sexist for including sports as a major subsection of this chapter. Now I'm still accused of being sexist, but for other reasons, because girls today are just as involved in sports as boys. Well, maybe not quite as much, but enough so that I have to mention them in order for this book to qualify as approved reading for school children under Title IX.

Seriously, though, we have advanced to the point in our quest for gender equity that girls, for the most part, have just as much opportunity to participate in sports as boys do. In many areas, girls have their own soccer, basketball, and softball leagues. And where the number of participants does not make this possible, girls are almost always allowed to compete with the boys in leagues that are co-ed (meaning "boys and girls play together" — not to be confused with "co-ed" as in "co-ed dorm," meaning "boys and girls *sleep* together").

Thus we have girls playing soccer and basketball with boys, playing Little League baseball, even some playing football. This is all great, except that coaches have had to reach for new metaphors to describe their players' inadequacies. You can't exactly complain that your starting pitcher throws like a girl when in fact your starting pitcher *is* a girl.

Another sports-related activity that appeals to many girls is cheerleading. (Okay, it may appeal to some boys, too, but not *my* sons.) For some reason, though, this particular activity doesn't get much respect from the jack-booted gender equity thugs. It's not even considered a "sport" under federal Title IX equity-in-athletics guidelines. I think that's an insult to those — mostly girls and young women — who participate in this physically demanding activity. I suppose you could argue that having nice legs makes a person non-athletic, but apparently no one's ever broken the news to Maria Sharapova.

So nowadays, whether you have sons or daughters, they're likely to be involved in some kind of sports. And our society tends to start them off young, with five-year-olds — and in some cases, four-year-olds — eligible in most parts of the country to sign up for soccer, basketball, and tee-ball. By the time a child reaches age seven, he or she could easily be playing three or four sports, with overlapping seasons. That's another one of those things, like explaining what a condom is, that you thought you wouldn't have to worry about until high school.

Throw another child or two into the mix, and you'll begin to think those guys on ESPN are amateurs. "All sports, all the time?" Who are they kidding? Try having three kids, ages six, nine, and twelve, with games on Monday night at 5:30 and 6:00

(so you have to run back and forth between fields), Tuesday at 8:00, Thursday at 5:00 and 7:00, and Friday at 7:30. Wednesdays and Saturdays are for practices. Sundays you have off, but only because you and eight other parents threatened to firebomb the coach's house.

What I've just described is a pattern that may be merely an inconvenience for a few years or become a way of life, depending on how athletically inclined your children are. As they move into junior high and high school, those who aren't as interested in sports tend to drift into other activities, like band, choir, and creating home bomb-building web sites. From a parent's point of view, all of these can be just as time-consuming as sports — more so, when you take into account court appearances. But at least they don't require you to sit outside, on metal bleachers, regardless of the weather, for three to four hours at a time. Death-row inmates would sue — and *win* — if subjected to that kind of treatment.

So what roles do *you* play, as family man and father, in relation to your children's sporting events? First of all, you are an *enabler*. The check you write for $150.00 at registration enables those children to participate. You write numerous other checks to outfit them with the proper equipment — gloves, cleats, shin guards, mouthpieces, sports bras, cups, and aluminum bats that cost as much as your first car, for starters. Between you and your wife, you see to it that they are there, on time — well, okay, not *too* late — for all practices and games. In short, if it weren't for you, they wouldn't be playing at all. That's probably why they resent you.

Secondly, you are a *spectator*. In the modern vernacular, this means not just one who sits and watches, but one who takes a far more interactive part in the proceedings. Your main duty, in your capacity as spectator, is to observe closely the actions of all participants — players, coaches and, especially, officials — and react vociferously to any perceived misstep. A secondary responsibility is to maintain a constant stream of instructions directed at your own child. If these happen to contradict the coach's instructions, that will merely test the child's loyalty, or perhaps her good sense.

Finally, you are a *volunteer*. Here again, I am not referring to the ultimate volunteer position, that of coach, but to the many other ways in which parents can serve their children's teams. Perhaps you can be a statistician, which will give you the opportunity to pad your own kid's numbers. Or you can help keep track of the equipment. Or maybe you can be a "team dad." (Better yet, volunteer your wife to be "team mom." Hey, it's not your fault she missed the meeting.) This is the person who coerces other parent volunteers to work in the concession stand or sell raffle tickets (persuade enough of them and you won't have to do it yourself), and who organizes the end-of-the-season team party, to be held at someone else's home.

Ultimately, though, your greatest contribution to the team's success may be one you are unwilling to make: volunteering to stay home during the games, so your child can relax and play without your yelling at him from the stands. Who knows, maybe he'll even have fun.

Please Shoot Me. I'm with the Band

Sports aren't the only activities kids enjoy these days. They just get the most publicity, because, frankly, our society generally considers athletic children to be superior to those who are not athletic. This is true only if we're talking about *my* children, who actually *are* superior. Otherwise, it's untrue, not to mention unkind and insensitive.

The fact is that many children — boys as well as girls — have interests other than sports: music, art, dance, drama. As a father, you should encourage your kids, including your sons, to be involved in these kinds of activities, despite any irrational concerns you may have about their future sexual orientation. If you fail to be supportive, your wife will accuse you of being a big, dumb, macho jerk — ouch! — and your children will feel they can't gain your approval unless they play sports. (Yeah, so what's their point?).

Although some of these non-athletic endeavors may be pursued individually, most require participation in groups, which of course is when they are elevated to the level of true "activity," as I am defining the term for the purposes of this chapter. Essentially, this means that parents must provide not only support and equipment but also transportation and, ultimately, an audience.

And these activities, as I've said, can be every bit as time-consuming as sports. When you're driving your child to and from practice four a days a week, whether it's for basketball or band makes no difference as far as your other responsibilities are concerned. And here again, having multiple children complicates matters further. Unless they're twins, they're not even likely to have the same activities at the same time, so you can easily find yourself spending your afternoons and evenings running a shuttle service from ballpark to dance studio to piano lessons. Or, rather, your wife will; that's why you bought her that neat mini-van. (Okay, she bought it, but you helped pick the color.) You can't even get two kids and one French horn in the back seat of your sporty two-door, which is what you like most about it.

Nevertheless, you do have an important role to play: that of *volunteer*. Of course you will be an enabler, as once again without your checkbook the kids probably couldn't participate at all. And you will certainly be a spectator, though in this case it isn't nearly as much fun, since yelling is generally frowned upon at a play, dance recital, or orchestra concert. (Actually, you're allowed to yell, but only in Italian.)

But volunteerism is incredibly vital to the success of these activities — much more so than with sports. Perhaps this is because the fine arts do not recognize such a strict hierarchy, with a coach in complete charge and everyone else answering to him (or her). The arts are much more collegial and collaborative, which may be why you don't see Bill Belichick or Nick Saban leading a dance troupe.

If you're a dad whose kids are into the arts, there are many volunteer tasks in which you can happily immerse yourself. You can build sets, paint scenery, or make costumes. You can polish trombones, hand out sheet music, haul pianos. You can erect platforms, hook up speakers, and drive the bus. Best of all, you can *raise money* — not to feed your family after you've spent your last dime on tutus, but to help support the choir or band or whatever.

In fact, raising money is probably the single most important thing you can do to support these activities, especially at the high school level. I don't know why, but in high school the sports teams always seem to be fully funded, whereas the band has to beg for scraps. You don't see the parents of the football players, for example, peddling candy or oranges. Apparently, their team has plenty of money — enough for all that equipment, three or four different uniforms, and pre-game meals at the local steakhouse. Meanwhile, if it weren't for your fund raising efforts, the band kids would be marching naked at half time, which might draw a bigger crowd but would become quite uncomfortable by mid-November. Thanks to you and the other parents, though, those kids won't have to be naked until the game is over and they're safely paired up in their parked cars.

As a family man, you will be called upon to sacrifice for the cause in the most horrific way imaginable: by taking the fund-raising merchandise to work with you. What, did you think your children's activities, which already occupy all your time away from the office, wouldn't intrude on your sacred work time as well? Welcome to the real world. And prepare to prostrate yourself before co-workers, most of whom need a candy bar about like they need another coffee break, just so your child can sing or dance or twirl in the latest fashions. Remember, though, if you sell six dozen boxes, you'll win a cool T-shirt, clearly identifying you as the big, gullible dope you are.

Of course, it's less humiliating if everyone else at your workplace is doing it, too. I mean, you're bound to be more comfortable hawking a ten dollar chocolate bar to someone who just last month sold you ten dollars' worth of cookie dough. Hey, it's all for a good cause, right? You don't want to see anyone else's kids playing musical instruments naked, either. If you did, you'd be on the Internet right now. And, besides, it's good for an organization when its employees have this kind of give-and-take, mutually supportive relationship. I know of one office that passed around the same ten-dollar bill for three years.

Scouting for Girls and Other Favorite Pastimes

The last category of children's activities consists of those that build self-esteem and teach valuable socialization skills through wholesome group interaction. And no, I don't mean encounter therapy, although depending on your children that may be indicated as well. I'm talking about such groups as the Boy Scouts, the Girl Scouts, and similar youth organizations sponsored by churches and synagogues.

Of these groups, the Girl Scouts have always had a special place in my heart. In fact, as a teenage boy, I was actively involved in scouting for girls. Even today, when some have come to question the relevance of such organizations, I still firmly believe that the Girl Scouts perform a valuable service for society. I order six boxes of the thin mints every year.

I was also a Boy Scout for a few years, though not a very good one. As a matter of fact, my bid to make Eagle fell short when my project was rejected. Seems the wheelchair ramps I built for the local retirement home were facing the wrong way. How was I supposed to know they weren't going to use them for jumping?

However, I spent most of my free time as a youth (definition of "free time": not in school, playing sports, or watching *The Six Million Dollar Man* on television) involved in church youth activities, mostly because that was where all the good-looking girls were. Now, you might think church is a strange place to pick up girls, especially for your average teenage pervert. But I couldn't help it: that's where they were, probably because that's where their parents wanted them to be. If you had a good-looking teenage daughter, wouldn't you rather she be at church with lots of her church friends than, say, behind the bleachers with six members of the football team? Hence the evolution of the modern church youth group.

What scouting programs and church groups have in common is that they exist for broader social purposes, rather than for some specific narrow purpose, like dancing or playing baseball. The Boy Scouts might offer merit badges in basketball and swimming, but it is *not* a sports organization. Those are only two of a wide range of activities in which individual scouts may become involved. I understand they can also earn merit badges in such things as quilting, Tibetan cooking, and small animal surgery.

By the same token, a church youth group might have a choir, but that is just one area of interest open to its young people. They can also do many other things, such as participate in community volunteer efforts, hold fund raisers like car washes and bake sales, go to youth camp, and sneak off to make out. Obviously, not all these activities are sanctioned by the group's leaders, but together they do manage to appeal to just about everyone.

Which brings me back to the point I was making above: that these groups are primarily social, existing mainly for the purpose of keeping kids off the street and out of trouble, while also introducing them to a variety of new skills and interests. In other words, they exist to keep kids occupied during their spare time.

Excuse me. *Spare time*? What was I thinking?

Having It All

Truthfully, most kids hardly have any spare time, nowadays. Things are much different now than when I was a teenager. These days Steve Austin is a professional wrestler, and there isn't a defense contractor in the world that could build a bionic arm for under $42 billion. Moreover, kids today have more activities to choose from than they've ever had, since the guilt syndrome I described earlier afflicts not just individuals but society at large. Faced with these multiple choices, many kids don't simply pick activity "a," "b," or "c." Instead, they go with "d," "all of the above."

So what do you do when your children play all the sports *and* are involved in band, and dance, and the school play, *and* are active in Scouts and the church youth group? This is actually quite common when kids are younger — elementary and junior high age — before they've begun to "specialize" (i.e., discover what they stink at). Once they get into high school, they'll discover they really only have time for one or two main activities, or that they stink at nearly everything.

In the meantime, you might as well resign yourself to sharing chauffeur duty with your wife nearly every night of the week. And you can forget about having dinner at home together as a family — except perhaps on Sundays, which probably ought to be set aside for just that purpose. But don't panic. You can always tape the football game and watch it sometime later, like when your kids are grown.

The main thing to remember is that you must never, under any circumstances, discourage one of your children from participating in any (wholesome) activity. That's because all these activities, however they may inconvenience you, serve to make your child more "well-rounded," which is a phrase we use to describe people who aren't outstanding at anything in particular. I mean, who wouldn't want to be the proud father of an Eagle Scout/starting second baseman who also sings and dances and won this year's "Agriculture and You" poster contest? Just think what this will mean to the child's future, when in order to get into the college of his choice he is required to field ground balls on the Appalachian Trail while doing a number from *Cats* and simultaneously drawing a tractor.

Besides, you never really know just what your children are going to end up being good at. Any one of these activities might lead to a lucrative career, or a college scholarship, or at least a $50.00 loan from a former classmate who actually *did* make it big. I mean, you may not be into the theater yourself, but do you have any idea what Brad Pitt gets for a single film? About what Albert Puhols makes in a season — and that's with his clothes on. (Pitt, I mean. I don't know if Griffey gets paid extra for taking his clothes off.)

So while you're hauling your kids around, spending interminable hours sitting in ball parks and auditoriums, and eating fast food, just look at it as a kind of retirement program, albeit a risky one. Because the truth is, at least one of your kids is going to have to hit it *really* big to make up for all the cash you've put out over the years in gas and maintenance on your vehicles, not to mention the hours you could have spent at home watching *American Idol.*

Hey, time is money.

Chapter 17

The Family Man's Guide to Eating Out

One of the great adventures in parenting is taking your kids out to eat at a restaurant, especially when they're small. The kids, I mean. The size of the restaurant doesn't matter. About the last place you want to take a toddler is where there are hundreds of sharp metal and glass objects within easy reach. In fact, it is my considered opinion that children under two should not be taken out to eat at all, except in cases of dire emergency, such as when you are traveling and have no other option, or when you are suffering acutely from what is sometimes known as a "Big Mac Attack." (Note: It is not my intention, in this chapter, to endorse any particular restaurant or product. However, interested parties should contact my agent to work out something for the next book.)

On the other hand, going out to eat is a favorite activity for many families. And if you have a large family, with several children, you may not be willing or able to leave any of them at home — especially if your regular baby sitter (i.e., your thirteen-year-old daughter) is in front of you in the buffet line. The focus of this chapter, then, is on how to survive the ordeal at the restaurant of your choice without being expelled from the premises and with your dignity, if not your wallet, intact.

Whose Turn Is It to Cook?

There are many reasons families with young children decide to eat out, despite the last attempt's inevitable fiasco. Foremost, of course, is a kind of collective amnesia, combined with that blind and irrational optimism without which no parent can function. (Don't you suppose David Berkowitz's mother still harbors the faint hope that he'll make something of himself one day?) In essence, you and your wife and your older children say to each other, "Yes, we know we were thrown out of Burger King last week when little Tommy squirted ketchup on two elderly patrons, then threw his half-eaten cheeseburger over the counter and into the fry vat. But it wasn't really all that bad. It was actually a pretty good throw for a two-year-old. And besides, he's grown up so much in five days."

Hmmm. If you really want to recall the true horrors of that fateful evening, just ask your pre-teen. Chances are, she's still writhing in embarrassment over the fact that you called Pepsi "soda pop" when ordering from the pimply-faced kid behind the counter, who just happens to live next door to the cutest guy in the eighth grade. I don't think she'll be tempted to gloss over the details of her little brother's rampage.

Families also go out to eat for many other reasons, such as to celebrate a child's accomplishments, or to honor Mom on Mother's Day or Dad on Father's Day. (If you have one of those ambiguous, post-modern, New Age families, or you're just contrary, you can try it the other way around.) You realize, of course, that all these so-called "holidays" have been cooked up by the card, gift, and restaurant industries just to separate you from your hard-earned cash. If you can afford it, though, they make great excuses to get out of cooking and doing dishes.

Which leads me to my next point: by far the most frequently cited reason for going out to eat is that no one feels like cooking. In today's families, it's not at all uncommon for both husband and wife to stumble in after a long and stressful day at work, gaze glumly around the kitchen, then turn to each other and say in unison, "Fast food." This pronouncement is generally met with cheers from the offspring, which when you think about it, ought to be insulting to the parent who usually cooks. In fact, though, the happy cries rarely penetrate that parent's dulled senses. All she can think about are heat lamps and disposable containers. (By the way, tell your wife not to worry — it's not her meals the kids don't like. It's that they don't come with a toy.)

You May Want to Consider Leasing

Unfortunately, as I indicated above, eating out several times a week can get really expensive. But to families with more money than time, it's a very attractive alternative to, say, not eating at all. (Of course, families with more money than time probably ought to consider some sort of trade off. But that's their business, not mine. I'm just here to make you laugh.) Families with more time than money should stick to traditional home-cooked fare, like fish sticks and Hamburger Helper. And for families with very little of either, there's always Spam on saltines.

The average family, though, can afford to eat out every now and then — at least, if we accept the definition of "afford" offered in Chapter 3. In our family, we don't always have the necessary cash right at hand, so we've had to develop more creative ways of financing the occasional meal out. Usually this involves some combination of raiding the kids' piggy banks, rifling through sofa cushions, and pawning the odd heirloom. Those car title loan places can be very helpful, too, especially at the end of the month. I recently discovered that my car is worth three Happy Meals, a double cheeseburger, and four small soft drinks.

Such methods may not be sufficient, however, if you wish to take your family out to a "dine-in," or what is sometimes called a "sit-down," restaurant. (You may have wondered at the etymology of the latter term. It was first coined to distinguish restaurants where patrons are seated for a full, leisurely meal from those where they "stand-up" the entire time — in other words, bars. Incidentally, the world's first "lie-down" restaurant, which opened in Manhattan in 1953, never really caught on. People got tired of going home with linguini on their foreheads.)

Recent surveys have shown that, to feed a family of four at a restaurant where the food is actually served to you on dishes made of a rigid material, you'll probably shell out about what the Pentagon pays for a toilet seat. Not that I'm equating the two, mind you. I'm sure the Pentagon gets its toilet seats much faster.

To address this problem, many of the better restaurants are now offering low-interest financing with on-the-spot approval for qualified diners. Just bring your Social Security card, the deed to your house, your most recent pay stub, and a copy of last year's W-2's, and in the time it would normally take to be seated, the *maitred'* can approve you for up to five courses. Be careful about getting in too deep, though. Have you ever noticed how many fancy restaurants occupy what used to be someone's home?

Fortunately, though, you and your family have choices. If your budget cannot support too many trips to *La Maison du Boeuf*, there's always "fast" food — so named because, in terms of nutritional value (though not caloric intake) it's about like eating nothing at all. Or you can opt for something in-between: the "buffet," or serve-yourself restaurant, which combines many of the advantages of the dine-in establishment — chairs with backs, metal flatware, distinguishable food groups — with the speed and convenience of fast food, at a comparatively reasonable price. Whatever you do, remember: it beats having to fix it yourself, especially since you don't even know the recipe for the special sauce.

As Long As It Isn't Half-Fast

The main attraction of fast-food restaurants is that you can get your food and get out in a matter of minutes. Unless, of course, you go during the breakfast, lunch, or dinner rushes, which last about two hours each and during which you may want to consider catheterization so you won't lose your place in line. But as long as you're willing to eat your meals at times when all other civilized human beings are either at work or asleep (or both), then fast food is a great convenience.

To further speed things up, modern technology has given us the "drive-through window," so you can get something to eat without even having to leave your vehicle. (Note: You can also accomplish this by looking under your child's car seat. Bear in mind, however, that restaurant food will probably be slightly fresher.) I don't really recommend the drive-through, though, for parents with small children. Using it will merely frustrate your *real* purpose: having half an hour to eat in peace while your kids will disappear into the playground. More about that later.

And whereas fast food used to mean just hamburgers and French fries, consumers now have a wider variety of choices. There are chicken places, for those who want a break from beef (or whatever); sub and deli sandwich shops, for those who prefer a lighter fare; even Mexican fast food, for those who are oblivious to their own flatulence. We all have our favorites. I personally like Wendy's hamburgers, McDonald's fries, and Burger King's little paper hats.

The smartest thing these restaurants have done is market themselves to children, calculating — rightly — that if the kids come, so will their parents. Actually, I suppose their reasoning goes even further: marketers are banking on the fact that, in most households, it is the children who make the really important decisions, such as what to watch on television and where to eat. Fathers are basically left with deciding which socks match their pants.

You can see this approach in the advertising directed at children during Saturday morning cartoons and on Nick at Nite. Such ads often feature a make-believe character — Ronald McDonald is the most obnoxious, er, I mean obvious — whose purpose is to appeal to younger children. Or maybe they use cool animation and special effects to capture the interest of older kids. These restaurants also love to use "tie-ins," advertising and give-away toys related to the latest hit children's movie or action-adventure film. Let's face it: you can get a hamburger anywhere, but only (name of restaurant here) can give you a plastic alien figurine with it.

Another brilliant marketing strategy was the creation of the "kid's meal," which goes by various names, depending on the establishment. The basic idea here is to take the items most parents would order for their children anyway — small burger, small fry, small drink — place them in a colorful container, throw in a ten-cent toy, and charge twice the price. That's precisely the kind of ingenuity that has kept this nation's economy strong, not to mention China's.

One more comment about those little plastic toys: don't throw them away. At a recent yard sale, we put eleven years' worth of accumulated "Happy Meal" toys into a box at five cents apiece. They were the first things to go. Altogether, we made just about enough to buy another Happy Meal.

Finally, there is the ultimate marketing weapon aimed at children: the playground. I don't know when the first playground was erected in conjunction with a fast-food restaurant, but they certainly have proliferated over the last few years. My children have become connoisseurs. They know every playground at every restaurant between our home and the places to which we regularly travel. They know exit numbers. As they plan our itinerary for each trip, they take into account all variables: weather (is the playground indoor or outdoor?), time of day (lighted or unlighted?), and food preference of the week (Burger King or McDonald's?). Then they let me know where we will be stopping, and when. I get to determine how long, as long as it's not less than an hour.

If you think I'm being facetious or that I'm merely weak-willed, then you obviously don't have any children over the age of two. As they grow into toddlerhood, please do yourself a favor and take my advice. When traveling long distances with children, the only reasonable course of action at mealtime is to stop at a fast food restaurant with a playground. So what if you're not in the mood for that particular kind of food. Go through a drive-through and get yourself a taco first if you must, but let the kids play. Given the enormity and maze-like structure of today's playgrounds, you probably won't set eyes on them for at least 30 minutes, during which time you and your wife can eat and maybe have a conversation without the kids there to interrupt. With any luck, you might even accidentally leave one behind.

Notice I said, "let the kids *play*," not "let the kids *eat.*" That's because, if you take them to a restaurant with a playground, not one of them will eat a bite, despite the fact that less than half an hour earlier two of them had slipped into starvation-induced comas. That's okay, though. Enjoy your own meal and don't worry about them. They're too busy throwing plastic balls into the parking lot to feel hunger at this point, anyway. Just be sure and get their food "to go," so you can give it to them later in the car, when they begin to complain again about being hungry. This should happen about the time you settle into the driver's seat and close your door.

One final note of warning. After many stops such as the one described above, you might think your children must be getting tired of fast food and generic playgrounds. *You* certainly are, and your wife is, too. Maybe, you rationalize, a nice sit-down restaurant would be a pleasant change of pace for everyone. If necessary, you can bribe the kids with dessert. They'll be fine.

Wrong. After being in a car for an extended period of time, which for them is more than ten minutes, the last thing children want is to sit down anywhere, dessert or no. They want a playground, and if you don't give them one, they'll make their own, right there in that nice restaurant, with you and twenty-three blue-haired members of the Ladies Garden Club looking on. You don't even want to know what they'll throw instead of plastic balls.

As Buffets Go, It's No Jimmy

Another type of restaurant that my kids love is the buffet. Here, patrons serve themselves from a "food bar" containing a variety of meats, vegetables, fruits, breads, and desserts, most of which are easily identifiable. Anthropologists tell us buffets have actually been around for centuries, with the earliest known examples dating back to ancient Rome. These were set up much like today's buffets, except feather dispensers and puke vats were located right on the premises. Nowadays, people have to go home for that.

The modern buffet seems to have evolved from the salad bars that used to be popular at steak houses. Managers discovered that patrons would pay more for the salad bar as a side item if they could also get things like fried chicken wings, baked potatoes, and ice cream — all of which completely negate the nutritional benefits of salad, but then no one ever said human eating habits are logical. Eventually, as the salad bar grew into the food bar, many of these steak houses — erstwhile dine-in establishments — became better known for their buffet lines than for their steaks. Apparently, their customers found the fried chicken wings much easier to chew.

The buffet-style restaurant has two main advantages, the first being selection. Today's buffets can offer as many as eight or ten different kinds of meat and twenty or more vegetables. And you don't even have to choose among them, the way you would if you were ordering from a menu or going through a cafeteria line. Rather than making a tough decision — do I want the chicken or the roast beef? — you can have the chicken *and* the roast beef. And the ham. And the liver. In fact, you can have a little bit of everything, though from what I've seen most patrons don't actually go that route. They have a *lot* of everything.

Which brings me to the second main advantage: quantity. Nearly all buffets advertise an "all you can eat" policy, meaning you can go back through the line as many times as you like, with the sole stipulation that you must be able to return under your own power.

The chief drawback to the buffet-style restaurant is price. These places tend to charge about as much per person as a lower-end dine-in establishment, and two or three times what a meal for one would cost if you went with fast food. The fact is, for what you'll pay at the typical all-you-can-eat buffet, you could probably get all the fast food you *care* to eat, and then some.

The quality of the food can also be suspect, though some places are better than others. I tend to judge a buffet line by its mashed potatoes. If the mashed potatoes are real and well prepared, that's a pretty good indication the management is committed to serving decent food. If the potatoes could easily be mistaken for the clam chowder, you probably don't want to eat there.

When it comes to going out to eat with children, buffets are often a good choice. You'll spend more than you would at a fast food place, but generally less than at a nicer dine-in restaurant. Some buffets even feed kids three and under for free, with a small surcharge for replacing the carpet afterward. Everyone can get exactly what they want — except, perhaps, you (you liked it better when it was a steak house), but then you don't count (haven't you been paying attention?). And there's always the dessert bar, which can serve as a powerful motivator in getting your kids to choke down those reconstituted mashed potatoes. Best of all, it really won't matter to you if your kids eat all their food or not. It's costing you the same thing, either way.

It's true that buffet restaurants generally don't have playgrounds to keep the kids occupied, but at least they will get some exercise going back and forth to the dessert bar. Also, it's worth bearing in mind that starch is a powerful natural sedative. This means that if your child takes two bites of anything on the typical buffet line, he or she will be sound asleep before you're halfway home.

Even so, I don't really recommend the buffet as a place to stop when you're traveling. But for an evening away from the kitchen and a break from fast food, it can be a nice change of pace. Just be sure to inspect the clam chowder for potato flakes.

One final issue worth mentioning in regard to buffet-style restaurants: how much to tip. I know the waiters and waitresses (PC: "servers" or "waitpersons") in these establishments probably expect the traditional fifteen per cent. But let's be realistic here. What do they do to deserve that kind of consideration? They don't take your order, bring you your food, or even insult you in another language. At least the counter girl at McDonald's brings you your food, even if she only has to walk five feet to do it, and you don't tip *her*.

To be fair, the "server" does keep her customer's drinks topped off and brings them clean plates, which in the case of some patrons can be considerable work. But is this really worth fifteen per cent? I think not. In my opinion, five per cent is fair, and ten is generous. However, if you frequent that restaurant and want to stay on a particular server's good side, you might consider coming across with the entire fifteen. After all, she may not have much opportunity to spit in your food, but you never know about the iced tea.

Garçon!

The last category of restaurant is the "dine-in" or "sit-down" type. Admittedly, this is quite a broad category, encompassing everything from little mom and pop eateries offering "home cooking" — isn't that what you're eating out to avoid? — to the most upscale establishments in New York and San Francisco. For our purposes, though, I'm talking mostly about those places that at least make a pretense of welcoming families. If you want to try the trendy new place, get a baby sitter and leave the kids at home. They probably wouldn't appreciate *Chez Sol's* kosher French cuisine, anyway — and Sol definitely won't appreciate the kids.

From the family man's perspective, dine-in restaurants have a number of disadvantages. They're expensive, and added to the expense is a big tip. Here, you are definitely expected to leave at least fifteen per cent, if not twenty, even if your server is hostile, arrogant, obnoxious, or incompetent, which covers just about all of them. If the service is especially bad, however, you may be able to get away without leaving a tip, as a form of protest, provided you don't plan on returning to that establishment until after your server has died or been deported.

The biggest drawback to the dine-in restaurant, though, is that you have to do quite a bit of waiting. You wait to be seated, you wait to order, you wait for your food. All of this can take up to an hour, provided the place isn't terribly busy. The management makes up for this inconvenience by charging you ten times what you would pay for fast food.

All of this is bad news if you have children. They're going to enjoy waiting thirty minutes for their food about like they'd enjoy having the Disney Channel disconnected. And at most of these restaurants, there's absolutely nothing for them to do, other than annoy the other patrons. This will be a challenge only for a very few minutes, as restaurant patrons *without* children tend to have very low annoyance thresholds.

Of course, some dine-in restaurants do attempt to cater to children, giving out comic books, crayons, and place mats featuring games and pictures for coloring. Unfortunately, unless the crayons are made of cookie dough, they won't keep a hungry child occupied for more than three minutes. Others offer games, like checkers and peg boards. My kids especially love these. The pieces make excellent projectiles.

The great advantage of the dine-in restaurant is that you are basically waited on hand and foot. Well, most servers don't actually use their feet, but I'm sure there are some who could. (Depending on the server, you may want to use *your* foot, but that's another matter.) Once seated, and provided little Timmy is not attempting to put the salt shaker in his sister's water glass, you can relax, peruse the menu, and savor the anticipation of a fine meal. Or you can use that time to do the amortization math in your head: "Let's see, three courses for five people over two years at eighteen-and-a-half per cent..."

There's also the fact that the dine-in restaurant offers the best food you're likely to get, except, of course, for the handful of times each year that you visit your mother. When you think about going out to eat, *this* is exactly what you have in mind: excellent food, attentive service, pleasant atmosphere. If you could get that at home, you'd probably never go out. You're not interested in playgrounds, coloring crayons, checkerboards, or plastic figurines — much less plastic food. You just want to enjoy your meal. Is that too much to ask?

Yes, it is. As a family man you must always remember that your children have the power to make your life utterly miserable. If you seek to please yourself at their expense, they will see to it that no one is pleased. If you attempt to please them, you may at least get a few moments of peace out of the deal.

Consider the following two scenarios. First, let's say you take the family to a nice dine-in restaurant. While waiting to be seated, you spend twenty minutes chasing your two-year-old around the twelve-foot-square waiting area. Once at your table, the little tyke is strapped into a high chair and given a cracker, which he promptly tosses onto the toupee of the middle-aged gentleman seated behind him. The five-year-old announces loudly that he has to go pee-pee. The nine-year old opens her menu, glances at it for five seconds, and says "Yuck!" From that point on, the situation deteriorates rapidly. By the time your food arrives, your stomach is churning too badly to eat it. Doggy bag, please?

Now let's say you take the family to a fast food place instead, one with a playground. You order and receive your food within ten minutes. Your kids remove the plastic toys from their kid's meal bags, then disappear into the maze of tunnels and slides. You and your wife have thirty minutes or so to enjoy — or at least ingest — your super-sized value meals in relative peace and quiet. Your stomach doesn't start churning until *after* you've eaten. When you think of it in these terms, it's really a no-brainer (which for most of us is a good thing).

This is not to say that you should never take your kids out to a nice restaurant. Of course you should, especially as they get older, if for no other reason than to teach them proper etiquette. Just be prepared to stop by the drive-through and pick up a couple of Happy Meals on the way home.

Chapter 18

Take Two Weeks and Call Me in the Morning

Every now and then — maybe once or twice a year — you will be called upon to take your entire family on a trip that may last up to a week or more. This is euphemistically known as a "vacation." My *American Heritage College Dictionary* defines vacation as "a period of time devoted to pleasure, rest, or relaxation." For the family man, a vacation is more likely to be a period of time devoted to marathon cross-country driving, interminable standing in amusement park lines, and chasing small children over natural rock formations.

That's not to say no one in your family will get a real vacation. If you plan well and spend enough money, your kids will no doubt derive great pleasure from the experience. (Notes: [1] "planning well" in this case means the kids get to choose what they want to do. [2] The amount of money you should spend on a family vacation is about ten per cent of your after-tax annual income, according to a study co-sponsored by the American Resort Hotel Association and the Federation of Gift Shops That Sell Incredibly Cheap, Tacky, and Expensive Souvenirs.)

Your wife may also get to relax a bit, assuming you are the primary driver, stander, and chaser, as you almost certainly will be. This is only fair, since she does the majority of the child-rearing throughout the other fifty-one weeks, while you watch sports on television. In fact, as hard as she works, you might consider just letting *her* take the kids on a vacation. You don't deserve one. While she and the kids are gone, you can stay home and watch sports on television.

Yes, I know. You're not going to get away with that. You're doomed to be stuck behind the wheel of the family minivan, trying to drive from Washington, D.C. to the Grand Canyon in three days, with stops in between at Niagara Falls, the Florida Everglades, the St. Louis Arch, and your wife's great-aunt Mildred's in Amarillo (see Chapter 5). Don't let the prospect of all that driving worry you, though. If you have any children under the age of six, at least you'll be able to stop and use the bathroom every forty-five minutes.

Of course, that's just one type of family vacation, what I call the "sight-seeing tour." There are many others, including the "outdoor adventure" vacation, the beach resort vacation, the theme park vacation, and the free vacation, also known as visiting relatives. These are the types with which I have had the most experience, and thus the ones I intend to talk about. If you want to know about vacations in Europe, Lake Tahoe, or the Caribbean, I suggest you watch the A&E network.

On the Road . . . Again

Some families think it's fun to see how many different places they can visit during one seven- or fourteen-day period. It doesn't matter if they have time to do anything once they get there, only that they were there. Catch a glimpse out the car window of the sun reflecting off Thomas Jefferson's forehead and you can say you've been to Mt. Rushmore. Spend an hour driving around the Mall and you've "done" Washington.

There are even those who seem to look upon travel as a kind of competition. How many states (or countries, or continents) did *you* visit this summer? These are the people who send you pictures of themselves spread-eagled across the "Four Corners," where Arizona, Colorado, Utah, and New Mexico meet; whose holiday newsletter reads like a travelogue: "Marge and I took the kids on a two-week vacation this summer. It was great! We visited North Dakota, South Dakota, Montana, Idaho, Colorado, Wyoming, and Vermont, with a brief stopover in Poland. Write and let us know what you've been up to!"

If this is your idea of a vacation, rest assured it probably isn't your kids'. Older children, especially, would almost certainly rather go someplace like Disney World or the beach, preferably without *you.* I mean, is it reasonable to think a teenager who can't stomach an hour with you at the mall will embrace the idea of spending fourteen days together in a van? So unless your kids are young enough to be dragged along unquestioningly, which is to say under age three, you're going to have to be extremely creative in your approach. Otherwise, you'll have to listen to them gripe the entire time, instead of only three-fourths of the time, like usual.

One thing you can do to encourage their willing participation is to plan the trip together as a family. Weeks before you leave, begin getting your maps out after dinner and tracing your intended route. Collect brochures and other information about the places you'd like to visit. Allow the kids to have some input in your itinerary, and always keep them in mind as you consider the relevance and educational value of various stops. For example, if you're traveling through Philadelphia, you'll definitely want to stop and see the Liberty Bell, while in Cleveland, you may want to take in the Annoying Fads Hall of Fame, which features exhibits honoring mood rings, pet rocks, the Macarena, and Regis Philbin.

There are basically two ways to plan a family sightseeing trip: geographically or around a central theme. In other words, you can decide to take in the sights that interest you in a given state or region, or you can try visiting, say, all the major Civil War battlefields, or bodies of water into which Ted Kennedy has driven his car. Or you can really bring the experience home to your kids by selecting places that have some relevance to your family's own history — for example, small towns where ancestors of yours were jailed, hanged, or placed in the stocks. You can always go back next year if you don't get to see everything.

The Great Outdoors: Nature's Bathroom

Another type of vacation is what I call the "outdoor adventure" — basically, camping out. You can also go hiking, rock climbing, canoeing, white water rafting, and/or mountain biking, as you have the time, desire, and funds. (Priced a mountain bike lately? Forget the bike — the mountain would be cheaper.) Or you can just lie around the camp site while your children beg food from neighboring campers and spread rumors of bear sightings (you should be so lucky).

Of course, there's camping out and there's *camping out.* Some people's idea of camping involves satellite television, phone service, indoor plumbing, hot running water, and a motor home spacious enough for a "Saved by the Bell" cast reunion. For these folks, a "campground" is generally visible from the interstate and has all the amenities: clubhouse, vending machines, Olympic-size pool, on-staff masseuse. Sometimes they can even park their "RV's" right on the beach, or next door to their favorite theme park. These are the people who "camp" because they prefer it to sleeping in a hotel or staying with relatives. Their relatives probably prefer it, too.

True outdoor types, on the other hand, prefer *real* camping: leaky tents, poison ivy, biting insects, and lots of woods — otherwise known as "nature's bathroom." This type of camping can make for the perfect family vacation, especially when you don't have the money to do anything else. You won't have to travel far, as there should be a suitable state park within an hour or two of your home. The camping itself isn't usually expensive — maybe ten or fifteen dollars a night for a site without water or electrical hookups (who needs those, anyway?). And all the activities are basically free, not to mention well worth every penny. About your only real expense, provided you already have most of the equipment, will be food and toilet paper. You may even be able to get by without the latter, unless it's winter, or the forest is all pine trees.

The best part is that you don't have to let the kids know you're only doing it because you're broke. You can pass the whole thing off as a great adventure, as well as an opportunity to commune with nature. Certainly your kids would rather go to Disney World, but how can Space Mountain compare with *real* mountains? Unless they're extremely sophisticated — i.e., over the age of three — they'll be suckers for that line of reasoning. You may even be able to convince your teenage daughter to go along without complaining, if you let it drop that the college's rugby team will be holding its annual summer camp in the same park.

Even if you can afford to do something else, a week of wilderness camping (translation: no hot water or flushing toilets) may be just the thing for your family. It will certainly get your kids active again, away from the TV set and video games. It will also get them to exercise, which can only be a good thing, considering your son's spare tire is starting to look a lot like yours. Best of all, it can really bring your family together, huddling for warmth in the middle of the night, as the rainwater slowly pools on the floor of your tent.

Speaking of which, if you're going to go camping — especially wilderness camping — you must be sure to have the proper equipment. You'll need a tent large enough for your whole family, and then another, smaller tent for yourself. You'll need a quality, waterproof sleeping bag for each family member, plus plenty of extra clothes for when the sleeping bags fill with water. You'll need a small ax for cutting firewood, a sturdy knife for trimming twigs, and a good supply of matches. You'll also need to make sure your car is full of gas, so you can be miles away before the park rangers discover the source of the blaze.

Some people like to take along modern conveniences, like kerosene lanterns and propane camp stoves. Not me. I prefer to cook over an open fire and go to bed when the sun goes down. At least, I like to get the *kids* in bed when the sun goes down. Then my wife and I can drive into town and see a movie. Those bear rumors probably aren't true, anyway.

The Sands of Time

If you have plenty of money, you can enjoy a truly memorable vacation by renting an oceanfront condominium and taking your family to the beach for a week or more. If you don't have plenty of money, you can do it anyway and put it on your credit card, which is what most people do. When the bill comes in and you have to balance the books, just file the expense under "off-budget" (see Chapter 3).

If all your credit cards are already maxed out, just choose a new one from among the dozens of offers you receive in the mail each week. That way, you can finance your vacation at a low 4.9 per cent introductory rate, for six months. Then, provided you pay it off within five years, your week at the beach will only have cost you $25,473.28.

Some people, wary of the cost or with antiquated ideas about debt and credit, try to combine beach vacation with outdoor adventure, by — you guessed it — camping out at or near the beach. This I don't recommend. For me, a week at the beach is made tolerable only by ready access to air conditioning and clean showers. I don't mind getting good and hot, as long as I have a place to cool off when I want to. And I don't mind getting a little sand in my crack, as long as the sand does not contain tiny sea creatures, and as long as I can rinse it off at the end of the day in comfort and privacy — both of which are in short supply at most campgrounds and state parks.

A better idea, for those who like to vacation at the beach but who worry about the cost, is "time-sharing," a late-twentieth century marketing concept whereby the same piece of real estate is sold over and over again to different people. In earlier decades, this was known as "fraud."

Today, though, the concept can allow you, along with thousands of other American families, to have the beach vacation you might not otherwise be able to afford, simply by paying monthly mortgage installments for the privilege of using the beach-front condominium you "own" for one week out of the year. Because other "owner" families must use the property, too, your week will be scheduled, by a committee of developers, lawyers, education consultants, and meteorologists, to fall either when your children are in school or during a class five hurricane.

As much fun as beach vacations can be, they have their disadvantages, as well. One of these I've already mentioned: the unholy union of sand and bodily orifices. Another is the fact that, if you have small children, you won't be able to relax at all. You'll spend all your time trying to protect them from being caught in an undertow, or eaten by sharks, or exposed to the sight of an eighty-five year-old-man in a thong bikini.

But the worst thing about spending an entire week at the beach is that there really isn't much to do. It's not like going to the beach just for an afternoon. Sure, it can be fun to soak up some rays and play in the surf, but what are you going to do for the other 164 hours?

Some people like to pass the evenings by sampling the local cuisine, especially fresh seafood. This takes us back to the problems discussed in Chapter 17, but with the added variable of sunburn. Others like to take in a movie, or go shopping. Let's be honest here: other than being dragged over the ocean floor by a giant wave and picking shell fragments out of your shorts, what can you really do at the beach that you can't do at home?

If you want to get the feel of the beach experience at a fraction of the cost, try this: pour two pounds of sand down your pants and take your family out to Red Lobster. Then go home and watch "Flipper" re-runs on Nickelodeon. It may not seem the same to the kids, but at least they won't have to look at some octogenarian's buttocks.

Variations on a Theme

A favorite type of vacation for many Americans, especially those with children — and most especially for those children themselves — is to spend several days at a major theme park. In recent years, we have even seen the rise of theme park "clusters," so that families can spend a week or more in one area and visit three or four different parks. This is a shining example of the convenience of modern society, as well as the remarkable efficiency with which large entertainment conglomerates can strip you of every last dime, not to mention every shred of dignity.

Today's theme parks are descended from the small amusement parks that began to gain popularity in the 1930's and 40's. Those parks usually featured a wooden roller coaster, a Ferris wheel, and a "Tunnel of Love." They were frequented primarily by young couples on dates. Too many trips through the Tunnel of Love, however, sparked the baby boom of the 40's and 50's, which in turn led to an increase in the demand for family entertainment. Hence the rise of the modern theme park.

The theme park, then, is basically an overgrown amusement park built around a central theme, such as Walt Disney films, or in the case of Six Flags, different eras in our nation's history. Sadly, a number of smaller parks have failed in recent years, unable perhaps to find their niche in the industry. There was Pig City, outside Ft. Smith, Arkansas, where various attractions emphasized the different uses of pork. It closed in 1997, after members of the Muslim community showed up outside the front gates, carrying placards that read, "Unclean! Unclean!" They were right, too. You should have seen the men's rooms.

Then Polka World, in Minneapolis, went under after four patrons were crushed to death on the "Roll Out the Barrel" ride. Finally, Recycling Land, near Portland, Oregon failed when park-goers riding the log flume realized that what was being recycled was raw sewage. Company attorneys argued that signs clearly warned patrons to "keep hands inside boat."

The more successful parks, however, rely on a family atmosphere and high tech rides, including ever more thrilling roller coasters. There are coasters on which you can sit, stand, or be suspended by your torso, and one in California on which you may assume the yoga position of your choice. There are coasters that follow the traditional course — up and down — and those that twist and turn through a series of loops. These last are not recommended for small children, pregnant women, or anyone who has eaten in the last 24 hours.

As family vacation destinations, theme parks can be a lot of fun, but you should certainly be aware of the drawbacks. First of all, if you go during the peak season, which is to say when it isn't snowing, be prepared to spend a disproportionate amount of your time standing in line. For some of the more popular attractions, you could have to wait as long as three hours, whereas the ride itself lasts only 42 seconds.

Another problem with theme parks is the expense. Two days for a family of five at one of the larger parks will not cost you quite as much as a week in a beachfront condominium, but the difference may be negligible. Add the cost of food (ten dollar hamburgers inside the park) and lodging ($200.00 a night rooms adjacent to the park), and you may find yourself spending approximately what *Toy Story 3* grossed in its first week.

There are, however, ways to reduce the expense. One is to go during the off-season, when admission prices and hotel rates are at their lowest. Of course, the off-season occurs when school is in session; that's why it's called the off-season. In order to take advantage of the lower rates, you'll have to take your kids out of school for the week — but don't let that bother you too much. Just add Epcot Center and Sea World to your itinerary and call it a field trip.

Some other ways to lower your costs: 1) Bring your own food, which you may have to smuggle into the park in a backpack or under a "Cat in the Hat" chapeau. 2) Instead of staying in a hotel, camp. A site close to the park may only cost $75.00 a night. (Another alternative: sleep in your car.) And, 3) the best idea of all: *don't go*. Take your kids on an outdoor adventure, instead. The attractions may be less thrilling, but they certainly last longer. The lines are shorter, too.

It's All Relative

By far the most common type of vacation for the family man and his family involves going to visit relatives. This is especially true for people who live hours away from their extended family and get to see them only on those rare occasions, such as holidays, when they are able to be absent from home, school, and work. Such people are often referred to by other family members as "lucky dogs."

Years ago, when families all lived and worked in the same general area, long distance travel was seldom necessary. Of course, back then, a vacation meant accompanying the vegetable wagon to the market on Saturday. In today's fragmented society, young people must often move far from home in order to find themselves, to find their own way in the world, to find a job that pays $75,000 a year. If they didn't travel when time permitted, they'd never get to see the family they left behind.

Which might be fine with you, but what about your wife? After all, you're the one who wrenched her away from the bosom of her family, carried her halfway across the country, and promptly begat upon her a family of her own (I just love Biblical language, don't you?). No doubt there are days when she longs to be the one crying "Mommy!" instead of always being on the receiving end. The least you can do is take her home a couple of times a year to visit her parents. All in all, that's probably better than having *them* come visit *you*, despite anything I may have said in a previous chapter.

All jokes aside, though, there *are* some advantages to staying with relatives while on vacation. For one thing, it's free, and that's a quality not to be overlooked, especially if that $75,000 a year job turned out to be more like $35,000. Note again the operative word here: *free*. That's as inexpensive as it gets. Camping is a *cheap* vacation; staying with family is a *free* one. You don't even have to bring your own food (though perhaps you might like to), and toilet paper is generally provided as well.

Your only expense will be the gas for the trip, and you may even be able to get your in-laws to pay for that, if you imply that their daughter and grandchildren might have to hitchhike otherwise. Not that hitchhiking would be much of a problem. After all, your wife is a very attractive woman.

You may also be fortunate enough to have relatives who live in places you would want to visit, anyway, like at the beach or near a large theme park. If not, begin suggesting now, to your parents or your wife's, whoever has more money, that they move to Florida when they retire, if not before then. Promise you'll bring the grandchildren to visit regularly. Heck, tell them you'll be glad to leave the kids with them for weeks at a time, if they insist.

(A personal note, on behalf of those families that do live in exotic locales: Earlier in our marriage, my wife and I lived near the Gulf of Mexico for several years. During that time, nearly every member of our extended family, on both sides, came to visit us at least once. Many came once a year. We were flattered by the attention, assuming they were actually coming to see *us*. Then we moved 90 miles inland. There are family members I haven't seen since, and I wonder to this day whether we were ever really related. I hope not.)

But I digress. If you plan on staying with family members for any length of time, I have several pieces of excellent advice. First, you may want to bring your own bedding. At least bring your own pillows, if only because a queen-size mattress won't fit on your minivan's luggage rack. Remember, there is no substitute for a good night's sleep, and you may find that hard to come by in unfamiliar surroundings. Thus, anything that provides greater comfort will be a blessing on par with discovering, on the last day of your visit, that you do actually have one more pair of clean shorts.

Of course, if you're visiting *your* parents, you may find yourself sleeping again in your own boyhood bed. That should be quite comfortable, assuming the younger brother who inherited it when you left home didn't leave anything large, lumpy, and illegal under the mattress. (Small, innocuous, and illegal is okay.) Just remember to be a gentleman and let your wife have the bottom bunk. (Hey! None of those jokes. This is a family book.)

Next, to the extent you're able, you should help out financially while staying with your family members, especially by buying groceries. I know this spoils the whole free vacation idea, which is probably the only reason you're there to begin with, but there are at least two good reasons to follow this advice: first, your hosts may be somewhat less likely to insist that you leave before your week is up, and secondly, when you go shopping you can buy some of the things you and your family enjoy. I mean, what if your Aunt Mabel and Uncle Fred, who live in Orlando but weigh approximately 300 pounds apiece, have nothing in the house to eat but Ruffles potato chips and Ho-Ho's? The least you can do is bring home some milk to go with those delicious snack cakes. Skim, of course.

Finally, don't wear out your welcome. This means you may stay with a given relative for no more than one week, and only once a year. Your wife's parents, obviously, are excepted from this rule. As the father of their grandchildren, you have the right to impose upon them at any time and for as long as you like, especially if they live on the beach. They should be happy just to have the grandkids there to visit them — and in most cases, they will be. It's you they don't want to see.

Time . . . Goes By . . . So Slowly

Wherever you decide to go on vacation, you probably face the daunting prospect of spending hours in a confined space with your kids, so you'd better think of some things to help pass the time. Listening to your five CD set, "Greatest Hits of the '70's" probably won't be an option, unless your vehicle is equipped with separate stereo units and a soundproof glass partition. If you're really lucky, you may own one of those vans with a built in TV/DVD player and individual headsets for each rear passenger. Then you can drive from Maine to Baja without having to engage any of your children in a single conversation.

Our mini-van, sadly, is not so equipped, but my wife and I did break down several years ago and buy a portable, AC/DC, TV/DVD unit that we strap down between the front seats for long trips. It doesn't have headsets, so my wife and I can hardly hear ourselves think — much less hear each other talk — while the kids are watching *The Lion King* for the 14th time (and that's just on one trip), but it's still better than listening to them complain.

Actually, my wife questioned the expense when I first bought the thing, so I told her I would take it back and give *her* the money if she could think of another way to keep all four kids quiet for an hour and forty-five minutes at a time. She thought for a moment, looked at the unit, and said, "It's really a pretty neat little TV." Smart lady, my wife.

If you can't afford that kind of technology, or if you still harbor the quaint notion that vacations are times for families actually to be *together*, and not just sitting in close proximity, then you may have some other ideas about how to spend those hours in the car. Some families like to sing; we did a lot of that ourselves, before the VCR, and still do occasionally between movies. Here's an interesting piece of trivia: on average, there are 3,412 bottles of beer between bathroom breaks. (Remarkably, this same statistic holds true for fraternity parties.)

Other families like to play car games, like the ones where you try to find letters of the alphabet on road signs, or spot Volkswagen Beetles, or identify road kill by phylum, class, order, and species. One of our favorite car games is "Twenty Questions." In this game, one player — usually a parent, since it's your car — picks a person or character, and the other players (the children) try to guess it by taking turns asking "yes" or "no" questions, up to a total of twenty. If they can't guess in twenty questions, you win, and they have to be quiet for ten minutes (I made that last rule up myself).

The trick to winning every time is to count "Are we there yet?" and "Can I go to the bathroom?" which are, after all, "yes" or "no" (mostly "no") questions. Then the kids will only have about four questions left in which to guess the character.

One last bit of advice: if you're traveling great distances with small children, try to drive at night as much as possible. Of course you won't be able to do this every night, because then you'd have to sleep during the day, while your infant and toddler frolic on the rim of the Grand Canyon. And driving at night has another disadvantage: you won't be able to see much of Mt. Rushmore, for instance, as you cruise by at 4:00 am. But at least you can say you were there.

Chapter 19

Scars of the Silver Screen

You don't have to drive halfway across the country or be gone two weeks to spend time together. Many families like to go out just for a few hours. I'm sure you'd like it if your family went out for a few hours, too, especially if they left you at home.

Fortunately, our modern, consumer-oriented society offers a variety of activities for families that have two or three hours to kill and a willingness to part with large quantities of cash. I'm going to talk about several of those activities in the next chapter, but here I want to focus on one of the most popular: going to the movies. I don't really know how to explain America's fascination with the big screen. I'm sure it has something to do with escapism, or perhaps with the Biblical proverb about the fool and his money. But we definitely *are* fascinated. Whether or not that makes us fools, I'll let you be the judge.

Like most Americans, you've probably been going to the movies all your life. When you were a kid, you went with your mom and dad. As a teenager, you went with friends and later with dates. In college, you and your buddies went to the student center to watch some second-run flick and throw popcorn at the screen. When you were dating, you and your wife liked to find some dark, deserted corner of the theater (okay, you still do). Even after your first child was born, you took her to the movies with you, where she slept right through exploding airplanes, small arms fire, and dirty dancing.

Then she learned to walk, and things were never the same. The movies became interactive. As Batman cruised through the dark city, stalking the Joker, you stumbled down the dark theater aisle, hunting something far more fearsome: the Toddler.

In time, she learned to talk and to comprehend speech, which brought about even greater changes. One day you were watching Jennifer Anniston or Angelina Jolie slink across the screen; the next day, the beautiful starlet was an animated Disney princess. Tom Cruise gave way to Oscar the Grouch. Sam Cooke crooning "I Hunger for Your Touch" became Barney the purple dinosaur singing "I Love You, You Love Me."

Of course, you and your wife may still go out occasionally, at least once every two or three years (see Chapter 2), and see an adult film — not an *adult film*, but a film for adults, something not animated or starring talking animals. But chances are most of your trips to the theater nowadays are family outings, to see family films.

As your children get older and become more numerous, this can present several problems. A few of these I've already touched on in Chapter 8, but I hope you'll bear with me as I reiterate a point or two and bring up a few new ones as well.

Whatever Happened to Good Old Running Dog Capitalist Cartoons?

The biggest problem with taking your family to a movie is finding a movie to take them to. I know a lot of films bill themselves as "family entertainment" or "fun for the whole family," but many of these are not what they claim to be — despite their rating. Any self-respecting family man knows never to rely on the rating system, which apparently is little more than a means for quantifying four-letter words and scenes containing frontal nudity. Make your own informed decision. Otherwise, you may spend the entire ride home explaining to your twelve-year-old daughter why it really *isn't* a good idea to take off your clothes while some guy you just met on a boat paints your picture.

To avoid this scenario, you should be very selective in the films you take your family to see. You might think it would be safe to allow your children to see films with a "G" rating, but as I said, that's no guarantee of anything. Several years ago, I took my kids to see a G-rated movie about ants, of all things. About halfway through, one of the ants makes an impassioned speech to his fellows, in which he proclaims, among other things, that "the workers control the means of production." Now, I'm pretty open-minded, but I don't know that I want my kids to get their Karl Marx from an animated feature. I can read *Das Kapital* to them at bedtime.

It's also true that if you limit your family to G movies, you'll only be going to the theater about twice a year — which would actually be a great thing for your budget. Over a five-year period, the savings could enable you to buy a summer home at the beach. But your kids would probably object and might even stage a full-scale revolt, taking over the den and demanding to watch The Disney Channel during the NBA finals. So you may want to expand your definition of "family movie" to take in PG films that you have thoroughly checked out.

Because that's really the key: checking movies out before you let your kids see them. You can do this yourself, though the cost may be prohibitive (goodbye, summer home), and you may even experience what scientists call "brain dulling," a measurable loss of intelligence that can cause you to forget such things as your boss' name and how to operate a remote control.

A better idea is to have friends check the movie out for you. Let them spend the money. Let them be the first to expose their kids to the amoral vagaries of some Hollywood producer who has long understood the connection between a parent's wallet and a child's hand. Take care, though, to choose only people whom you trust implicitly, other parents whose tastes and standards exactly mirror your own.

Okay, you probably don't know anyone like that, so an alternative is to stand outside the theater when the movie in question is letting out. Watch the faces of the parents as they walk by. If they're blanched and wide-eyed, or show other symptoms of shock, consider another film, like *The Sound of Music*, now playing at Harry's Old Fashioned Ice Cream Parlor and Film Emporium, admission one dollar. Just tell your pre-teen son there are ninjas at the end.

All Dogs Go to Star Wars

Once you've determined that there are in fact films worth seeing, your next step is to choose one. This will not be as easy as it sounds, especially if the ages of your children vary widely. Remember, we're talking here about taking the *entire* family. Thus, in addition to resolving the kinds of conflicts I describe in Chapter 8, you must also weigh the desires of older children against the needs and capabilities of younger ones.

Up until your oldest child is about twelve or thirteen, you can probably get by with taking them all to see an animated film. The better offerings usually have enough of a story to interest more mature children, along with plenty of loud music and slapstick comedy for the little ones. For the adults, I suggest an MP3 player with headphones and a download of my new self-help audio, "Twelve Steps to More Successful Living." (Step No. 9: Don't waste time going to movies.)

Problems arise, however, when older children want to see a live action film that may not hold a toddler's interest. Take the more recent Star Wars installments, for instance. Children six and up will spend the entire two hours glued to their seats, completely dazzled by the special effects. Any younger than that, though, and they're likely to become bored after the second robot loses its head, which is to say four minutes into the movie. Then they'll want to get up and wander around the theater, looking for discarded popcorn and candy, or perhaps for a plot.

You may also have problems with siblings of different sexes. Even among cartoons, there are definitely guy movies and "chick flicks." My eleven-year-old son, for example, may have enjoyed *All Dogs Go to Heaven* when he was five or six, but now he'd much prefer something like *Mutant Biker Dogs from Hades*. He doesn't mind animation, as long as the gore and severed limbs look real, just like in his computer games.

My daughter, on the other hand, at age thirteen, would probably still pay to see *All Dogs Go to Heaven*. Her favorite movie is *A Little Princess*, which her brothers would not watch if they were stranded on a desert island with only that one DVD. He'd use the DVD player to crack open coconuts, instead. In another couple of years he might be interested in a sequel, but only if it stars Selena Gomez in a bathing suit.

If you have older children of different sexes, then, it may sometimes be difficult to please them both. When you can't, one answer is to rotate movies — one for her, one for him. Then again, it may be that once your kids reach a certain age, you'll just have to give up the idea of family movie outings altogether. Then you can take your daughter to movies she likes and your son to movies he likes. Or — and this is the best idea of all — you can leave them both at home and go see a real movie with your wife.

Your Total Is $112.75, Sir

The thing I find most galling about taking my family to the movies is the cost. It's not so much that I can't afford it. I long ago established an "off-budget" category specifically for that purpose. (See Chapter 3.) I suppose it's just sour grapes on my part. I admit, I *do* harbor some resentment toward the fabulously wealthy actors, producers, and studio CEO's who so merrily gouge the rest of us, and I'm mildly insulted at their audacity.

I mean, where do they get off charging $11.00 for a 70-minute movie? *Eleven dollars*! You can get a suit dry-cleaned for that, or buy 2.5 Happy Meals, or pay the library fine on a book four months overdue. But that's not the most surprising thing. Far more astonishing is the fact that we pay it, with pleasure, and consider it a privilege.

I can remember when evening admission to a first-run feature film was about two dollars and fifty cents. Of course, I can remember when you could get a used Volkswagen Beetle in pretty good shape for about $750.00, so my information may not be the most current. Still, it just seems a bit sinful to spend that much money on something so fleeting, especially when just $19.00 more will get you the WWF on pay-per-view.

If you're going to take your entire family to the movies, then, you had better be prepared to drop a bundle. Even if smaller children get in free or at reduced rates, admission alone is probably going to cost upwards of $40.00. You can lower your cost, however, by going to a matinee — at most theaters, any showing that starts before 6:00 PM. This will save you about four or five dollars, which you may then use to purchase a small soft drink.

Which leads me to my next point: the $40.00 you spent on tickets was the *good* news. Once inside the theater, you find yourself in a bizarre world where the same candy bar that costs 50 cents at the convenience store is now somehow worth $4.50, and a 12-ounce soft drink that would go for 99 cents at McDonald's now fetches five bucks. And somehow they really *are* worth those prices. Because worth, or value, is a product of demand, and for me nothing creates the demand for a Snickers and a Sprite like walking in the door of a modern multiplex cinema.

Amazingly, this is true even if I can barely walk at all, having just polished off a Number 6 (three beef enchiladas, a bean burrito, and a chimichanga) at El Rancho del Gordo. I step into the theater, I smell the popcorn, I see the candy lined up inside the display case, and immediately two things happen: I have to go to the bathroom, and I know intuitively that there is no way I will be able to get through the next 90 minutes without ingesting at least 1000 more calories. At about one cent per calorie (I'm convinced that's the formula theaters use to calculate food prices), that's $10.00 just for me.

Someone once explained to me that overcharging for food is how cinema owners make their money. Of course. It's not as if they make anything on their $11.00 seats. Five hundred of them. In each of 12 theaters. Four times a day (not counting matinees and midnight showings). But, hey, this is America after all, and I don't suppose I should begrudge anyone a profit, especially when that profit is responsible for all the marvelous luxuries we theater-goers enjoy, such as seats with broken armrests and cola-covered floors that grab hold of your feet like something out of *The Abyss* (another good example, I suppose, of movies becoming interactive).

The problem — and the bill — becomes greater when you factor in a family of four. Or five. Or six. Everything I just said about the demand for food and drink goes double for my kids, especially since they probably didn't even *eat* their kid's meal tacos. This means each of them will need approximately 1500 calories *just to stay alive* during the movie, which translates into one medium box of popcorn, one large candy bar, and a large soft drink apiece. That adds up to — well, you do the math.

Of course, there are some ways to save money on snacks, and I'd be remiss if I didn't conclude this chapter by mentioning a few. One is to tell your wife, on the way to the theater, that she looks as though she's recently put on an extra pound or two. She may not speak to you — or relate to you in any other manner — for several days, but you could come out as much as $10.00 ahead at the concession counter, which you could then put toward a divorce attorney.

A better idea is to bring in snacks from outside. I know most theaters actively discourage this, but until they resort to strip searches, my family and I will continue to defy their petty rules. If you're talking about more than just a couple of candy bars in mom's purse, though, you're going to have to be somewhat creative.

For example, if you have small children you can always use the diaper bag. Just make sure you keep track of which little brown things are the Tootsie Rolls. Or you can wear shoes two or three sizes too large and fill the toes with M&M's, though you may be the only one who eats them. And a plastic bread bag filled with popcorn will fit neatly inside your son's baggy jeans. You probably won't be able to include your teenage daughter in the fun, though. If she dresses like most girls her age, she couldn't hide a stick of chewing gum anywhere on her person.

The worst thing about bringing your own snacks is that it's very difficult to smuggle in liquids, much less ice and cups. You might try using the baby's bottles, unless of course you don't have a baby, in which case you'd look pretty silly. And if the teenager at the gate bothers to check, you may have to explain why the milk looks like cola. (Answer: protein enriched formula.) Another strategy is to take the money you saved on candy and popcorn and let the family splurge on soft drinks. That should get you out of the theater for under $70.00.

Or you can simply insist that everyone drink water, which will mean frequent trips to the fountain — if anyone can find it. But hey, that's a good project for you, while you're out in the lobby chasing the toddler.

Chapter 20

Games People Plié

I promised at the beginning of the last chapter that I would talk about other forms of family entertainment, too. After all, not everyone is into movies, and even those of us who are probably don't want our children spending too much time in theaters. Then they might begin to confuse film with reality, believing for example that there really are such things as friendly ghosts, or that gorillas actually do speak English. This could lead to a terribly skewed perception of the world. Everyone knows gorillas speak Norwegian.

Come to think of it, what kind of a family activity is going to a movie, anyway? That's no way to spend time together. You can't see each other because it's dark, your attention is focused on something completely extraneous, and if you do attempt to have a conversation some stranger may threaten you with bodily harm. It's like trying to bond at the public library, during a brownout, except that going to the library would be free. Surely your family deserves something more personal, or at least something cheaper.

That's why you might want to consider some of the other activities I'm going to talk about in this chapter. Taking your family to a ball game may not be less expensive than taking them to a movie — okay, it's about four times as expensive — but at least you're visible to each other and can talk all you want without risking injury, unless you happen to be taunting Metta World Peace. Participation activities, such as bowling and miniature golf, aren't cheap, either, but they do provide excellent opportunities for you and your loved ones to interact as you argue over the score and whose turn it is to putt. Plays, concerts, and art exhibits, on the other hand, often *are* cheap, even free. But you may have to pay in other ways, such as when your son decides to move to Los Angeles and become an actor, otherwise known as a waiter at Denny's.

Taken at the Old Ball Game

There's nothing quite as American as taking your family to a professional or major college sporting event. Warm summer evenings at the baseball stadium, crisp autumn football Saturdays, snow-covered walkways outside the basketball arena — these are the stuff memories are made of. After four or five such outings, you may even be able to remember when you had money to buy groceries.

The major leagues, of course, represent the highest level of competition, and I think every father ought to take his kids to a big-league ballpark or arena at least once. Aside from the games, the edifices themselves are generally well worth seeing, though they're all starting to look a bit alike these days. Indeed, sometimes it seems every new stadium or arena is being built to the same specifications: a ring of luxury skyboxes for the shockingly rich, overlooking thousands of chair-back seats for the merely wealthy. The rest of us watch the game on television, or catch the SportsCenter highlights.

But if you're like most family men, you can probably afford to take your family to a game every now and then, especially if you follow the advice in Chapter 16. In fact, I understand that many major league venues now have their own car title loan franchises on the premises, known as "Tickets for Titles." Be advised, though, that to get decent seats your car must be no more than three years old and have fewer than 50,000 miles.

And then there's food. Everything I said in Chapter 19 about movie theater food prices holds true here as well, except that at the ball park they have *real* food, like hot dogs and chicken-on-a-stick. You can't get nutrition like that just anywhere, but you're going to have to pay dearly for it — about two or three cents per calorie, on average. Don't think for a moment, though, that you'll be spending all that money with nothing to show for it at the end but a case of gastroenteritis. No, sirree, your six-dollar soft drink comes with a plastic cup you can actually take home. In fact, if you want to wait around a few minutes after the game, you can probably take home several hundred of them. Just don't hoard them all for yourself. Set aside a few for wedding gifts.

Another great thing about big-time sporting events is the outstanding role models they provide for children. This may be especially true for boys, but these days, with the rise of the WNBA and women's soccer, it's becoming true for girls as well. I mean, would you rather your daughter grow up to be like Madonna or like Mia Hamm? Mia Hamm made a commercial with Michael Jordan. Madonna (allegedly) slept with Dennis Rodman. Enough said.

For boys the question is even more *apropos*: whom would you rather your son emulate, Tom Brady or Luciano Pavarotti? Granted, Pavarotti could probably whip Brady in a fair fight, especially if they were sumo wrestling, but that's beside the point. I have nothing against opera or the performing arts in general; in fact, I'm going to devote a separate section of this chapter specifically to that topic. But I'm not ashamed to admit that I prefer football. So do most other American men, which is probably why the Met doesn't seat 95,000. So I think by and large my readers will agree with me that it's okay if our sons grow up to be large and bearded, with a penchant for ill-fitting black suits, as long as those suits say "Raiders" across the front.

At the ballpark, stadium, or arena, your children can mingle freely with their larger-than-life heroes (just don't allow your teenage daughter to mingle too freely) and perhaps even take home a memento they'll cherish for a lifetime. And I'm not talking about the stick the chicken came on. I mean an autograph, a personal signature in a star athlete's own illegible hand, on an object such as a baseball or the T-shirt you just bought for $35.00 at the souvenir shop. At the very least, your son or daughter will have the opportunity to spend 90 minutes waiting outside the player's entrance for the privilege of hearing those three magical words, "Not now, kid." Don't worry, though. They can catch their idol at the mall this weekend and get that autograph after all, for only another $75.00.

When they can't be rejected by them in person, your children can read about their favorite athletes in the newspaper every day. Most major dailies devote considerable space to sports coverage, including game analysis, up-to-date statistics, and feature stories. If your kids don't find anything about the players they admire in the sports pages, suggest they try the police blotter.

Contributing to Delinquency in the Minors

If, on the other hand, you're sick to death of athletes who are greedy, self-centered, obnoxious, and felonious — and those are just the bench warmers — you might want to try taking your family to a minor league or small college game. It's true, as I said, that everyone should have the big-league experience at least once, but for pure fun and family entertainment, nothing beats sports at the lower levels.

To begin with, the stadiums are much smaller, so there really isn't a bad seat in the house, unless you happen to be right in front of the guy who has one too many beers and loses his chili dog down the back of your shirt. (Remarkably, it looks pretty much the same as it did when he bought it.) And the ticket prices are much more reasonable — typically about ten or twelve dollars a seat — so you can enjoy the game without having to worry about losing your car. The chicken-on-a-stick still costs the same, but at least you can afford to eat, since you haven't had to liquidate all your assets just to pass through the turnstile. You may, however, be liquidating for days afterward.

It's also true that lower-level sporting events are much more accessible to most people. Unless you happen to live in one of 30 or so large cities, you may have to drive hours to see a big league or major college game, whereas the only Americans not within 90 minutes of a minor league or small college venue are hiding from the FBI in remote mountain cabins.

The best thing about minor league sports, though, is that most of the franchises are dedicated to maintaining a family atmosphere. At many of the newer or newly renovated baseball parks, for example, you will find playgrounds, rides, and other attractions for small children. Older children often are allowed out on the field before and after the game to mingle with the players, managers, and mascots. Your kids can even get autographs, as most minor league players will stay as long as necessary after the game, patiently signing anything you thrust at them, including body parts. They haven't yet learned to be surly, aloof, or obnoxious. That comes with experience.

The same thing holds true for other non-"big-time" sporting events, like minor league hockey and small college basketball. The games themselves can be just as exciting, but without many of the side-shows common at higher levels: bench-clearing brawls, shouting matches between coaches and players, obscene gestures directed at the fans. Of course, I realize those are the main reasons some people go to the games to begin with. If that's true in your case, then I suggest you consider leaving the wife and kids at home, or at least make them wear blindfolds and earmuffs. When people laugh and point, just explain that they're training to become NFL referees.

Aside from all that, sports are simply good clean fun for the entire family, unless you happen to be sitting too close to Bob Knight. They provide a kind of unscripted drama not found anywhere else. Absolutely no one knows what is going to happen, other than a few Las Vegas bookmakers and Don King. That's the beauty of sports, and that's what makes them better than movies, where everyone knows exactly what's going to happen, except apparently for the 250 pound biker seated directly behind you, who also doesn't appreciate your running commentary. You'd never have to worry about that at the ballpark. He'd be too drunk to care.

Bowling for Dullards

Movies and sporting events can both be entertaining, but there will be times when your family wants to be a little more active — when you want to *do* something rather than just *watch* something. Fortunately, there are things you and your family can do together that are perfectly wholesome, only take a couple of hours, and don't cost too much ("too much" being defined for our purposes as "not exceeding the remaining credit limit on your six cards combined").

One perennial family favorite is bowling. This is a game that can be enjoyed by people of all ages. Even toddlers are able to push the ball down the lane using both hands, though it may not strike the gutter with quite as much force as your own errant attempts. That's because you've mastered the concept of follow-through, if not that of accuracy.

I'm not sure just when bowling was invented, but I understand that it goes back at least several centuries. There is mention of "lawn bowling," a form of the game played outside (duh), in several 15th-century manuscripts, and one of Shakespeare's lesser known sonnets refers to "A gentleman, who putting on his airs, / In funny shoes doth score his strikes and spares." Some historians even claim that the game was played by the ancient Mayans, who used the severed heads of enemies as balls. Recently discovered hieroglyphs seem to indicate that participants often experienced problems finding a head whose nostrils fit their first two fingers comfortably.

Modern bowling isn't nearly as barbaric, unless I'm the one playing. As recently as the 1940's and 50's, bowling was considered a diversion for the lower classes, played in dark and dingy "alleys" that often doubled as beer halls. Today's alleys, in contrast, are clean, stylish, and well-lighted beer halls — but with a family atmosphere, which makes them little different from ballparks.

The great thing about bowling, then, is that you can take the whole family, and everyone can play. More importantly, everyone *will* play, including the children. I mean, what child, whether toddler or teenager, is going to pass on the opportunity to propel a heavy object into a stationary target that not only will fall over but will make a loud noise upon impact? Your wife also will play, because it's the only game she can beat you at, other than golf, tennis, billiards, chess, backgammon, gin rummy, and arm wrestling. And you, of course, will play because you're paying for it, and because the shoes look great with your pants.

The hardest thing about bowling, other than actually knocking down the pins, is trying to keep score. I've been assured by a prominent physicist I know that you don't have to have a degree in differential equations to keep score in bowling. Still, I'm dubious. I guess I'm going to have to learn, though, since I've observed that the one who knows how to keep score generally ends up winning. In our last outing, my eleven-year-old, by his calculations, beat me 287 to 5.

Another game families like to play together is miniature golf, an abbreviated form of the popular sport that allows putting only. It was popularized in the 70's and 80's by the famous "Putt-Putt" courses, and soon every wide spot in the road with pretensions of being a tourist attraction had its own imitation based on a local theme — hillbillies, sea monsters, *Mafiosi*. Most courses have 18 holes, with a variety of twists, turns, dips, and angles. Some holes even feature built-in obstacles, ranging from simple curbs to revolving windmills to animatronic figures.

Though poor at real golf, I've always been pretty good at the miniature version. Perhaps this is because I'm so accustomed to playing around obstacles, like trees, large man-made lakes, and other people's houses. Whereas another golfer might become unnerved at the thought of having to time his putt so that the giant clown's mouth is *open*, I am completely unaffected. I only wish those trees would open up occasionally.

Miniature golf is a great activity for children because it doesn't require as much skill as regular golf or as much strength as bowling. Your kids will not hit into the rough or strike water, and they will ultimately feel the satisfaction at each hole of seeing their balls drop into the cup. You may periodically have to remind your pre-teen son, as he prepares to tee off, that the club in his hands is a *putter*, that the distance to the pin is only ten feet, and that he is in fact *not* Tiger Woods. But other than that, you and your kids should have a great time together. Be generous in your score keeping and they may not even beat you too badly.

Which brings me to my last point: if you decide to do something active like this with your family, just remember you're putting a lot on the line. Your children will expect you to be able to beat them at bowling or miniature golf or whatever at least until they're old enough to walk. Your sons especially will also expect you to beat your wife with some regularity. (Beat her at the *games*, I mean.) If you can't, I suggest you negotiate: in return for her letting you win, you can agree to take the entire family to the ballet next time. It won't be nearly as much fun, though. No mechanical clowns.

What Do You Call a Man with No Arms and No Legs Hanging on the Wall?

In the introduction to Part Four, I noted that women often feel strongly about the need to expose children to a wide variety of cultural activities, including plays, orchestral concerts, the ballet, the opera, and art exhibits. I then went on to make snide remarks about men who feel the same way. I now realize that I was being sexist, narrow-minded, and insensitive, which is so out of character. The fact is that many men are also interested in the visual and performing arts, and they too wish to share those interests with their children. If they have any.

Even if you're a typical semi-literate, country-music listening, professional-wrestling watching, red-blooded American male, you have to admit your wife has a point. Your children *do* need to be exposed to the arts, if only so the boys can be reminded just how much they prefer football. Ultimately, this will give them a greater appreciation for the finer things in life: the gracefulness of the ballet, the beauty of classical music, the heights to which a paper airplane (formerly known as a "program") can rise when launched from a real balcony. Movie theaters don't have balconies anymore — or programs either, for that matter.

Of course, one of the drawbacks to taking your kids to a performance or a museum is that you have to go yourself, unless you can get out of it by feigning illness. If your wife isn't buying that, try taking calcium supplements in the hope of inducing a kidney stone. It may ultimately be less painful than the leading lady's ten-minute soprano solo, which sounds as though she herself is trying to pass something. Or, as a last resort, you can always get yourself kicked out for throwing paper airplanes off the balcony.

Once you're resigned to the idea, however, bear in mind you probably shouldn't begin with a black tie event. Those tend to be very expensive and can last up to three or four hours. Your kids wouldn't sit still that long for an Avengers sequel, much less for *Madame Butterfly*. And they won't be able to understand why there are no hot dog vendors, or why the bathrooms have couches.

It's much better to start your kids on something like a "Pops in the Park" concert. I take my family to one of these every Fourth of July. A local symphony orchestra sets up in a large park and plays a mixture of classical and "pops" while families picnic on blankets and listen to country music on their headphones.

I think a similar approach is wise when it comes to the ballet, the opera, and the theater. Most of these offer special performances for school-age children, which are usually abbreviated and sometimes edited to make them more appealing to young audiences. The dancers, for example, may wear super hero costumes, or the baritone may offer his interpretation of Coldplay's latest hit.

Another cultural activity your children may enjoy is going to an art gallery. Here they can view the paintings and sculptures of the masters, and you can attempt to explain to your son why nudity is acceptable as long as it's considered art, and why the magazines you found under his mattress last week don't qualify. They'll also gain a better appreciation of color and form, which will be useful when they pick out your next Father's Day tie.

The problem with museums and galleries is that children are not confined to a single seat and may therefore tend to run wild. This is how the Venus de Milo ended up in her current condition. Of course, your children may not actually be confined to a single seat at the opera, either, which could explain why Brunhilde's ax is missing. But that's another story.

The last time I took my three boys to an art gallery, they escaped my grasp and went weaving in and out through the exhibits. By the time I caught up to them, they had dodged into a closed area, knocked a workman off his ladder, and spilled a gallon of red paint on his canvas drop cloth. As I was apologizing profusely to the owner, another patron, seeing the mess, offered him $25,000 for it.

In closing this chapter, let me say to all you manly fathers of strapping young boys that just because your son grows up loving the arts doesn't mean he'll turn out to be a sissy. Maybe he'll just become the kind of well-rounded young man who doffs his football helmet at halftime to play clarinet in the marching band. Maybe he'll even go on to be a professional musician, which is almost as good as being a professional athlete but with much less chance of a concussion.

Chapter 21

Readiness Is All

No matter where you're going, if children are involved, the hardest part is always going to be getting ready. Gone are those carefree days when you and your wife could decide on a whim to go out to eat or to a movie. Now you must plan as if you were NATO preparing to invade a small country.

Before your children were born, you and your wife could even take spur-of-the-moment trips out of town on weekends. Want to go to the mountains? To New York? To a city five hours away to visit an old college roommate? No problem. Just throw a few things in a bag Friday after work and take off. You could be ready to go literally anywhere in the world in 30 minutes. Even your wife required only two hours.

Now the planning stage is more likely to consume two days. Do you have enough diapers? Bottles? Extra nipples (for the bottles, I mean)? Sipper cups? Hair ribbons? Stuffed animals? Do you have the requisite four pairs of shoes per child — dress, casual, play, and wet-weather? Have you packed at least 14 pair of undershorts for each boy? (And that's just for a weekend.) You know you're truly a family man when you can't get ready to go anywhere without making a last-minute stop at Wal-Mart.

Unfortunately, the problem grows exponentially with each additional child. If it takes about 15 minutes to get one child dressed to go out, understand that getting two children ready will require approximately 45 minutes. If you have three children, you should count on spending an hour and a half. And so on. With four kids or more, pizza delivery and pay-per-view start to look pretty good.

Of course, once you reach that watershed number of three children, you and your wife are outnumbered anyway, and life thereafter is pretty much an exercise in futility. When you had one child, the two of you could take turns getting her ready. With two, you could each take one. Now, no matter which two you tackle first, they'll always find a way to undo everything you've done before you finish tending to the third, perhaps by dipping themselves in chocolate or creating body art with their mother's lipstick. And those are the teenagers. Toddlers are much worse.

Dressing to Excess

My wife seems to think that when it comes to getting the kids ready to go somewhere, the labor should be divided along gender lines. That's fine for her, since we have a daughter and three sons. Moreover, our daughter is thirteen and can thus pretty well fend for herself. This leaves me with the three boys, two of whom are still quite small. The eleven-year-old can get himself ready, true, but then he must sit absolutely motionless on the couch until we're actually ready to get in the car, or else he'll look as though he's been lost in the woods for six days and attacked by coyotes.

The other two are a different matter. The only way I can deal with them is literally to sit on one while dressing the other, then swap. While this is going on, my wife pitches in by glancing pointedly at her watch and sighing impatiently.

So I've had a bit of experience with getting children dressed — more, probably, than most men. I know, for example, that dressing an infant is much like dressing a Barbie doll, if the Barbie could pull its arms away and flop over on its stomach. (Not that I've dressed many Barbie dolls, you understand. This is just for the sake of analogy.) Dressing a toddler, on the other hand, is more akin to trying to squeeze a small pig into a spandex body suit. Despite your best efforts and intentions, neither the child nor the pig is going to look anything like the models in the magazines.

The situation becomes even more complicated when you're going to be away overnight. Please understand that when I say "overnight," I mean for one night or fourteen. It really doesn't matter, as far as your preparations are concerned. Because the fundamental rule of traveling with children is that you need just as much stuff for a one-night stay as you would for a two-week vacation.

Take clothes, for example. Surely, you say, you don't need to pack as many clothes for one night as you would for a week. Of course you don't — as long as you're willing to run the risk that your child may be cold, hot, wet, uncomfortable, overdressed, underdressed, or out of style. To avoid calamity, you must pack at least eight different outfits, along with matching shoes, socks, and hair bands, not to mention an adequate supply of undergarments.

Likewise, you need no fewer than five sleeping outfits, because who knows what the weather will be like, or where the child may be sleeping, for that matter. For all you know, you could be lost for days in a snowstorm, even though it's May, and you're going to Florida.

Getting Loaded

And speaking of sleeping, that opens up a whole new category of "stuff": sleeping bags for the older kids, porta-cribs for the little ones, and of course everyone must have his or her very own pillow. As I suggested in Chapter 18, it's pretty much impossible to sleep anyplace without your own pillow. These are things you're going to have to take regardless of how long you plan to be gone.

Moreover, they're all things you have to find some way of getting into the car. I've noticed that packing a car trunk or the luggage compartment of a van is one of those endeavors in which some men seem to take inordinate pride, like grilling steaks or (allegedly) winning at fantasy football. And there's no question loading does take a certain amount of ingenuity, logic, and creativity, especially if you have a large family. Because inevitably, just as you have finally gotten everything in its ideal place, so that all fourteen bags are arranged precisely in your trunk like the pieces of an ancient mosaic — thus reflecting your superior mental acuity and technical competence — your wife will be so unkind as to point out that you forgot the porta-crib.

And that's just *going*. I've found it takes even more ingenuity to pack for the return trip, since I have never once, in my entire married life, gone away with my family and not come home with more than I had when I left — even taking into account things I left behind, some of them on purpose. That's because it's impossible to go anywhere in the world nowadays without buying something, except to the homes of family members, where they *give* you things instead. In my case, these are mostly things I don't want, like old play clothes and used crockery. But my wife *does* want them, which means that once again I will have the opportunity to bring my considerable trunk-loading skills to bear.

But I digress. My point is that all of this is true whether you're going to be gone overnight or for an extended period, and as a result it takes just as long to pack for a short trip as for a longer one. I first noticed this during the holiday season a few years ago. Two days after returning from a week-long Christmas vacation, my family and I were preparing to leave again, to celebrate New Year's at the home of some friends in a neighboring city — an overnight trip.

To my chagrin, I found myself loading into our van exactly the same equipment I had spent 90 minutes unloading just 48 hours earlier. My wife had washed all the clothes — I deduced this from the smell — and put them back into the same bags, which consequently seemed to weigh about the same as they had when I unloaded them. The porta-crib sat in the baby's closet, right where I'd put it. Even the hanging garment bag appeared not to have been touched, although I suppose it held different clothes.

At that point I realized it would've been far easier if we'd driven directly to our friends' house, unloaded all our stuff, then gone home for two days. If they were real friends, they might even have done our laundry.

Another fascinating aspect of vehicle loading is what I refer to as the law of diminishing returns, as it applies to automobile storage space. When we owned a four-door sedan, anytime we traveled overnight it would be completely packed. I mean, I couldn't have wedged another pair of play shoes in with a can of W-D 40 and a crowbar.

Then, recognizing that we needed more room for our growing family, we bought a minivan. The first time we took a trip in it, it was as packed as the sedan had ever been. There was barely enough room for the children (which isn't necessarily a bad thing). So our next van had a luggage rack, to which we eventually added a car-top carrier. Same thing. I'm convinced that if we went on vacation in a diesel bus, pulling a U-Haul trailer, we would find some way to load both of them to the gills. With any luck, though, we might be able to put the children in the trailer.

Planned Parenthood

To make going anywhere with your family as painless as possible, whether you intend to be away for a few hours or a few weeks, you should begin planning well ahead of time. For an evening out, this may mean deciding two or three days earlier where you will go, what time you will leave, and how long you will stay. Overnight trips should probably be planned at least two weeks in advance. And for vacations of several days or more, you should start making plans months beforehand. This will enable you to find the best air fares and hotel rates, so that you will lose only a few thousand dollars, and not your entire life savings, when you have to cancel at the last minute because the four-year old has chicken pox.

Understand that when I talk about "planning" I mean that you place the event on your calendar and begin making all the necessary arrangements. At times this may seem like overkill, but rest assured, it's not — not when one or more children are involved.

Say, for example, you and your wife decide it would be nice to take the kids to the new Disney movie. Does that mean you can just pick up and go one Friday evening or Saturday afternoon? Of course not. That would defy all the known laws of parenting and subject you to prosecution for neglect — how could you possibly be meeting all of your children's needs if you don't spend four hours getting ready for a two hour movie? — not to mention lawsuits brought by other resentful parents.

Instead, you must first coordinate with all of the children's other goings-on: school programs, sports practices and games, doctor's appointments, birthday parties, church youth activities, etc. — not to mention your own schedule and that of your wife. Then you must make sure you have everything you need for a two-hour family outing, which may include but will probably not be limited to the following: diapers, diaper wipes, bottle, formula, Tylenol, asthma inhaler, first-aid kit, eye glass repair kit, compass, copy of Dr. Spock's child-rearing book, set of Mr. Spock's pointy Vulcan ears, handcuffs, pepper spray, and antacid tablets. Finally, you must go by the automatic bank teller and withdraw $100.00 in cash, which will leave you with a balance of $23.07 for the remainder of the month, even though it's only the 11th.

Once again, the entire process becomes more complicated when you're going to be gone for at least one night. About the only way to cope in that situation is to have a thorough checklist. In fact, you really need *two* checklists — a planning list and a packing list.

Your planning list includes all the things you must *do* before you leave. For example, if you're going to be on vacation for a week, you might want to stop your mail and newspaper delivery, make arrangements for garbage pick-up, and find accommodations for your pets. You might also want to leave a key with neighbors, in case they need to get into your house for any reason, such as they're having a big party and your stereo equipment is much nicer than theirs.

The packing list, on the other hand, contains all the items you'll need to take with you on the trip. I've already mentioned a number of these, but let me just say here that you should be very careful not to leave off anything of vital importance, such as your son's allergy medication, your golf clubs, and a sufficient number of traveler's checks, which are for your wife to use while you play golf. You should also remember to pack things for the trip itself, such as books, snacks, and industrial strength earplugs.

If all this sounds like far too much trouble, you may be tempted just to stay home. Don't. Families need to go places together. Children need to be exposed to a variety of stimuli — and I'm not talking about the Internet. You and your wife need to get out of the house and away from your jobs, if only for a few hours. Most importantly, you all need a break from the daily routine — which you will nevertheless welcome like an old friend when you return from your "vacation." (I believe that's why vacations were invented: because they make being home seem so pleasant for weeks afterward.)

In any case, once you're on the highway, in your fully loaded vehicle, with the miles stretching out before you, you'll experience a sense of freedom not found anywhere else, except perhaps in those few moments between finally getting the kids to bed and falling asleep snoring in your recliner. So make your plans, draw up your lists, pack your car, and prepare to hit the road. You'd better hurry, though. I think Wal-Mart closes in a few hours.

PART FIVE:

Other Duties as Assigned

It's been said that the three most dreaded words in the English language are "some assembly required." That may well be true, but the *four* most terrifying words, without a doubt, are "other duties as assigned." If you're not familiar with that phrase, you obviously haven't read your job description all the way through, perhaps because you became suicidally despondent after the first five pages. This little item is usually tucked in at the very end, right after "clean toilet after each use" and "give supervisor daily foot massage."

Your role as a family man comes with its own job description, too (see preceding 21 chapters). And tacked onto the end of that list is the same ominous item: *other duties as assigned.* That means, in addition to being a loving and sensitive husband, an involved father, and (in many cases) the primary breadwinner, you must also perform every other function that no one else in your family — or in the community, for that matter — has any intention of being roped into.

Such functions include serving the children of your community as a youth coach or scout leader, supporting and enriching your own children's educational experience, keeping your home and automobiles spruce and in working order, and keeping *yourself* spruce and in working order. You may also, in your spare time, write a novel, formulate a responsible foreign policy, and learn to play the cello.

One final note before you read on: you may, at this point, be feeling a bit overwhelmed by all that goes into being a family man. Don't sweat it. Remember, no one really expects you to do all these things, or to do any of them perfectly — except, of course, for your wife. And your children. And your parents. And especially your wife's parents. But other than that, you'll find the world a pretty accepting and forgiving place. Just make sure you take North Korea into account when you're working on that foreign policy.

Chapter 22

A Man's Work Is Never Done

As a family man, one of your most important duties — other than helping your wife in the kitchen, taking your children to ball practice, bringing your wife flowers, teaching your teenagers to drive, budgeting your family's finances, selling candy bars to raise money for the band, and occasionally finding time to earn a living — is to keep your house, your yard, and your automobiles functional and reasonably attractive. It's not a bad idea to keep your*self* functional and reasonably attractive, too, but we'll get to that in Chapter 25.

I mentioned in Chapter 4 that working on your house or yard can be a great way to get out of doing "women's work," like cleaning and laundry. Unfortunately, there will be times when you just have to work on your house or yard things whether you get out of anything else or not, not to mention whether you want to or not. In fact, if you're like me, there will be plenty of times when it's the yard work itself you'd like to get out of — but probably not so much that you'd be willing to do laundry instead.

The Art of Being Shiftless

Even though I've used the term "women's work" to describe what is traditionally called "housework" and to differentiate it from the kinds of "man's work" I'm going to talk about in this chapter, I recognize that in our society the lines have become increasingly blurred. Just as men can learn to do laundry, clean bathrooms, and prepare meals, so women can learn to cut grass, trim hedges, and install gutters. In fact, it's actually very important that your wife to learn how to do these things — in case something happens to you, you know. And of course the only way for her to really learn is by doing them. Repeatedly. I estimate that, for her to become truly proficient at mowing the yard, for instance, she'll need to do it at least once a week for the next 15 to 20 years. Just make sure she's finished the laundry first.

If you can't get your wife to do your work for you, then try your kids. They're slightly more likely to do what you tell them, and they can't punish you quite as effectively for asking, either. And remember here, too, the blurring of gender lines. Whether you have boys or girls, once they reach the age of eight they can be put to work cutting grass, for starters. Later on, children can graduate to hedge trimming, car washing, and performing minor repairs. Your role will be to supervise, preferably from the porch, with a glass of cold lemonade. If it's really hot, you can move your command post into the living room. That's why it has windows.

But the best way to get out of "man's work" is to use the time-honored excuse that you don't have the right tools. If you can convince your wife of this, you should be able either to a) buy a new toy, or b) hire someone else to do the work. Either of those is good for you.

For example, if you have a normal size yard and own a lawnmower, you probably aren't going to be able to use the "I don't have the right tools" excuse. But if you have an unusually large yard (definition of "unusually large": can't be mowed during half time), you may try saying something to your wife like, "Gee, honey, I really need a big riding mower for a yard this size." If she buys that, you should either get your new riding mower or else be allowed to hire the neighbor boy to mow the yard for you. Either way, you win.

Another example: say your dryer quits tumbling, and your wife is convinced it can easily be fixed. "It's probably just a slipped belt," she says, having Googled the matter thoroughly (just one reason I hate Google). "You can fix that," she says.

In this situation, the proper response is to remove the back panel of the dryer, stare thoughtfully at its insides while rubbing your chin, and say something like, "Sure, honey, this would be easy to fix if I had a linear hydraulic separator. It's not like you can fix one of these things with a crowbar and a Phillips-head screwdriver, you know." She takes the bait: "How much is a linear-hydro-thingamajigee?" she asks. "About $200.00," you reply. Bingo! Since the repairman will only charge $190.00, you will now be able to do what you should have done all along: *hire a professional*, who can probably take care of the problem in 15 minutes... using a crowbar and a Phillips-head screwdriver.

You may also be able to hire a professional if you can persuade your wife that you lack the *knowledge* to do a particular job. That shouldn't be a hard sell.

For instance, I used to change the oil in our vehicles myself. A few years ago, I grew tired of spending half an hour lying on my back, on concrete, just for the privilege of skinning my knuckles and having hot oil drip on my forehead. So I began taking our cars to one of those nifty 10-minute oil change places, where I could spend the same half hour sitting in an air-conditioned waiting room reading a 1987 issue of *Car and Driver* ("Road Testing the Yugo!"). Of course it's more expensive, but to me it's worth every dime.

But how to explain this to my wife without admitting that I've merely become lazy and profligate, which would be the truth? Fortunately, I was able to convince her that, on these new cars, everything is controlled by computer, so you can't have just anybody messing around under the hood. As far as changing the oil is concerned, that's complete bull, but she bought it — perhaps because she has learned the hard way not to underestimate my ineptitude.

Big Toys for Big Boys

Of course there are men who actually *like* to do things themselves. We even have a name for them, but I can't print it here, even though it's in the Bible. Some of these guys are genuine "hands-on" types who have real mechanical ability and simply like to use it. Others find working in the yard or painting the house or installing new shock absorbers relaxing, which is something I can't fathom. To me, sitting in my recliner watching a football game is relaxing. Anything else is just plain work.

Then there are those who just like to get new toys — er, I mean *tools*. These are the guys with riding mowers — make that "lawn tractors" — that can pull an eighteen-wheeler out of a ditch, weed-eaters capable of taking down small trees, and leaf-blowers that create entire weather systems. They're also the ones who have expensive gadgets for every job: power paint sprayers, eighty-two foot extension ladders, portable battery chargers, and so forth. With what they spend on equipment, they could probably afford to hire the neighbor boy full time and keep a professional handyman on retainer. They might even be able to afford to *buy* a retainer, which, if you've been to the orthodontist lately, you know is another matter entirely.

If you're one of those guys, then to you I'll simply say, "Have fun, and be careful." Some "toys" can literally hurt you, as more than a few men have discovered to their sorrow. (They've also discovered that a lawn mower really doesn't need 150 horsepower.)

A greater danger, though, is addiction. As with all forms of technology, having powerful tools or fancy gadgets can lead to dependency, so that the owner is incapable of functioning without them. There's my former neighbor, for instance, who mentioned to me one day in passing that the motor on his leaf blower had burned out. When I offered to let him borrow my *rake*, he looked at me as though I had suggested he sacrifice his teenage daughter to the yard gods — which probably wouldn't have worked, anyway. I seriously doubt she was a virgin.

In any case, it's important that you not become a slave to your tools. Remember, even the fanciest of new toys can get old very quickly, as we parents are reminded each Christmas morning. Yet once you have the tool, you are then obligated to continue to perform the task, no matter how tedious it may become. Using your new toy may be fun for a while, but the day will almost certainly come when you'll wish you could hire someone to do the job for you. Sadly, you won't be able to. You'll have the right tool.

So I would discourage you from buying anything you don't absolutely need, or that is more powerful or performs more functions than you really need. That new power drill may look really cool, but understand that if you buy it, your wife will have a list of drilling-related projects waiting for you when you get home. Buy the drill only if you are prepared to spend the next eight Saturdays building shelves, hanging pictures, and installing various fixtures. Otherwise, I suggest you develop a kind of Zen-like acceptance of your tool-deficient condition. You'll get to watch a lot more football that way.

The Yard Beautiful

I don't know about you, but working in the yard has always been one of my least favorite chores. So naturally I moved to a part of the county where the grass grows nine months out of the year and bought a house on a three-acre lot. Now I have to set aside one day of the week to do nothing but yard work. It's a bit like having another part-time job, except I don't get paid. Of course, I can't be fired, either, but I certainly wish I could.

The situation has improved somewhat as my children have gotten older. Now they can help, which isn't nearly the same as doing it for me, but I'm hoping we'll get there soon. I also have to admit that there are times when I enjoy the solitude of sitting on my big lawn tractor (yes, I got a new toy out of the deal, but don't worry — it's only 125 hp) and riding around in circles for three hours. There are weeks when that's about the only time I get to myself, and I use it to ponder such weighty philosophical questions as, "How many angels can dance on the head of a pin?" and "Is Kurdistan a real country, or did the Three Stooges just make it up?"

But that still doesn't mean I'd rather work in the yard than sit in my air-conditioned den and watch football. And for those of you who feel the same way, I'd like to offer a few suggestions for keeping the work to a minimum. (Note: If you're one of those guys who delights in having the lushest, greenest, most perfectly manicured lawn in the neighborhood, you may want to skip the next few paragraphs. Go outside and aerate, or something.)

Of course, as I've already stated, it's a given that the best strategy is to get your children to do all the work for you. If they're not old enough, or you're merely afraid of them, the next best thing is to hire someone. But assuming neither of those is an option, for whatever reason, then here's how to make the job as easy as possible on yourself.

First, remember that if it's green and grows in your yard, it's grass. Others may have some fancy name for it, like *weeds*, but as far as I'm concerned, it's grass. This is a point of view that has saved me a lot of work over the years. I see my neighbors spending hours in their yards planting grass seed, spreading fertilizer, aerating, and so forth, and I am truly relieved not to have to worry about any of that. Why should I? I have perfectly good grass, already. It grows. It's generally green in appearance. What more could I ask?

Second, you should mow your yard regularly. Now, this may sound like a contradiction — wouldn't mowing regularly be *more* work? Not necessarily. The problem with occasional or sporadic mowing is that the grass can get too high in between cuttings. This can turn a relatively stress-free one-hour job into a three-hour ordeal of restarting the engine, pulling out your hair, and cursing everything in sight — kind of like your Friday afternoon commute.

Regular mowing will also help ensure that your neighbors never circulate a petition calling for you to be kicked out of the neighborhood. So take my advice and mow your yard at least once a week, unless of course your prayers are answered and your region is stricken by a terrible drought.

Finally, don't worry about grass clippings. Raking is a complete waste of time and serves no purpose other than to pander to the anal tendencies of your more intrusive and obnoxious neighbors. In the first place, if you take my suggestion and mow regularly, you shouldn't have a problem with excessive clippings. And if, on occasion, you notice large clumps that are visible from the road, just run the mower back over them a time or two. Anything not visible from the road shouldn't be an issue. About the only real danger is that your wife may complain about people tracking grass into the house. But isn't that why you bought her a vacuum cleaner?

Above all, never use any sort of bagging or catching system, even if you have one of those ridiculously expensive riding mowers with the rear-mounting device. You'll spend so much time stopping to empty the bagger that you might as well be cutting the grass by hand with a pair of safety shears and disposing of each blade individually in a hermetically sealed envelope. Just follow the advice above and your yard will look fine, at least to anyone driving by at 55 or 60 mph.

Goodbye, Old Paint

If you're like most family men, then you and your wife have already agreed on the division of labor when it comes to maintaining your home: she is responsible for deciding how the house should look, and you are responsible for making it look that way. Thus, your duties may include painting, wallpapering, and minor remodeling, while hers will include deciding on a color, selecting the wallpaper, and deciding what constitutes "minor."

I actually hate to paint about as much as I hate to cut grass. The good news is that I can generally stretch a five-hour job into a three-day project, thus making it seem as though I'm working much harder than I really am. This would elicit sympathy from my wife, if she had a sympathetic bone in her body, which she doesn't. Not for me, anyway. For lost kittens and children with skinned knees, yes. But for a man who has to paint the hallway during the NBA playoffs, no. Especially if he's been putting off the job since the Bird and Magic era.

What I despise most about painting is all the preparation — taping off windows and molding, covering floors and furniture. I also don't like cleaning up afterward. Just how many gallons of water does it take to get the latex paint out of a three-inch brush, anyway? I don't know about you, but anytime we paint a room, our entire community goes on water rationing for a week.

And, come to think of it, I don't care much for the trim work, either. I find all that dabbing and intricate brushwork to be extremely tedious. But give me an open expanse of wall and an enormous roller and I'm good to go.

Fortunately, my wife and I are very compatible in this area. She's good at the preparation, and she actually doesn't mind the trim work, especially painting the baseboards, perhaps because she's closer to them. I don't suppose she really enjoys the cleanup, but she's willing to do it if it means having a room painted. All I have to do now is get her excited about the roller thing and I'll never have to miss another game.

All things considered, I think I'd rather hang wallpaper than paint. Of course, I'd almost rather just hang than do either. But wallpapering isn't too bad, if you use the pre-pasted kind. And if you have the right tools. And if your room doesn't have too many corners. And if you can get your wife to do nearly everything but place it on the wall — measure, cut, wet, and wipe. While all that's going on, you can usually manage to convey the idea that you're really doing the bulk of the work by sighing heavily as you put each piece in place. You might even be able to take a short TV break while she's measuring, cutting, and wetting the next piece. In fact, if it's football you're watching, you could conceivably paper an entire room in this manner without missing a down.

I have some other work-saving ideas I'd like to share with you, but be advised that certain details may not be entirely under your control.

For instance, when painting it's always a good idea to choose a color as close as possible to the old one. This way, you may be able to avoid having to apply more than one coat. Trouble is, you're probably not going to have much say on the issue of color, perhaps because your wife knows *your* choice would be based solely on its work-limiting potential. It's going to be her call, and the main reason she's painting to begin with is to change the existing color as drastically as possible. So you can pretty much count on having to cover Cranberry Red with Pale Autumn Sunshine — a minimum of four coats.

A similar rule holds true for wallpaper. The larger the pattern, the harder it's going to be to match the edges as you go around the room. So it's best to look for a paper with a simple pattern or none at all. Pre-pasted sheets of a solid color would be ideal. But your wife will never go for that. Her response will be, "Then we might as well just paint." So what you want to do, when she brings home the sample books, is to observe the size of the pattern in each of her top choices. If you see anything over two inches, just tell her it's "too busy." Most women will buy that, as for some reason they don't like their rooms to look "too busy." I only wish they felt the same way about husbands.

As for remodeling — major *or* minor — and other home repairs, I have only one piece of advice: *don't do it.* Hire a professional. Even if you manage to pull off some minor project without totally screwing up and costing yourself three times what you would have spent on a pro, you're only setting a bad precedent and further fueling your wife's unrealistic expectations.

Say you succeed in installing new sliding shower doors, for example. Good for you. The next thing that happens is that your wife makes a giant intuitive leap and assumes that you are therefore capable of laying tile. This is bad for you. About the only thing that can save you at this point is the mantra I taught you earlier. Repeat after me once again: "Sorry, honey. I just don't have the right tool." (The first guy who makes a tasteless joke here gets sent to his cubicle. In this book, only *I* get to make tasteless jokes.)

Baby, You Can Drive My Car

There was a time when all family men could perform minor automotive repairs and routine maintenance. Thank goodness that time has passed. My father was a member of that generation, as was yours, I'm sure, and he taught me how to do such simple things as change the oil, do a tune-up, and rebuild a carburetor. Thus, no one was happier than I when tune-ups became electronic and carburetors ceased to exist. About the only thing I can do now is change the oil, and as I mentioned, I've even been able to get out of that, for the most part.

It seems to me the question one must ask when faced with any project is, "How likely am I to screw this up, and how much is it going to cost me if I do?" This obviously applies to all sorts of home repairs, but it is especially relevant where cars are concerned. Because, other than the house itself, nothing you own is as expensive as your car. If you attempt to repair your clothes dryer, for instance, and make a royal mess of things, you may have to purchase a new one. But a new dryer doesn't even cost as much as a set of tires, much less a major front-end overhaul. The most expensive appliance in your home is probably your refrigerator, which costs much less than, say, a new transmission, though, in all fairness, a transmission doesn't keep food nearly as cold.

So when it comes to doing work on your car, remember that the stakes are high. If you damage the car's computer system while attempting a do-it-yourself tune-up, you're looking at some major expense — not to mention the contemptuous looks and derisive comments of the automotive service technicians when you take it in. Maybe you don't mind being insulted by some kid who dropped out of high school last week to spend more time working on his '82 Camaro, but I have to admit it bothers me. That's why I avoid those places whenever possible, and I recommend that you do, too, unless you're just going in for routine maintenance, or looking for your daughter's boyfriend.

Unfortunately, having your car regularly serviced by trained automotive technicians is the key to keeping it running smoothly. It will also help you avoid the humiliation of taking it in only when you've done something really stupid, like driving it for two years without adding oil. Admittedly, regular maintenance can get to be quite expensive. Even an oil change runs $25.00 or more these days, with transmission service, alignments, and brake jobs costing a lot more than that. Personally, I believe the resulting peace of mind is worth every penny, but then again, I'm a highly paid professional with a virtually unlimited off-budget expense account, otherwise known as a wallet-full of credit cards.

If you find the expense a bit overwhelming, perhaps you can make some compromises — changing your own oil for instance, while letting the pros handle everything else. You might even want to try installing a battery or replacing a distributor cap. But unless you really know what you're doing and have the right equipment, I wouldn't advise going much beyond that. The result might be the temporary loss of your vehicle and another metaphorical trip to the woodshed with some smirking Neanderthal in grease-stained coveralls.

Of course, there are guys who work on their cars just because they like doing it. Perhaps they find it relaxing after a long day of pushing paper or sitting in sales meetings. While I have a lot of respect for these guys, I basically put them in the same category as the ones who like to garden or do woodworking: I think they're all completely insane. But I wouldn't mind having one for a best friend. That could potentially save me hundreds of dollars a year.

One thing I don't mind doing myself, in terms of vehicle maintenance, is cleaning, though that may come as a surprise to my wife. I'm certainly not obsessive about keeping our cars clean, but I do believe they ought to be washed and vacuumed regularly, at least once every three or four years. This ensures that we are able to recognize each car by its color, so we can always find it in a crowded parking lot.

I know there are those who like to wash their cars once a week, perhaps because they have a brand new car, or maybe they just have some sort of weird fetish. These are people who, in my opinion, have entirely too little else to do. I think there ought to be a law that anyone caught washing his car more than twice a month be required to perform some kind of community service — like digging wells to replenish the water supply, or maybe something involving a pooper-scooper.

The bottom line is that, if your yard is too well-manicured, or your house too well-cared-for, or your cars too clean, the rest of us will hate you. Unless, of course, you have teenage children who are visibly doing all the work, in which case our teenage children will hate you. So it really doesn't pay to spend all the extra time required to do more than the bare minimum. You'll be amazed how many hours this frees up for playing golf and watching sports on television. Best of all, you may even be able to squeeze in a few extra moments with your family — as long as they're not too busy working in the yard.

Chapter 23

Still Looking for a Few Good Men

I've already talked at some length about a father's responsibility to be involved in his children's lives (see Chapter 16). In this chapter, I want to discuss the ultimate in parental involvement: *leadership.* As anyone who has ever served as a little league coach or scout leader can attest, youth organizations are always looking for knowledgeable, responsible, caring people to help mold young minds. In a pinch, however, they'll probably settle for you.

Being a youth leader has many advantages. For one thing, you can get into events free, which, if your child is involved in two or more activities, could save you upwards of $500.00 a year. For another, you don't have to worry about your child coming under the influence of some foul-mouthed drill-sergeant-type, or some idiot who doesn't know what he's doing, unless of course you yourself are one of those things.

But the best thing about being a youth leader is that you get to act like a kid for several hours each week without having to feel guilty about it. It's for a good cause. Yes, it's true that if you're the adult in charge, you must behave like an adult to a certain extent — knowing where you're going, for example, or taking care of the logistical details, or making sure no one is seriously injured, especially yourself. But the bottom line is that, when you take a group of kids camping, hiking, or fishing, guess what? You get to camp, hike, and fish, too — provided you weren't tied up with 20-pound test during the night and left in your tent while they went off to the lake.

When it comes to sports, being a youth leader can even provide the opportunity to live out a few fantasies. At this point in my life, I have more or less come to terms with the fact that I will never hit one out of Yankee Stadium. But on a little league field, with a 200-foot fence, facing a ten-year-old who throws 45 when he's got good stuff, I'm Ken Griffey, Jr. Granted, I don't get to take BP very often, because the kids need that time, and because I could hurt somebody (or so I flatter myself). But every now and then, I have to get up there and go yard, just to show I can. With luck, it probably won't occur to these impressionable young lads until they're at least 13 or 14 just how pathetic and immature that kind of behavior really is.

One of the basic requirements for leadership, then, is *competency*. Simply put, if you're going to teach someone else how to do something — field a grounder, pitch a tent, track moose — then you need to know how to do it yourself, or at least be able to pretend you can. This will give you a degree of credibility with the kids and with other parents, provide a sense of confidence as you approach your duties, and perhaps — though probably not — keep you from occasionally making a complete fool of yourself.

Don't think, though, that knowledge of the activity in question is the most important qualification a youth leader can have. I'm sure you've been around a coach who supposedly knew his stuff but still wasn't effective — no doubt because he didn't have the sense to do it the way you would have.

No, you need more than just knowledge to be a good youth leader. You must first of all be doing it for the right reasons; and more importantly, you must have the patience of Job, or at least the patience of a man whose wife has had him rearrange the living room furniture 17 times and still isn't sure how she wants it. Because everyone involved in the endeavor, including the kids themselves and *especially* their parents, will try your patience to the utmost. So if you don't want to lose your temper and smack someone, you're going to have to be able to keep your cool. And if you *do* want to smack someone — well, I can't think of a better place to start than little league.

The Importance of Being Earnest

The first step in becoming a youth leader is simply being willing to take on the responsibility. Because it *is* a great responsibility, as well as a major commitment of time and energy. For this reason, most parents aren't willing to take on any sort of leadership role. Instead, they'll spend that time and energy criticizing *you.*

Of course, there are those parents — usually fathers — who are perfectly willing, even eager, to help, but whom you may not want to have anything to do with your child. These are the guys who use Scouting to live out their *Deliverance* fantasies or think coaching Pop Warner makes them Vince Lombardi. Here's a tip: if your child's coach ever outfits the team in "Winning Isn't Everything — It's the Only Thing" tee shirts, it may be time to consider a change.

I think the ideal youth leader would be much like the ideal public official: humble, self-effacing, reluctant, yet willing to serve as needed. Of course, the percentage of youth leaders who actually fit this description is about the same as for politicians — approximately zero. But at least, as parents, we can see to it that qualified leaders are sought out, then elected or appointed by committees, rather than simply self-anointed. This may keep a few ego-maniacs from carving out their own little fiefdoms and subjecting our children to an abusive, win-at-all-costs mentality, at least until they get to middle school.

Granted, the committee approach doesn't always work, either. I know of one community whose youth football coach was very successful for a number of years, until he was removed by the parents' committee for using foul language. When the team suffered through consecutive losing seasons, he was asked to return — but only after he assured the committee he'd @#$!%# changed.

So if you want to make sure your children are well coached, and that if they're going to be cursed at, at least they'll be cursed at effectively, your best bet is to coach them yourself. Don't be intimidated because you think others may know more about the sport than you do. Of course they do, but so what? At the level we're talking about, knowledge of children is much more important than knowledge of the game. Thus, anyone who is a good parent can, with a bit of training, also become a good youth coach. (Note: if that last stipulation eliminates you, go back and re-read Part Two.)

This doesn't mean you don't have to know *anything* about the game. You just have to know more than the kids. Since most of them — even those who have played before — know virtually nothing, you're probably on pretty safe ground. It's the parents you're far more likely to have trouble with. They may not know any more than their kids — whom do you think the kids learned from? — but the difference is they'll *think* they do. More about that later.

The Star Makers

Another great thing about coaching your own kid is that he or she will get to *start* every game. Maybe even be a star, if you can manipulate events skillfully enough — by letting him pitch and play shortstop, for example, or letting her shoot every trip down court. Obviously, this won't work if your child is a horrible athlete. (Although I must admit that I've seen some parent-coaches on whom that point was clearly lost.) But as long as the child is reasonably skilled, your decision shouldn't raise too many eyebrows, except from the other twenty parents who think their kid ought to be the one taking all the shots.

In fact, if your child is a halfway decent athlete, and you're the coach, he or she is virtually a lock for post-season honors. This phenomenon first came to my attention when I was playing little league many years ago. One season we had an outstanding pitcher, who completely dominated the other teams, and a pretty decent third baseman who also led the team in hitting. (Okay, I confess: I was that third baseman.) The coach's son played a solid but unspectacular shortstop. At the end of the season, when the all-star team was announced, our team had two representatives: the pitcher... and the coach's son. Perhaps this is what people mean when they say stars are born, not made.

It was at that point in my life that I decided to be a youth coach. Not that I want my sons to make all-star teams unfairly, but I don't want them to be slighted, either. If they're deserving of the honor, they should get it. If not — well, I'm sure I can always swing a deal with the other coaches. I know they want their sons to be on the team, too.

The same principle holds true when it comes to Scouting or any other activity. The leaders' children always get preferential treatment. Even the most fair-minded leaders can hardly help but regard their own children more highly than other people's children, and who can blame them? I personally don't even care much for other people's children, unless they're my own nieces and nephews, or dominant pitchers.

(I'm being entirely facetious here, of course. I actually love working with children, which is the sole reason I've been a youth coach for the past nine years. My son's recent all-star selection is purely coincidental.)

The obvious conclusion, then, is that if you don't want your child to get short shrift, be a youth leader. You don't even have to be the head leader. You can be an assistant leader, whose main duty is to see that the head leader doesn't slight your child. This way, you can have all the advantages mentioned above without the headaches of actually being in charge. You may even find yourself feeling very comfortable in this kind of role. It's a lot like being a husband.

Memorizing the Serenity Prayer

Perhaps the most important character trait in a youth leader is patience. This is because no one involved in the activity is ever going to do exactly what you want — not the kids, not the parents, not the officials, not the other leaders or even the board members. Just remember that the purpose of the activity is for the kids to learn and grow, not for you to prove how much you know or how great a coach you are. Since you don't know anything and couldn't coach the Miami Heat to a YMCA title, putting things in that sort of perspective should come as a great relief.

Also bear in mind that youth sports are not primarily abut winning. Well, okay, they're sort of about winning. But much more important are the intangible qualities developed through friendly competition: the will to succeed, the desire to excel, the ability to high five. When your five- and six-year-old soccer team loses 14-0 to the team of eight-year-olds whose birth certificates were conveniently lost, don't criticize your kids' performance or rail against the injustice of the system. Instead, use the opportunity to teach them a valuable lesson: that if their parents had had the foresight to lose *their* birth certificates, they could be mopping up with the four-year-olds right now.

By far the most important thing you can do as a youth coach is to develop in your young charges a sense of *sportsmanship*. This is a quality too often missing in our society, from trash-talking NBA point guards to brawling little league skippers. Teach your kids to be gracious in victory and serene in defeat. This will ensure that, as they go through life, they will be noted for their serenity.

Of course, they can't learn sportsmanship without your good example. Be certain they'll be watching your every move, hanging on every word, even noting facial expressions and body language. If you're constantly using bad language, arguing with the officials, and demeaning the opponent, you can hardly expect them not to do the same. And the "I can do it because I'm the coach" argument won't work, any more than the "I can drink because I'm an adult" argument will keep your teenager from experimenting with alcohol. If you want the kids on your team to be good sports, *you* have to be a good sport. I suggest you begin yoga classes or some other form of serenity training right away.

I say all this because coaches who put too much emphasis on winning are more likely to be bad sports, and to be impatient with their players when they don't perform up to expectations. The truth is, at the youth level, winning and losing have much more to do with your players' inherent abilities than with your coaching. So unless you're familiar with the talent level of all the kids in your league, and can manipulate the process so all the best players are assigned to your team — which is a great idea, if you can arrange it — then you're simply looking at the luck of the draw. Take what you've been given and do your best to teach them some skills and instill in them correct values. Regardless of whether you win the league or go 0-16, your reward will be the same: a cheap, three-by-five plaque presented at the end-of-the-season pizza party.

Boorishness, Thy Name is "Ryan's Dad"

Youth leaders occasionally have grandiose visions of just what they can inspire their charges to accomplish. Such expectations are almost certain to be frustrated. Despite your great knowledge of baseball, you're never going to be able to hit and run with tee-ballers. And your Cub Scouts may handle a two-mile hike okay, but they're not going to be able to climb Pike's Peak, no matter how many times you show them clips from *Cliffhanger*.

The key to working with kids is to meet them where they are and try to make sure they're a little further along when they leave you. Be patient. Five-year-olds don't even know where first base is, much less how to turn a double play. Your job at this level is not even really to "coach," but to teach. Focus on the fundamentals, like fielding, throwing, and eating a mouthful of sunflower seeds without swallowing the husks. If, at the end of the season, all the kids on your team know to run to first base after they hit the ball, you've accomplished something. If they can actually hit the ball, you're a genius.

Above all, never berate or verbally abuse the children in your care, especially not so anyone can hear you. Screaming and profanity have no place in youth sports or other activities. They're for the freeway, on your way home.

Ultimately, though, dealing with kids is the easy part. The parents are much more difficult. In fact, according to a recent survey, conducted by me while watching pee wee football practice one evening, the main reason more parents don't get involved with youth activities is that they don't want to have to deal with the other parents. Then, of course, these same parents come up to the coaches at the end of the season and wonder why their kids didn't make all-stars.

That's not to say *all* parents are a problem. Only nine-tenths of them. But the worst by far are the "little-league parents," whose sole aim in life, other than making *your* life a living hell, is to advance their children's interests to the exclusion of all others. These parents can generally be identified by garb (team T-shirt and hat, button with child's picture), location (as close as possible to the playing surface), and posture (hands cupped to mouth, screaming contradictory instructions to their children on every play). They have grossly inflated opinions of their children's abilities, sometimes to the point of hiring an agent. And they won't hesitate to let you know when they feel their children are being treated unfairly (definition of "treated unfairly": only getting to play as much as the other kids). To make matters worse, their children often have little skill, perhaps because the parents spend more time badmouthing the coach than practicing with them in the back yard.

Of course, we all tend to overestimate our children's abilities, but the difference is that, as coach, your perceptions become reality for all practical purposes. That's why your son is a starter and a lock for the all-star team, whereas that troublesome parent's child is sitting on the bench. If he (or she) were willing to take on the responsibility of leadership, then his child might be playing instead of yours. This, let me remind you, is precisely why you should be coaching the team in the first place.

It might even be said that a youth coach is an erstwhile little-league parent who has gotten tired of standing on the sidelines complaining and decided to take matters into his own hands. Understanding this, you ought to be able to tolerate the poor saps, perhaps even sympathize with them. But you don't have to like them. And you are allowed to be glad they're not coaching the team. After all, if they can't recognize at a glance that your kid is infinitely more talented than theirs, how much could they possibly know about the game?

One. Two. Three. Kill the Referee

And then there are the officials.

The antipathy between coaches and officials is well documented, but as someone who has been both, let me say a word or two in defense of officials: some of them are actually trying to do a good job. There. That's more than two words, and it comes from the heart. Regardless of what I say from this point on, I don't know how anyone can accuse me of not giving officials a fair shake.

As I said, I've been a youth official myself, as well as a player and a coach. I don't recommend it. It's basically a thankless job with ridiculously low pay, and the abuse you receive would make a prison inmate blush. And that's just from the children. Many parents seem to think monitoring the officials is the main reason for watching the game, and they're quick to detect and comment on every perceived error, inconsistency, and physical imperfection: "Hey, four-eyes, you need your prescription checked!" "Is that your nose, or is your head trying to clone itself?"

Given these realities, it certainly makes sense to ask why anyone would want to be a youth league referee or umpire. I know when I was in college I did it for the money, but only because the blood bank wouldn't let me donate more than once a week — which shows just what kind of desperate characters we may be dealing with.

I'm sure many officials will take issue with me on this. No doubt they'll claim to be acting out of civic-mindedness, a sense of duty. "After all," they might say, "without us, there wouldn't be any games." True enough. That also explains, incidentally, why there won't be any organized sports in Heaven.

Others may simply enjoy officiating, enough so that the negatives are inconsequential. But I'm convinced that underlying all this high-sounding rhetoric is a much darker motivation: *the god complex*. After all, in what other capacity can one have so much control over the immediate happiness of so many people all at once? In what other venue is one's word absolute law, even when visibly in error? Certainly not at home. In our society, only sports officials have this kind of power, even if that power is limited to a specific location and period of time. And those who can't be college or professional officials can get the same sort of rush calling youth games.

I think this is the primary problem coaches have with officials. We're accustomed to thinking we're always right when it comes to our sport, and the officials *know* they're always right, so the entire enterprise can become little more than the setting for a colossal clash of egos. We resent it when officials don't know what they're doing but pretend they do, or when they won't admit they're wrong. Of course, we won't admit we're wrong, either, but that's mostly because we're not. If we were going to be wrong, we'd be officials instead of coaches, and get paid at least a little something for the time we spend on the field.

It's a fallacy, in any case, to assume officials know more about the rules of the game than coaches just because they're officials. In actuality, coaches are *much* sharper. Officials have to concentrate on only *one* aspect of the game — officiating — whereas I've never known a coach who couldn't do his job and the referee's at the same time.

Men Behaving Badly

Finally, if you're going to be a youth coach, you must learn to get along with the other coaches in your league. This may not sound too difficult at first. After all, you've probably been on good terms with those guys for years. Your wives may be close. *You* may be close. But there's something about competition that seems to bring out the worst in us, and in how we see others.

It doesn't matter if the guy in that other dugout has lived next door to you for ten years. He may have loaned you his lawn mower when yours was in the shop, given your kids rides to school, helped you build your deck. You may know him to be a great benefactor to the church and a pillar of the community. He may be one of the finest men you know — off the field. But when it comes down to game time, and your team is pitted against his, he becomes the enemy, and you are utterly convinced that he will lie, cheat, or steal to get the upper hand.

Just remember, he feels the same way about you. And sadly enough, you're both probably right.

Believe it or not, I've seen life-long friends come to blows over a tee-ball game. It was cool. Okay, it wasn't cool, it was pathetic, though it *was* a pretty good fight. But my point is that, even though it won't always be easy for you to get along with the other coaches, you have to do it anyway. A youth sports organization can function only when those who know the most about the game — and we've already established that's the coaches — work together to make the contests fairer and more enjoyable for everyone involved. Whether fine tuning the rules of play to fit a certain age group or determining the way teams are selected, all coaches should have equal input — in a spirit of cooperation, not one of contention. This will prevent scenes like the one I describe above from being acted out on the field. The parking lot, of course, is another matter.

In any case, regardless of how you may feel about another coach or official, be careful to monitor your behavior in front of the children. Remember, there's never any excuse to use bad language or become physically violent. If we allow youth sports to deteriorate into that kind of ugliness, next thing you know, we'll have some cable network wanting to televise the whole mess. And then where will we be as a society? Perched on the edge of our couches, of course, watching tee ball on pay-per-view.

Chapter 24

No More Teachers' Dirty Looks

Before your children started school, you couldn't possibly have anticipated how much time you'd spend helping them with their studies and other school-related projects. You probably don't remember *your* parents being that involved, and if they were, it generally meant you were in big trouble.

But times have changed. Now parents can expect to devote hours after work to helping kids with homework, attending PTA meetings and parent-teacher conferences, manning carnival booths, and building floats. You may even find yourself visiting the school frequently during the day, especially if your child's teacher is young and attractive.

There are many reasons for this increase in parental involvement. The first, I think, is the kind of guilt I describe in Chapter 16. Parents aren't home as much with their kids, so they try to compensate by doing other things that show their concern, like attending little league games and PTA meetings. You may not have had time to build your son a tree house — which is okay, because you bought him one at Sears, instead — but you can show how much you love him by helping build a float for the junior high homecoming parade. (This year's theme: "Legends of the Luau.") I'm sure he'll be thrilled, as well, to see you in your grass skirt, hula dancing on the back of the float with all the other guilt-ridden fathers.

Another powerful motivator is fear. As a society, we've had it preached to us for years that education is the key to success in a competitive global economy. (I was hoping to work that phrase into this book somewhere.) We're scared to death that if we don't spend hours every night helping our kids with their homework, they'll end up in dead end-jobs as hamburger flippers, grocery baggers, or television talk show hosts. Many of us also believe, at least subconsciously, that our regular presence at the school and willingness to volunteer for every project give our kids an advantage with their teachers. Undoubtedly, that's so. But wouldn't it be nice if they were sharp enough to make good grades on their own? The truth is, they are — if we give them the chance.

Ultimately, though, greater parental involvement is made necessary by the fact that schools don't seem to have the resources they once had. Or maybe they just don't have the resources we would *like* them to have, and think they need. In any case, when school systems don't have money for new computers, playground equipment, lockers, or health class manikins — probably because they spent it on teacher pay raises and football equipment — it's up to the parents to pitch in. Hence PTA membership drives, bake sales, candy sales, fall carnivals, and so forth. I mean, which would you rather do: pay higher taxes, or sit in a dunking booth for two hours one Friday evening in late October? (You don't have to answer right away.)

If you have at least one child of school age, you already know what I'm talking about. If your children are still young, now is the time to prepare yourself, perhaps by boning up on your math skills or acquiring a wet suit. Because when your child starts school, so will you — and it won't be half as much fun as the first time around.

Homework Patrol

Here is a typical weekday evening at my house:

My six-year-old son and I arrive home from soccer practice at 6:45, about the same time my wife and thirteen-year-old daughter are getting in from gymnastics. I just have time to give him and his three-year-old brother a bath and maybe grab a quick bite to eat — or maybe not — before heading back out to pick up the eleven-year-old from football practice. That means it's 7:45 by the time he gets home, whereupon he takes a shower and eats his warmed-up food while I put the two younger ones to bed. It's now 8:30 and time for me to kick back and relax after a long hard day, right?

Wrong. It's now time for HOMEWORK.

Certainly it's not this bad every single evening. Sometimes soccer practice is over by 6:15. Sometimes the older kids are able to get their homework finished in the afternoon, before they have to leave for their activities — and, more importantly, before I get home from work. Sometimes there are snowstorms and hurricanes that prevent them from going to school at all. But those instances are all about equally rare.

Most days, they just have too much homework to finish it all in the hour between getting home from school and heading back out. Other days, they could have finished it but played with Lego's or watched Nickelodeon instead. So we're in the dining room doing homework nearly every evening from 8:30 to 9:30 or later. This is time when I would really rather be doing something constructive, such as watching *Monday Night Football*, or *CSI*, or even *The_American Philatelist* on PBS.

I don't recall having this kind of homework burden when I was a kid. I was almost always able to get most of mine done before I even left school for the day. Granted, this meant I was doing my math homework during English, English during science, and so forth, but I found that if I did this throughout the day, the most I would ever have to do at home was the assignment for one class. And I could usually get that done on the bus the next morning. Of course, I didn't learn much in the process and was never able to escape the vicious cycle I'd created. But if anything, that merely prepared me for the rest of my life.

As I progressed though school and began to have more and more work outside of class, I also found I was being given more and more opportunities to do it right there in school. "Study Halls," these were called, with "teachers" assigned to monitor them, and they were listed as classes and built right into my schedule. I always thought this a profoundly sensible idea. After all, only one assistant football coach can teach driver's ed. The others need something to do, too.

It's not that I'm opposed to children being given work outside of class. I expect my children's academic courses to be rigorous, and I recognize they must learn the values of hard work and time management. I'm also aware that our public education establishment is under some pressure to pile the work on, so we can keep up with the Japanese and the Canadians and the Finns (as if any of *them* ever invented stock car racing, or pizza delivery). But, honestly, when I look at the amount of work my kids bring home, I sometimes have to ask myself: just what are they doing *in* school?

I remember when the kids were younger. My wife and I used to have them in bed by 8:00, after which we could settle in for a relaxing evening of mindless television. Sometimes we'd even talk to each other. Now we're lucky if we get to watch the late news, and we rarely have a conversation that isn't somehow related to the children and their school activities. As for anything else — well, the romance experts say that foreplay really begins several hours before bedtime. Now if only my wife were turned on by social studies.

My most heartfelt wish is that the culprits in this case — the teachers who pile on the homework — also have school-age children whose teachers give *them* ridiculous amounts of homework, too. If my day is going to run non-stop from 6:00 am to 11:00 pm, and my nights are going to be cold and lonely, I want theirs to be that way, too. Of course, those teachers might not spend as much time as I do trying to help their kids grasp difficult concepts. That would be totally out of character.

Another problem I have with my kids' homework is that I'm often intimidated by it. This is a difficult position to be in as a parent, because of course we're supposed to know everything, at least about school subjects. We may be completely ignorant when it comes to fashion, music, romance, and prevailing social norms, but we're expected to know all about polynomial equations. Personally, I think I'd have more success trying to figure out just what the heck Kanye West is talking about.

It's always the math that gets me — even second and third-grade math. I know you engineers and computer programmers will have a hard time identifying. But I was one of those people who learned just enough math to make a decent grade on the test, then promptly forgot everything. I never learned to *think* in mathematical terms. No doubt that's why my salary, compared to yours, doesn't equate.

English homework I can do, but heredity being what it is, my children rarely have trouble in that subject. After math, it's history, social studies, and science — all of which require me to remember facts that were obscure when I learned them and haven't become any more relevant since. And of course, there are a lot *more* facts now — about thirty years' worth.

When I can't help, the kids naturally turn to their mother, who is much smarter than I am to begin with. Thus, my role as a member of the homework patrol is gradually diminishing. My fondest hope is that as humanity continues its relentless march into ever-greater realms of knowledge, I may one day be able to watch Monday Night Football again.

Parents, Teachers, Accountants

Each fall, our children bring home flyers announcing the new school year's PTA membership drive. These flyers change from year to year, but they invariably do two things: extol the virtues of the organization ("Where would our school be without the PTA?") and offer great rewards for students whose parents join ("Free pizza party for the home room that signs up the most members!") All of which raises a number of pertinent questions, such as what exactly does the PTA *do*? Where does all the money go? And, if it's the parents who are signing up, why do the kids get the free pizza?

Don't get me wrong. I'm not at all opposed to the PTA. My wife and I join every year. We pay our dues. My wife has even served as an officer, a peculiar form of masochism that modern psychology has yet to explain. I believe firmly in the basic ideal of the organization, which is that, for schools to be effective, parents and teachers must work together. I'm just not sure that's what the PTA is about anymore.

What it really seems to be about these days is *raising money*. Why else all the urgency of the membership drive? How many of those who join will actually participate? And does the school really care how many participate — or just how many join? After all, everyone has to pay the same dues, whether or not they ever attend a single meeting.

Here are some even more pointed and relevant questions (I know you expect no less): Why are the schools themselves — read *school administrations* — so involved in the whole process anyway? It seems to me that the PTA — the *Parent Teacher Association* — should be something related to, even auxiliary to, but separate from the school itself. I can imagine circumstances in which the PTA might find itself at odds with the administration, when the best interests of the children are at stake. That might be difficult when the PTA president is the assistant principal's wife.

The obvious answer is that schools tend to see the PTA as a golden goose. Consider the projects that money raised by the PTA typically goes to sponsor: playground equipment, lockers, gymnasium bleachers, art and music supplies, library books, hair nets for the cafeteria staff. Is it my imagination, or are those all things the school should be providing in the first place? Things our tax money is supposed to buy? (Except, possibly, for the hairnets, which I would gladly have paid for myself when I was in school, even though they significantly decrease the protein content of the food.)

Honestly, shouldn't PTA funds be going for true extras, things the school system seems genuinely unable to provide?

Things like additional computers, television monitors, updated laboratory equipment, and competent administrators?

The sad fact may be that in this modern age of waste and inefficiency, school systems can hardly afford to provide anything other than the building itself and personnel to staff it. When I was a kid, schools were built with lockers already installed; these days, they may very well *be* extras. But then again, for many schools, so are usable whiteboards, classrooms that don't leak, and toilet paper.

So what's next — the toilets themselves? Will we see the day when schools are built without adequate restroom facilities where our children can go to smoke in peace? When bathroom fixtures are thus considered "extras"? I can see the ad campaign now: "Give to the PTA, so tomorrow's leaders will have a place to flush their butts." I think that's where I personally will draw the line. The implied metaphor strikes too close to home. I don't want to be reminded how much of my money has already been flushed down the toilet by one bureaucracy or another.

Noteworthy Accomplishments

One of the more unpleasant duties you may be called upon to perform in connection with your child's schooling is to attend a conference with the teacher or principal. Granted, these aren't always negative. Many schools nowadays hold regular parent-teacher conferences just to keep parents informed. Still — and maybe this is due to my own past experiences — I find it hard to shake the belief that if a teacher asks to talk to a parent, it can't possibly be good news.

As a child in school, I knew of no worse feeling than having the teacher give me a note to take home to my parents. And if the purpose of the note was to request a conference, that was even worse. Even if all the teacher wanted was to tell my parents what a great student I was — as if *that* ever happened

— I would feel sick to my stomach for days, despite staying away from the cafeteria.

I get that same sick feeling when one of my kids brings home a note requesting a conference. I know I have good kids, and if one of them had done anything really awful I'd be reading about it in the paper, not a note from the teacher. I also know parent-teacher conferences nowadays are often totally innocuous. Many teachers are simply required by their contracts or by system guidelines to have a certain number of such conferences each year. Still, I can't help feeling that no good can come of it.

To help those with similar misgivings, I therefore offer the following guide to preparing for that worrisome parent-teacher conference. This should help take some of the guesswork out of the process. Moreover, knowing in advance what you might say or do in certain situations will help to relieve the stress. Please bear in mind, though, that if you find yourself having to use this guide too often, you probably need to refer back to Chapter 8.

First, *grill the child* thoroughly. Granted, he or she may be just as much in the dark as you are concerning the proposed conference; that's why I use the word *grill*. Spend some time with your child going over his or her recent performance and behavior in school. Ask direct and probing questions designed to elicit enlightening responses, questions such as, "Does this have anything to do with the big-screen TV you bought last week?" "Have any of your classmates had to leave school recently with bleeding head wounds?" "Have you been abusing the gerbils again?"

Secondly, *review the child's recent work*. Most children bring home graded tests and other assignments on a regular basis. Sometimes parents are even required to sign these papers and return them, via the child. If your child has not been bringing anything home lately, that in itself should indicate a problem, and may in fact *be* the problem. With a little luck, you may find some of these papers stuffed into a notebook, or wadded up in the bottom of a backpack, or folded neatly into a jeans pocket. Also check the lint trap of your dryer. Once found, these documents may provide some clues as to the nature of the upcoming conference.

If you can't find any such incriminating evidence, and thus still can't figure out why the teacher has asked to meet with you, then it may be to your benefit to *prepare an all-purpose alibi.* This is a story that will help to explain any situation with which you may be confronted, even if you find it shocking, disturbing, or embarrassing. A very common all-purpose alibi these days, for instance, is that you and your wife both work full-time outside the home. "Yes, Ms. Jones, I can see how you would find it upsetting that Matthew keeps putting the gerbil's little paws in the electric pencil sharpener. It upsets us, too. But you see, his mother and I both have demanding careers, and we haven't really had the chance to teach him not to torture rodents." Then end the interview with a promise to do better. If "We'll see that he doesn't do it again" seems to imply too great a commitment, then just go with "We'll talk to him about it."

Finally, if all else fails, *change your name.* Then you can claim to be not the child's parents but merely his legal guardians, maybe even his foster parents. This will enable you to put some distance between yourself and the child, so that you need not take any direct responsibility for his actions, thus sparing you a great deal of pain and embarrassment. You can merely look at the teacher as she describes his offensive behavior, shake your head slowly, shrug your shoulders and spread your palms, as if to say, "What can we do? It's the system, you know?"

Of course, there's always the possibility, as I mentioned above, that the teacher wants to meet with you for a *good* reason, such as to announce that your child has been chosen to be the first kindergartner in space. In this case, you may feel a bit guilty about overreacting and possibly traumatizing your child. You may also want to rethink the whole name change thing.

Perpetual Mardi Gras

Finally, as the parent of a school-age child, you will be called upon to volunteer for every project that comes along, from building a float to manning a carnival booth to chaperoning a dance. This may sound like a lot of fun, on the surface. It isn't. Don't expect to relive the good times you had going to parades, carnivals, and dances when you were a youngster. You had fun then because someone else was doing all the work. Now you are that someone.

Perhaps not everyone reading this has experienced all these activities. Unfortunately, I have.

For example, my children's elementary school regularly enters floats in area parades, and the individual classes can become quite competitive. So I've spent more than a few evenings building frames out of two-by-fours on top of some old trailer, then wrapping those frames with "chicken" wire, apparently named after the fathers who aren't there helping. Covering the wire with tissue paper flowers is a task we usually leave to the children, which is another way of saying their mothers do it. Generally speaking, it isn't manly to do anything with tissue, at least not in public.

Another activity I occasionally get roped into is working a booth at the school's fall festival. Or spring fling. Or end-of-school bash. Or back-to-school carnival. Here I find myself spending three hours at some tedious and demeaning task, such as crouching behind a cardboard cut-out of the ocean, attaching weighted plastic fish to the magnetic "hooks" children drop over. Or dodging darts thrown by five-year-olds while attempting to blow up balloons. Or donning a Freddie Krueger mask to jump out of a closet in the "haunted house" and yell "Boo!" at a pack of pre-teen boys, who then kick me in the shin and run away. Is this what I went to college for? Most certainly not. They didn't even offer those kinds of classes when I was in college, though I suppose some do, nowadays. The athletes have to major in something.

My wife and I have also been asked on occasion to chaperone the odd junior high school dance. And I use the word "odd" advisedly. If you've never been to one of these — as an adult, I mean — you really ought to go. In my place. Please.

Today's dances are nothing like the ones you remember from high school and college. Instead of a crowded room, full of people dancing, laughing, and talking, the scene looks more like the prelude to some medieval battle, with opposing forces massed on either side — boys against one wall, girls against the other. You may find, in the darker corners of the room, a few defiant or simply hormone-crazed couples making out, but that's about the only male-female interaction you're going to see.

So to get things going, my wife and I will get out on the floor and dance. This takes a great deal of courage on our part, since it isn't easy to do the hustle to rap music. But eventually we'll be joined by a few more couples, mostly other parents. And I suppose it's worth it, since we're modeling appropriate social behavior. Personally, though, I'd much rather be in a dark corner making out.

What bothers me in each case is not the activity itself but the underlying purpose: once again, to raise money. Which takes me back to the point I was making earlier, that other than actually sitting in class, nearly everything our children do in school in somehow tied to fund raising. We have the PTA membership drive and the other activities I've mentioned, plus all the direct selling our children — and by extension, we ourselves — are expected to do throughout the year: candy, oranges, turkeys, gift-wrap, hemorrhoid cream. Even at school athletic events, admission can be as much as ten dollars per person, though I've never personally seen a high school game that was worth more than a buck-fifty.

I know there's a good reason for all this fund-raising, which is that school administrators make far more money than the truck drivers, nurses, and factory workers whose children they purportedly educate. But once again I can't help but wonder where all my tax money is going. To Bermuda over Spring Break would be a good guess.

And it's not that I don't want to be involved in my kids' school activities. I love and support my children. Honest. I want them to do well and their school to prosper. I also want them out of the house for seven hours each day. I don't even mind helping with a few fund-raisers, because I know they're for a good cause. I'm sure those administrators really need their island vacations.

But I resent it when I feel like the school is taking advantage of me. Then again, I suppose that really shouldn't come as any great shock. Like everyone else, I had twelve years to get used to the idea.

Chapter 25

Weakened Warriors

The family man's final duty is to himself — to keep himself physically fit, mentally sharp, and emotionally stable (relatively speaking). I say "final duty" not because it's the least important, but because it often seems to take a back seat to other more pressing needs, such as earning a living and raising a family. That's why many family men, after seeing their children successfully out of the nest and retiring from their professions, promptly drop dead.

But it doesn't have to be that way. You can make an investment in your long-term health and sanity by taking a few hours to yourself each week — and perhaps the occasional four-day weekend. This may seem self-indulgent, and may indeed take you away from other important responsibilities, but ultimately you will have more energy, be more productive, and live a longer and healthier life. With luck, you might even live long enough to become a burden to your children.

One of the best ways to achieve such enviable longevity, according to the experts, is through regular exercise. There are other methods, of course, like cryogenics and experimental drugs available only in South America. But those tend to be prohibitively expensive, and besides, you can't really have much quality of life when you're frozen stiff. Just ask Al Gore.

Not only will exercise help you live longer, studies have shown that it also sharply reduces stress, as the examples of former world-class athletes such as O. J. Simpson and Tonya Harding clearly illustrate. Other studies have shown that exercise can even increase one's mental capacity, which explains why so many aerobics instructors later go on to become rocket scientists.

The problem with exercise is that most of us hate doing it. It's dull, it's repetitive, and worst of all, it really hurts. A surprising number of men would rather just die young, which is probably why so many of them do. The trick is to find some physical activity you enjoy and will therefore engage in regularly, something like running, tennis, cycling, or golf. Or if you want a little more adventure, try mountain biking, rock climbing, or white water rafting. That way, you won't have to think of it as "exercise" at all. You can think of it as recreation, or just having fun, or rediscovering your inner child. Just hope that your inner child, once discovered, isn't in a full body cast.

Intimations of Mortality

One of the least wise decisions any man over the age of forty can make is to participate in contact sports. A contact sport is defined as one in which someone else's body might possibly make contact with your own, or in which any part of your body other than the soles of your feet may come into contact with a hard surface. As you can see, this definition includes not only the obvious contact sports like football and hockey but also basketball, baseball, softball, racquetball, and Indian leg wrestling.

Like many American men, I grew up playing contact sports, mostly in the dining room next to my mother's china cabinet. My friends and I even made up new sports, like "kill the guy with the slide rule," and found ways to introduce contact into sports that have traditionally been more genteel. For instance, we added a rule in doubles tennis stating that a player may use his racket to strike any opponent who gets too close to the net.

However, I have outgrown my thirst for that kind of action. It happened just last spring, in fact, when I realized that my basketball skills had deteriorated to the point where twelve-year-olds were being picked ahead of me at the rec center. Around the same time, a close friend of mine was badly injured over-sliding second base during a church league softball game. Actually, all of him but his left foot over-slid the bag. The foot stayed at second.

Unable to ignore such obvious intimations of my own mortality, I simply quit playing. Everything. In my opinion, it's just not worth it anymore. When I was in my twenties, and even in my thirties, I occasionally got a charge out of showing the young dudes I could still bring it. Now it's painfully obvious I can't, and there's no thrill in that. I don't need the competition fix as I once did, either. I get enough of that these days just listening to other parents talk about their children's meager accomplishments.

So I figured I would quit while I was ahead, and while I could still walk without a limp. But I continue to be amazed at how many other men my age and older keep right on playing. And I don't mean just rec league basketball, or church softball. Some of them — some of <u>you</u>, no doubt — are playing adult baseball, sandlot football, even rugby. Personally, I think you're all lunatics. The only football I'm going to play from now on will be in the front yard with my sons. I'll make the oldest one sit out, though. He might hurt me.

Other Sports and Things That Aren't

The best way to get the exercise you need, then, is to find something that involves a degree of physical exertion but no contact. This way, you can get all the benefits of exercise without having to worry about irreparable damage to vital body parts. Moreover, because it's a sport — or at least a game — you can have fun doing it and thus avoid the drudgery so often associated with "working out."

I suppose a relevant question at this point might be, "what qualifies as a sport, and what is merely a game?" I'm glad you asked. This is a distinction that will forever be argued in locker rooms, watering holes, and therapists' waiting rooms across the country. Those who consider themselves purists might contend that only the most physically demanding of activities deserve to be classified as true "sports," while others will want to include less strenuous pastimes such as golf, bowling, and lawn darts. I personally have my own criteria, which I suppose will identify me as a purist. I stand by them, nonetheless, happy just to be pure at something.

My definition, then, is as follows: a sport is a physical activity that requires substantial exertion of the muscles and produces copious amounts of perspiration, and in which one participates for fun up until the age of six, after which the sole objective becomes to win. Please note that an activity is *not* a sport if:

a) it can be played well by fat guys (football being the notable exception);
b) one can do it competitively while wearing slacks;
c) anyone over the age of 45 has ever been world champion;
d) after participating in it regularly for five years, one experiences no significant decrease in weight, blood pressure, cholesterol, or the urge to eat an entire box of donuts at midnight; and
e) it involves doing anything with animals other than riding on them.

Thus, some of the most popular "sporting activities" of our day, including the aforementioned golf and bowling, are not really sports at all but rather *games* or *pastimes.* Horse racing and rodeo are sports; auto racing and hunting are not, however much avid hunters may style themselves as "sportsmen."

Don't get me wrong. I'm a big fan of hunting, which I think is an excellent and worthwhile pastime. And even if I didn't think so, I'd still say I did, because the last people I want mad at me are the ones with closets full of high-powered semiautomatic weapons. But hunting is not a sport. You can do it for hours, wearing long pants, without breaking a sweat, even if you weigh 350 pounds.

I also don't mean to suggest that only true sports can provide health benefits. Golf, for example, is a wonderful activity involving moderate physical exertion in a peaceful, outdoor setting. That alone can be stress-reducing, which explains why the average course lake contains approximately 312 woods, 273 irons, and a few dozen or so putters, according to a recent study by Ball Divers, Inc.

Even hunting can be relaxing, and it has other benefits as well. Judging by the daily headlines, some men find the urge to shoot something nearly irresistible. Even though I *do* get a little choked up when I think about Bambi's mother, common sense leads me to one inescapable conclusion: better her than me.

So I'm not suggesting you take up rodeo just because it's a real sport and what you like to do isn't. As I said before, choose something you enjoy that will get you moving around for a few hours a week, allow you to have some fun, and not inflict violence upon yourself or others. It's okay to inflict violence upon defenseless animals, overpriced sporting equipment, or carefully maintained putting greens. Just be careful not to ruin your slacks.

In the Presence of Aerobes

Then there are men who exercise the old-fashioned way: by doing some dull, monotonous, repetitive physical activity. Other than their jobs, I mean. These are the runners, the cyclists, the weight lifters, the guys who do aerobics in their dens to Richard Simmons videos. Some of them are quite competitive, entering races and so forth, while a few just like to be seen in tight shorts, but the vast majority simply enjoy being in shape.

I suppose there are many family men who, like myself, have turned to running or some other form of exercise as a way of staying trim now that their days of playing competitive contact sports are over. These men are smart, and I say that not just because I'm one of them (though that would be reason enough), but because the benefits are considerable.

In the first place, as I've already indicated, these kinds of aerobic activities present little or no risk of serious injury, compared to contact sports. (Note: "Aerobic" is Greek for "in the presence of *aerobes*," which are ridiculously fit individuals such as health club employees and your workout partner — "aer" meaning "air" and "obes" meaning "head.") I suppose you could get hurt while running or cycling, if you're a klutz or a moron, or if you're doing it on Mt. Fuji. But the chances are really pretty slim. I mean, when was the last time you saw a guy leave a bike-a-thon with a Grade III concussion, or get thrown out of a 10K for high-sticking?

Moreover, aerobic activities are better forms of exercise than golf or bowling because they are actually forms of exercise. Your heart rate increases. Your muscles expand and contract. You perspire. Driving around a golf course in a little cart may be more fun, but it isn't going to do anything for your fitness level. Walking the course and carrying your bags is an improvement, but it's still not the same as jogging three miles or pumping iron for an hour. That, by the way, is why you rarely see golfers with their shirts off, not that you want to.

Aerobic exercise doesn't take as much time, either. A round of golf can occupy an entire day. Who has time for that, other than doctors, lawyers, accountants, bankers, insurance salesmen, stockbrokers, real estate agents, high school gym teachers, and the 50 million or so other men who make a lot more money than you do? A good, brisk run takes only 20 or 30 minutes — less, if you can convince yourself early on that you've pulled a hamstring.

And that's not taking into account the expense. A single round of golf on many courses costs as much as a good pair of running shoes, which of course can be worn over and over again, in between sitting for months in the back of your closet.

Then there is the greatest benefit of all: the exercise-induced euphoria often known as the "runner's high." That's a very fitting label, although I'm not going to tell you how I know. It's none of your business. And the phenomenon is quite real, as numerous studies have shown. The act of vigorous exercise releases "endorphins," which according to the latest scientific research are little men carrying small battery-operated devices, who proceed directly to your brain's pleasure centers and there perform unspeakable acts. The end result is that you feel good, sometimes for hours, or at least until you get home. There's nothing else you can do to achieve this state that isn't illegal, immoral, or just darned unlikely.

Finally, vigorous aerobic exercise not only makes you feel good, it makes you feel good *about yourself*, whether you deserve to or not. I mean, let's be realistic here. I'm sure there are plenty of guys who are complete jerks, who cheat on their wives, who lie and connive at work, who pick up small kittens and swing them around by the tails — but they work out all the time, so they feel great. They have tremendous self-esteem, whether anyone else esteems them or not. Don't let that bother you. Remember, the same thing will work for you.

Adventures in Male Pattern Bonding

Sometimes the family man just needs to get away for a few days — away from the pressures of home and work, away from the soccer games and PTA meetings, away from all those sports on television. At these times I suggest you do something manly and adventurous, like camping, hiking, or white water rafting. Because when you get home from your little jaunt, and your wife gets ahold of you, you're not likely to feel real manly again for at least a couple of weeks.

I also recommend you go with a few friends, if for no other reason than in case you fall into a river. Having friends along also gives you someone to talk to, someone to cut firewood, someone to cook breakfast. And all of you together can enjoy the kind of deep emotional bonding experience you'll be embarrassed to talk about for years to come.

Seriously, though, I think there are a number of advantages to be gained from the type of excursion I'm talking about, rather than something like one of those fancy getaway golf weekends.

First and foremost is expense. Unless you're mounting an expedition to Borneo, camping and hiking just don't cost that much, especially if you already have the equipment (see Chapter 18). If you don't have your own equipment, you can always borrow it from some poor jerk whose wife won't let him go. Be sure to return it to him afterward. Once your wife talks to his, you won't be needing it next year, either.

Another advantage is that you'll have an opportunity to commune with nature, as well as with the more adventurous side of your own personality. True, you can do this to a degree on the golf course, but it's not the same. Hacking your way through dense undergrowth to find your way back to civilization is a bit more intense than hacking your way through rhododendrons to find your Titleist 4.

Then there's the camaraderie that develops during something like an all-guy camping trip. It's been my experience that men will say things to each other around a campfire they wouldn't say in any other setting, except perhaps on death row. That's why the friendships you make on these trips are ones that last a lifetime. (Though I suppose the same could be said for death row.)

But the best part is, your wife won't want any part of it! If you're going to an expensive golf resort, you had darn well *better* be taking her, along with a sheaf of those pre-approved credit card applications. But she won't be nearly as thrilled at the prospect of spending four days in the woods with a bunch of guys who refuse to shower and who feel free, under the circumstances, to pass gas at will.

My buddies and I — four of us — have our own annual adventure weekend, which involves going up into the mountains and spending four days hiking, climbing around on rocks (an activity we later describe to our friends and co-workers as "rock-climbing"), and eating pork and beans from the can. We also take a white water rafting excursion, which allows us to spend the rest of the year thinking of ourselves as "river rats" — innocuous looking, perhaps, as we toil in our cubicles, but dangerous nonetheless.

My friends and I become extremely close during this time. We open up to each other about everything, including our wives, our relationships, and our relationships with our wives. We say things we would never say at home, things like "these beans taste awful," and "hey, toss that hatchet over here."

The result is a highly cathartic experience. I return home each year feeling purged, and not just from eating all those beans. My relationship with my wife and kids is better, my performance at work is better, I feel healthier, and yes, to be fair, my bowel movements *are* much more regular. I don't know if it's the adventure, the communion with nature, the camaraderie, or a combination of all three, but at the end of those four days I'm a new man. Which is a good thing, because everyone was getting pretty tired of the old one.

Till We Meet Again

In conclusion, then, let me review. As a family man, you have a great many responsibilities, quite a few of which have been enumerated in the pages of this book. But the point of this last chapter is that you must first be attentive to your own needs — just as soon as you've seen to the needs of your wife, your children, your boss, your co-workers, your clients, and a large number of complete strangers. By following this formula, you should live to a ripe old age, or at least long enough to finish this book, which is all I personally care about, when you get right down to it. If, with your last few breaths, you are able to recommend the book to someone else, that's a bonus as far as I'm concerned.

Of course I'm only joking. I think we've reached the point in our relationship where we can engage in a little good-natured ribbing, don't you? Never mind that we don't actually *have* a relationship, and that the ribbing is all one sided. Tweet me something obscene if you like. The point is, over the course of these twenty-five chapters, I've come to care deeply about you, about each one of you family men, and I wish you only the best, including good health and long life. After all, I'm planning to write a lot more books, and — pardon me for being sentimental — I want you alive to buy every last one of them.

About the Author

Rob Jenkins is a popular regional columnist who writes regularly for *The Gwinnett Daily Post*, *The Rockdale Citizen,* and *The Newton Citizen.* His essays on family life and living in the South have also appeared in *The Atlanta Journal-Constitution, The Knoxville News-Sentinel,* and *The Carrollton Times-Georgian,* as well as in the book *Georgia: A Backroads Portrait.*

He speaks frequently to civic groups, on college campuses, and at writers' conferences. A father of four, Rob lives in Lawrenceville, Georgia with his wife Bonnie and their children.

CPSIA information can be obtained at www.ICGtesting.com
Printed in the USA
LVOW040004060912

297583LV00004B/1/P

9 780978 774486